The One-Eyed Doctor

'You are requested to close the eye(s).' (*Standard Edition*, vol IV, p. 318).

THE ONE-EYED DOCTOR: SIGISMUND FREUD

Psychological Origins of Freud's Works

*Jay Harris, M.D., and
Jean Harris, Ph.D.*

JASON ARONSON
New York & London

Harris, Jay, 1936-
    The one-eyed doctor, Sigismund Freud.

    Bibliography: p. 244.
    Includes index.
    Contents: Bk. 1. Reconstructing the creator's
childhood.
    1. Freud, Sigmund, 1856–1939. 2. Psychoanalysts—
Austria—Biography. I. Harris, Jean A. II. Title.
[DNLM: 1. Psychiatry—Biography. WZ 100 F889HB]
BF173.F85H33   150.19′52 [B]   81-65787
ISBN 0-87668-453-3 (v. 1)   AACR2

Manufactured in the United States of America.

Contents

Introduction   *1*

**1. An Image-based Method of Literary
     Biography**   **7**

Method and Theory of Reconstruction   7
The Primal Scene and Other Basic Terms   8
The Revised Primal Scene   11
A Chronology of Freud's Childhood   11
Freud's Primal Scene Imagery   14
Early Childhood   17
Later Childhood   19

2. Reconstruction of Freud's Infancy   **23**

The *Non Vixit* Dream   27
End of the Transitional Era   33
Julius's Death and Funeral   37
The *Riding on a Horse* Dream   38

**3. Reconstructing Anal Origins of Freud's
     Creativity**   **43**

Some Reconstructions from Freud's
    Self-Analysis   45
The Method of Reconstruction   48
The Scar   52
The *News from the Front* Dream   53
Crying at the Cupboard   57
Ending of the Anal Phase   62
The Screen Memory   64

Departures, Separations, and Losses   66
The Dream of *My Son the Myops*   67

4. **The Primal Scene: Revisited and
    Oedipally Revised**   **74**

    The Trip from Freiburg to Leipzig: Freud's First
        Oedipal Revision   76
    The Trip to Vienna   81
    Freud's Attachment to Oedipus   82
    Symptoms of Oedipal Origin   86
    Dreams of Travel to Rome   89
    The Revised Primal Scene in Freud's Childhood   93

5. **Three Oedipal Dreams**   **97**

    1898   97
    The Positive Oedipal Revision of the Primal
        Scene: The *Hollthurn* Dream   101
    The Negative Oedipal Revision of the Primal
        Scene   111
    The Dream of *The Open Air Closet*   111
    The *Count Thun* Dream   120
    The Creator's Resolution of the Oedipal
        Dilemma   143

6. **Freud's Latency**   **145**

    The Dream of *The Botanical Monograph*   147
    Peace on the Battlefield: Freud's Middle Latency   156
    A Failure of Repression in Latency   157
    The Dream of *The Bird-beaked Figures*   157
    Preadolescence   161
    Preadolescent Derivatives in Freud's Creativity   165
    The Dream of *The Uncle with the Yellow Beard*   166

7. **Early Adolescence**   **173**

    Masturbation and the Young Creator   178
    The Dream of *The Three Fates*   180

Functional Phenomena in the Dream of
    The Three Fates 181
The Adolescent Beginnings of Freud's Writing 190
Some Aphorisms of the 15-Year-Old
    Sigmund 193

8. Middle Adolescence **196**

"Screen Memories": A Prelude 198
"Screen Memories" 200
Freud's Adolescent Love for His Muse:
    Gisella Fluss 204
Formation of the Screen 206
The Screen-building Letter of September 18, 1872 210
The Natural Scientist 214

9. Late Adolescence **218**

Ichthyosaura 218
The Sublimination 224
Trieste 225

10. Adult Origins of Freud's Creativity **228**

The Threshold of Maturity 230
The Dream of *Dissecting My Own Pelvis* 232

References *244*
Index *247*

Introduction

This book traces the development of Sigmund Freud's creative life, through a biographical reading of *The Interpretation of Dreams*, *The Psychopathology of Everyday Life*, "Screen Memories," and Freud's letters to Wilhelm Fliess. These writings all derived from the self-analysis Freud carried out from 1897 to 1899. Other primary sources used are the letters Freud wrote to Emil Fluss and to Edward Silberstein during his adolescence and early adult life. In his writings, Freud left a full and detailed account of his genetically developing identity themes, special alternate resolutions to phase-appropriate dilemmas, and his ultimate penetration and self-analytic reconstruction of them. In penetrating his own romance of alternative origins (his fantasized family romance), Freud discovered the genetic vitality of the dynamic unconscious. In *The One-Eyed Doctor*, the authors have attempted both to reconstruct an image of Freud's developing psyche, and to use this portrait as a full and particular illustration of the creator's syndrome discussed in *The Roots of Artifice* (Harris and Harris 1981). Freud's discovery of the dynamic unconscious is a major and historically recent key to understanding individual and social relations. It is not, certainly, the only tool we have for understanding personal and social events, nor would anyone argue that it should be used in isolation in a reading of history or current events—yet its importance should not be underestimated. Recently however, a group of commentators has begun to argue on the basis of new information about Freud's life that human psychic experience in general, and Freud's own experience in particular, is determined less by genetic development than by social, political, and historical forces. We have attempted to replace the notion that the genetically developing psychic life exists reactively and autonomously in its time with the monolithically determinist theory that psychic life exists to be affected by its time. The focus of this controversy revolves around Freud's previously censored letters to his adult friend Wilhelm Fliess and his previously unpublished letters to his adolescent and early adult friend Silberstein. Thus, a central task of this introduction must be to comment on the ways in which this new Freudiana may be interpreted. The validity of psychoanalysis is at issue, for as the power of psychoanalytic traditionalists like Anna Freud wanes, the dispute between the new and old positions has become increasingly open and public. The new group believes that Freud preferred to avoid reality factors in accounting for psychological causation. What is more, this group seems to feel that the psychoanalytic conservatives have held to the intrapsychic supremacy of the Oedipus complex as the major organizer of human conflict in order to maintain their own position in power as the direct inheritors of Freud's wisdom.

Taking the social point of view, and summoning evidence from the new Fliess correspondence, these psychobiographers argue that Sigmund Freud's emotional life crystallized around the alleged immoral seductions of his father, Jacob. They assert that, in denying this essential reality, Freud came to view psychological causes as arising *intra*psychically rather than *inter*psychically. Freud's view of oedipal mythology, his contention that Oedipus's guilt arose intrapsychically, has been attacked as a denial of the fact that the fault lay within Laius, Oedipus's father, who according to legend seduced and slew Chrysippus, a young boy. In this reading Oedipus avenges his father's fault.

This deduction becomes the keystone of the argument that authority in society in general, and in the conservative psychoanalytic community in particular, has been used to seduce, rape, and subordinate new generations of psychoanalytic practitioners. The argument based on Jacob's faults assumes that classical psychoanalysis has neglected to give reality factors, particularly social forces, their proper causal significance in understanding the development of human conflict. It further assumes that Freud set up the split with social reality himself, by turning away from the information which his own self-analysis provided concerning his father's abuse and seduction of Freud, of Freud's mother, and of Jacob's earlier wives.

While the new information about Freud may be used to support these hypotheses, it also illuminates and strengthens the contentions about psychodynamics and Freud's life made in this book. Despite his caveats and protests to the contrary, a rich portion of Freud's legacy is the open book of his life. So lavish are the details that almost any hypothesis could be supported by selecting among the data of his life, yet from our point of view, the chronological march of organizing imagery compels hypotheses concerning the subjective integrity of Freud's developing identity.

One of the facts that lends itself to new hypotheses about the nature of Freud's development is that Freud's birth date was falsified by his parents, pushed ahead by two months from March 6 to May 6, 1856. Thus, Freud appears to have been conceived out of wedlock by his parents. Great effort and possibly social conspiracy went into the concealment. Investigators of Freiberg's official records have found also that while Jacob migrated to Freiberg with his children Emanuel and Philipp in 1840, the children's mother, Sally Kanner, is not listed in the records for that year. What is more, Rebecca Freud appeared as married to Jacob in 1852 only to be delisted by 1854 (Balmary 1982, p. 36).

It might be argued on the basis of this evidence that at the age of 16 Jacob seduced his wife-to-be Sally Kanner, later abandoning her. From this it follows that after marrying Rebecca in Freiberg, he seduced another 16-year-old girl, Amalie, abandoning Rebecca in the aftermath of this dalliance when Amalie became pregnant. Finally Jacob seduced his children. Such hypotheses follow from Freud's preliminary formulation, documented in the Fliess letters written during the mourning process and self-analysis undertaken in the aftermath of Jacob's death, that his father had sexually molested him when he was a young child.

Yet these hypotheses are insufficient. Just as dramatic as this seduction theory is Freud's conclusion—or realization—that his seduction by his father was a fantasy. This turning away from the belief in his own seduction, it is argued, is the critical point in the turning away of psychoanalysis from the concept that motivation originates in social reality. We maintain, to the contrary, that Freud's discovery of the organizing effect of fantasies on intrapsychic life was a momentous discovery. It is for this reason that the following chapters trace the intersection of Freud's developing, subjectively conceived, imagery and fantasy formation with the events of his life as he grew up.

In his adult creative work and in his search for the origins of his own mental process, we shall see that Freud relied on imagery to guide him in the regressive journey through sedimented experience to the underlayers of his consciousness. In *The Interpretation of Dreams*, for example, he traced his search for the origin of his fantasy that he was special to the imagery of a caul—or veil—in which he was wrapped at birth. This was an image suitable to represent the screening which took place at the origin of his life, separating his birth from the actual facts of conception through an artifice imposed on the circumstances. The image of screening at the beginning of life condenses the division between the extrauterine debut into psychic life and the earlier facts of his prehistory.

In his search for his origins Freud came upon his "family romance fantasy" and rediscovered the myth of the alternative parents. For the creator and for the neurotic, Freud averred, the romance of alternative origins holds great attraction. It is part of our thesis that for Freud the alternative couple, the King and Queen of his own prehistory, was embodied in the persons of Joseph Pur, the one-eyed doctor of his childhood, who was also the mayor of Freiberg, and Monika Zajic, Freud's nursemaid and member of the family that owned the house where the Freud family lived. Both of these attending Christians must have known Freud's prehistory—the details of his conception.

In this book we mean to show how the one-eyed doctor motif became the emblem of Freud's creativity and the organizer of his dreams. By following the development of the image themes of Freud's childhood, that is, by reconstructing his subjective ontology, we can recover Freud's development as a creator. Biographers must be conscious of the lens of the binocular microscope they are using in their biographical work. The social vision we have of other persons objectifies the image, leaving the subjective life out of account. This is the point at which the social point of view seeking to identify the mythos of a man in *the* world diverges from the psychoanalytic view of the man in *his* world.

Reconstructing through Images

The Interpretation of Dreams culminated and documented Freud's late-adult maturational identity changes. The 40-year-old, entering into a process of maturing consciousness, relinquished the objective certainties that had organized his personal identity. He began an identity change through regression in the service of the ego that took in the various life-stage roots of his subjective consciousness. The adventure of his psychic life closely resembled the course of a dream. A dream begins with a regression that is followed first by a flare of imagery and then by a progressive phase of new objectification. The psychic life, during an identity-altering period, follows a regressive path until some essential change occurs, and then it follows a progressive path, consolidating and objectifying the change in basic identity structure. Thus ran the course of Freud's self-analysis from 1895 to 1900; it was an initially regressive movement comprising, ultimately, a process of identity-altering maturation.

Freud the writer needed to experience this whole process with special clarity. He was, he felt, fabricating his own identity as a psychoanalyst. Exploration of the subjective roots of his identity required that he plumb the depths of his own prehistory as artist and creator. This brought him into contact with his family romance fantasy. As a psychoanalytic scientist, Freud needed to recognize his own origins thoroughly in order to distinguish subjective personal history and development from experience that was more universal, more common to most people. Eventually the need for objectification became a major motive for analyzing other persons.

Reconstruction of Freud's progress toward and through *The Interpretation of Dreams* depends on contextual analysis of his imagery patterns. For example, Freud's dreams are a source of pure imagery. Anyone reading the dreams must be struck by the repetition of the same images in the manifest content of diverse dreams. Even the associations to his dreams, brimming with stories, jokes, references, and quotations, become more than familiar, more than repetitious. Obviously identical themes lie beneath the surface of this prose. At times they break through instantaneously, like a sea serpent gulping for air before it plunges back to its proper depths.

As the repetition of the same images in different, dynamic contexts implies, images adopted as integers of experience during one era of development acquire an added and overlaid meaning as they are progressively condensed with new imagery derived from focal conflicts in later periods of development. Thus the individual image has an array of significance according to the developmental depth of the sedimented layer of experience encountered in Freud's work, for Freud's creative regression as a mature creator required that he use his imagery to guide him into the earlier worlds of his consciousness.

1

An Image-based Method of Literary Biography

Method and Theory of Reconstruction

The method of reconstruction we use consists in noting repeated and significant image elements in Freud's writing, considering the nature of the associational context as the images relate to Freud's experience in a particular stage of his life, and extrapolating the subjective experience that gives rise to the image organization through the agency of age-appropriate pressures of psychosexual drive organization. The method is rooted in theory. Freudian theory assumes that these basic drive organizers relate to the psychosexual zones themselves: the drive aims for zonal satisfaction while the image of the drive is represented as an immutable *primary fantasy*.

Stimulated by pressures from the external reality, the earliest and most basic derivatives of the drives form bedrock, structuralized images integral to wish and fantasy formation. These images are foundation stones in the formation of psychic structure. We will call images of primary fantasy *bedrock images*.

The drives that give rise to bedrock images develop out of a maturational readiness for drive to be expressed in an age-appropriate way. This same readiness also gives rise to an ability to experience reality in a new set of perceptual patterns, which here shall be called a *construct*.

Conscious experience is composed of drive registrations and registrations of perceptions. Bedrock fantasies act to absorb and channel drive pressure, serving as basic defenses against the primary fantasies becoming conscious. Successive bedrock imagery develops into a hierarchy so that a personal, life-story (long-term memory) is formed from the succession of basal experiences. The basal imagery of each stage is general enough to coalesce into the imagery of each new phase yet specific enough to act as a locator in personal history.

The creator's work is the realization of bedrock imagery. In Freud's case, there is less compromise of the drives with reality and less derivative imagery than is usual. As a creator, Freud found it necessary to explore his drives and to reconstruct the way in which his mind synthesized reality. As with other creators, Freud's closeness to his drives lends the products of his thought a greater generality.

Freud's dreams are a particularly fertile source, for his dreams often link expressions of experience with bedrock imagery. This lends his dreams a universal quality. The reason for the ready application of Freud's dreams to the experience of mankind is that Freud's dearest, most dream-inciting wish while writing *The Interpretation of Dreams* was to understand the origin and meaning of psychic life. These are the dreams of a creator about his work.

In the famous *Non vixit* dream, for example, Freud recreates and rediscovers the basic experience of the infant coming to recognize and manipulate his own consciousness: "people of that kind only existed as long as one liked, and could be got rid of if someone else wished it" (*Standard Edition*, vol. V, p. 421). This is an apt description of the kind of wishful infantile experience that is linked to the satisfaction of the drives in the infantile period.

The Primal Scene *and Other Basic Terms*

The Freudian theory describes development in a standard vocabulary. What follows is a discussion and redefinition of standard terms designed to facilitate the present reconstruction. It may be that the redefinition will contribute to psychoanalytic theory as well.

The *primal scene* is an early basal-image organizer. The term as employed here is refined somewhat from the ordinary usage. Often *primal scene* means a sexual scene between the parents witnessed or overheard by the infant or child. It is said to have significant repercussions in the child's development because of the unusual intensity of feelings that the scene evokes; these repercussions induce identifications with the role of each parent as perceived and fantasied in the scene. The problem with this definition is that it does not emphasize the particular period in psychogenetic development in which the scene develops determining significance. Thus in Freud's study on the *Wolf Man* (*Standard Edition*, vol. XVII, pp. 3–122), the scene is believed to have occurred within the second year of life and then to have taken on an added retroactive significance at the onset of the oedipal period. In this book the primal scene is viewed as a universal construct—readiness to experience reality according to predetermined patterns—originating in an inevitable neuropsychological event and occurring sometime in the second year of life. For the sake of terminological clarity, *primal scene* will refer in this work to a necessary neuropsychological development that brings psychological infancy to a close. The sexualized primal scene of the oedipal period is referred to as the *revised primal scene*.

The primal scene brings an end to the era of infantile thinking. The resolution of the primal scene is a new era of consciousness, the verbal era. Before the primal scene, during the era of what Winnicott called transitional thinking, the infant feels that reality exists as an extension of his own subjective effort. It is the time of life when creative effort is felt to make the world. Gesture creates motion. At the end of a motion is a new visual image of reality.

The primal scene arrives as a radical experience that reorganizes the components of consciousness. The primal scene is an experience of the parents relating to one another in a way that totally excludes the infant, despite supercharged wishes, effort, and insistence of the part of the infant that he be included in the parental experience. The primal scene is an experience of the failure of transitional thinking to have any effect whatsoever on the making or shaping of reality.

A person destined to be a creator resists the delineating culmination of the primal scene. Vestiges of transitional thinking persist in the productions of every creator. Every creator fixates to the transitional era, resisting the full resolution of the shattering of infancy. Resolving the primal scene is realizing that the parents are separate people, and that the child too is a separate person. Like the normal person, the creator comes to this conclusion. But, at the same time, a creator like Freud also concludes that it is possible to circumvent this conclusion under special circumstances. In other words, a future creator devotes himself to the proposition that he can still effect the shape and nature of reality through special effort.

Observation and realization of the parental encounter, whatever the actual content of the experience, trigger the formation of new psychic structures in the observer. The process of observation itself becomes the significant feature of the primal scene experience. Unable to affect the primal scene, the infant finds his pre-existing organization of consciousness overwhelmed. Only the sense of being an observer remains intact. This sense forms the core of the infant's first representation of himself as a separate object in the world. If reality is immutable, the identity of the observer is now experienced as flexible. The change, tantamount to construction of identity, neutralizes the drives, lessens frustration, and provides new means for seeking satisfaction.

In the aftermath of the primal scene, the primary world of infancy, with its illusion of gestural effort becoming reality, becomes a buried organizer of consciousness. A new, essentially verbal framework reorganizes the conscious processes. The future creator becomes devoted to recreating the one element in the primal scene available to his control, namely the formation and realization of his own identity. This has the effect of binding the identity of the nascent creator closer to the raw neuropsychological origins of consciousness. For the future creator, the imagery of the primal scene remains more permanently available than it does in other people. It more closely approximates the aims of the drive. What is more, the creator fixedly recreates the initial method of seizing

consciousness in the face of frustrating stimuli that would ordinarily call for a lapse in conscious process. Thus, if the future
creator has actually seen the parents coming together in copulation
during his later infancy (which is not erotic in early understanding
of copulation), such imagery may well become the foundation of his
sense of identity in the process of formation. The fixation to
creative resolution of the primal scene makes reality seem a mutable
factor in every developmental revolution in consciousness.

We shall be considering the nature of Freud's primal scene
experience at some length, because the first act of constructing his
own consciousness had to become the prototype of all creative acts.
In the first closure and fusion of conscious identity accomplished in
the resolution of the primal scene, Freud managed to include the
earlier infantile circumstances of his existence. As we shall see, his
act of consciously organizing was thus imbued with the sense that he
was a special creator who could overcome external adverse opposition, as his parents had done, through his own efforts at creation.

The Revised Primal Scene

The age of 4 is a period of biologically predetermined revolution in consciousness. The negative and positive oedipal conflicts
that arise in the fourth year accomplish a double hierarchical
revolution. The primal scene imagery organizing the subjective
consciousness of early childhood is now revised and reformulated
as symbolic phallic-zone imagery. This imagery enters into the
construction of the mother and father directed versions of psychic
life that submerge earlier primal scene imagery and consciousness.
The subjective organizing imagery of the negative and positive
oedipal fantasies is *revised primal scene* imagery.

A Chronology of Freud's Childhood

Sequencing and dating events in Freud's childhood is essential
to their reconstruction. Many seemingly minor inconsistencies in

the chronology were originally introduced by Freud himself. He had a habit of altering and distorting dates and ages by small, but consequential amounts. This habit appears to betray his incomplete knowledge of the facts about his own birth date. Many of Freud's distortions were picked up by various biographers from sources such as *The Interpretation of Dreams* or letters of Fliess, and taken as fact. Other distortions have been recognized, corrected, and explained. The distortions in dates have the greatest effect on those events that bear on Freud's early childhood. For months in early childhood are like epochs later in life. None of Freud's biographers give exact dates of the birth of Freud's siblings, except for Julius, the first sibling, and Anna, the second. For the purpose of reconstruction, exact dates are used here whenever possible, and approximate dates derived from the best consensus among his biographers whenever necessary. At times, Freud gives clues in his imagery about the age of important events. This helps to decide where to place ambiguous events. Biographies used for the reconstruction are listed in the reference section at the end of this volume.

Freud was born on March 6, 1856, in Freiberg, in a strongly Catholic, predominantly Czech section of Austria. His mother, Amalie, was just 20 years old when she married, and she must have been two months pregnant when she was married, as Sigismund was born little more than seven months after the marriage. Freud's father, Jacob, was 41 years old when Sigismund was born. From his first marriage, Jacob had two sons: Emanuel, born in 1834 (22 years old when Freud was born), and Philipp, born in 1838 (18 years old). Emanuel and his wife had two children, John and Pauline. John must have been about 18 months old when Sigismund was born; Pauline was approximately Sigismund's age.

Jacob Freud and his father, Schlomo, were both wool merchants. Jacob's sons, Emanuel and Philipp, Emanuel's wife, and Amalie, all worked in the family business.

A rabbi as well as a merchant, Jacob's father died during Amalie's pregnancy. The child was given his Jewish name, Schlomo. His grandfather's name was to be an honor to the infant. Schlomo, derived from *sholom*, means *peace*, as well as *hello* and *goodby*. It represents, in a sense, the continuity of life. Freud means *joy*, as Freud was later to be well aware.

The infant Sigismund was cared for by Monika Zajic, a woman in her early forties and a member of the family which owned the building in which Jacob, Amalie and Sigismund rented a single room. Monika was already employed by Emanuel and his wife to care for John and possibly Pauline when Sigismund was born. Thus Freud's sense that Monika worked for his parents, as his exclusive devoted nursemaid was something of an exaggeration and infantile transitional-type illusion. Nevertheless, this religious Catholic woman does seem to have taken it upon herself to save young Sigismund's soul. Quite possibly this related to her knowledge of the illegitimacy of Freud's conception.

Freud's first sibling was Julius. Julius died of dysentery at the age of 6 months. For dynamically significant reasons Freud misapprehended the birth and death age of Julius (see letter #71, Kris 1954, p. 221). Schur (1971) gives Julius's date of death as April 15, 1858. Since Sigismund was born March 6, 1856, he was already 2 when Julius died. Thus Freud was 19 months old when Julius was born, rather than 11 months as Freud himself thought. In other words, Freud distorted Julius's birthdate by pushing it back into the preverbal period of his infancy. We may infer that Sigismund produced a split in his ego by renouncing a portion of his experience. Freud's pushing his own age backward revealed his 2-year-old's symptomatic splitting of his ego.

Sigismund and Julius were both breast-fed. We can conclude from this that the infant Sigismund must have connected losing the breast with the origins of Julius. Amalie Freud became pregnant with Julius when Sigismund was 10 months old. The nursing infant must have experienced the physiologic and psychological change in his mother during the ensuing months. Quite possibly his breast-feeding ended at 11 months. Thus Sigismund would have reason to associate Julius's conception with his own loss of the breast. Freud often refers to an infantile poverty or gluttony of need in connection with his feelings toward Julius. The infant Sigismund must have observed his mother breast-feeding the infant Julius, at a time when he, Sigismund, was capable of conscious apperception and realization that he was no longer privy to the breast.

Julius contracted dysentery toward the end of March in 1858, soon after Sigismund's second birthday. No doubt the young Sigismund had received coins and presents on his birthday. Julius became ill in the psychic aftermath of the celebration of the end of Sigismund's infancy. Young Sigismund was aware of the illness and his awareness, as we shall see, was expressed in residual imagery from this period. The family must have believed at first that Julius had eaten the wrong food, possibly something poisonous, or that he had developed an infection, perhaps through poor infant care. Eventually, Freud fixed the imagery of Julius's illness symptomatically within the attribution of bad or dangerous mushrooms.

Undoubtedly, Dr. Joseph Pur was called in to care for Julius. Monika Zajic too must have been caring for Julius. Thus the pair we will see as the primal couple of Freud's family romance alternative life of the imagination must have presided over the death of Julius as they had presided over his birth. Dr. Pur was the Mayor of Freiberg. There must have been papers to fill out, and memories of other papers which had been filled out. The recriminations, and there must have been recriminations, must have come to rest with the Christian natives of Freiberg on one side, and the unholy Jewish interlopers on the other. This social split, perhaps reinforced by economic difficulties the family was beginning to encounter in their business as wool merchants, must have condensed in 2-year-old Sigismund's identity formation, and must have had the same fate as the memory of the experience with Julius; it must have been banished by primal repression to the newly created dynamic unconscious of the preverbal period in his life.

Freud's Primal Scene Imagery

It may be assumed that major perceptual events during the primal scene period, from about 1½ to 2, leave their imagistic imprint on the sense of new identity that arises in the aftermath of the primal scene. In the case of Freud, it is hardly possible to exaggerate either the effect on his development of the birth of his brother Julius, when Freud was 19 months old, or of Julius's death when Freud was 25 months old. Freud, like most creators, developed a strong fixation to transitional thinking. He believed that he had created Julius, and he believed that he destroyed him as well. These beliefs were contained within a series of images that recurred in Freud's dream life. These images, ghosts of Freud's infancy, remained permanently vivid and alive in the genesis of Freud's dream imagery.

The reasons for Freud's intense transitional fixations are manifold. Given Freud's talent for new learning, it is reasonable to suppose that he was constitutionally endowed with an unusual degree of neurologic facilitation. Conceivably, this would render his first mental structures stronger and more developed than the average. What is more, several factors predisposed Freud's parents to treat him as a special person capable of unusual production. He was the first child of his father's third marriage. The father's own beloved father had just died. Thus Jacob Freud wanted his son, Sigismund, as he was then called, to represent renewal in every sense. Sigismund was, moreover, the first child of a young mother who was heavily endowed with the capacity to love and admire her child. Neurologic factor, paternal expectations of renewal and maternal admiration must have combined to make Freud's every infantile production seem wonderful and unique to the parents and to their child. Finally, the artifice of treating Sigismund as if he were two months younger than his actual chronological age made his precocity extraordinarily clear.

Julius was born at a time when the young Sigismund was predisposed to experience him as an extension of his own subjective life. Experiencing Julius as an extension of, and simultaneously as an intruder into, the satisfaction he was making with and taking from his mother focused young Sigismund's sense of existence. Then during the primal scene months, as Sigismund struggled with the fact of his separateness from his parents, Julius died. This death acted as a correspondence to Sigismund's transitional wish to make and unmake the conditions of his satisfaction. But Julius's death also had an antithetical effect: it showed Sigismund that he too could lose consciousness, be annihilated and, in effect, become a casualty of the primal scene. In this way Julius's image was inextricably linked with Sigismund's transitional wish to transcend the primal scene, as it was also linked to inevitable submission to the primal scene. Julius became an image of a perpetual tension in Sigismund's sense of identity.

Creating and destroying Julius came to signify both Sigismund's sense of self-creation and his fear of sinking back into primary chaos. Thus, as we shall see later, Freud embodied his irrational wish to be the creator of reality by investing key persons with extraordinary significance in his work. The examination of Freud's creative processes undertaken in this volume shows that there was always a man whom Freud treated as an extension of his most primitive ideas and who played a part in Freud's sense of the genesis of his work. Such a figure maintained Freud's access to his own primary process, acted in fact as a kind of channel of regression-in-service-of-creation. Freud maintained a complementary relationship to this figure when he was writing. It was a dangerous relationship, for the other man was marked for eventual destruction. The irrational nature of the other man was finally to be exposed, and the man was to be made to disappear much like the ghost, Julius, of Freud's past.

The primal scene, as imaged by Sigismund's relation to Julius, was the first determinant of Freud's overall disposition to become a creator. In reconstructing Freud's preadult life, this book shows that Freud's primal scene experience affected the nature of the resolutions in all subsequent stages of development.

The failure to close the early visual world out of consciousness renders the individual with a transitional fixation liable to the return of primary processes. On the one hand this facilitates creative regression; on the other it increases the likelihood that later experience will be overwhelming. All subsequent developmental conflicts will be intensified by early primary process imagery, making ordinary resolutions more difficult.

An individual such as Freud who develops what may be called a *creator's syndrome* chronically views life crises as amenable to unusual resolutions. In all his subsequent stages Freud failed to resolve his dynamic conflicts completely; instead he developed imaginative solutions. These solutions can be traced through their imagery to stages in Freud's development. As a biography of a creator, this book views Freud as an individual deeply afflicted with an identifiable syndrome. In this sense Freud is revealed to have had no choice but to go on being a creator throughout his life.

Early Childhood

Amalie became pregnant again at the time of Julius's fatal illness; the germs of death and the seeds of life were introduced almost simultaneously. We can reconstruct that Freud's primal scene imagery of his parent's cohabitation and exclusive possession of each other must have occured around Sigismund's second birthday when Julius was radically ill. Sigismund, Julius, Amalie and Jacob all lived in a single room, and shared the momentous biological events.

As the spring latened and Amalie's new pregnancy became apparent, it must have been welcomed as a compensation for the loss that had occurred with Julius's death. Sigismund must have experienced relief from the biological intensity of these events and the long winter as he began to spend more time out of doors with his nurse and with his playmates, John and Pauline. In *The Interpretation of Dreams* he recalled the fields and flowers and forests of Freiberg with a 2-year-old's special intensity.

The Freud family's disaffection with Monika Zajic appears to have deepened during Amalie's new pregnancy. Emanuel's wife was also pregnant at this time. Since Julius had died, the Freud family must have experienced doubts about her competency. Monika, for her part, seems to have experienced doubts about the Freud family's moral and religious concern for their children's souls. During the period of this pregnancy, Freud recalls that Monika took him to church frequently in an attempt to save his soul.

In a key screen memory, Freud reports that Monika was incarcerated for having stolen from the Freud family. Monika's alleged imprisonment is treated in the memory as being equated with becoming pregnant and confined. Freud's mother told him that Monika was imprisoned for stealing coins which belonged to Julius and Sigismund. We may take this partly as a piece of reality distorted by family mythology themes. For it is hard for us to believe that Monika Zajic, Christian daughter of the owner of the house in which Jacob and Amalie lived, was incarcerated for simply stealing coins from babies. Taking up a reconstruction of Balmary's (1982), we must concur that Monika deposited Sigismund's coins in the church collection box as part of her campaign to save Sigismund's soul. From the point of view of Jacob and Amalie, she must rather have been attempting to steal Sigismund's soul. In this same light, attributing Julius's death to Monika made her a thief of life. Monika would have to be dispatched before the new infants were to be born.

Reconstructing further from these themes of the Christian–Jewish split we see that the Freud family also attributed its increasing financial difficulties to Christian resistance to the prosperity of Jewish merchants. This imagery too may be condensed in the official Freud family version that Monika had stolen from them. A prior event, loaded with screen memory significance, occurred when Sigismund was about 2½. Sigismund had a fall and lacerated his chin, and Joseph Pur, the one-eyed doctor, so designated by Freud, was called to attend to Sigismund. Thus the one-eyed doctor and the Christian nursemaid attended once again at a moment in which life and bodily continuity were threatened. As our analysis of this incident will show, its memory screens a highly condensed set of images and fantasies concerning the nature of the mother's new pregnancy, and the meaning of life and death.

Monika was banished around the time when Anna, Freud's sister, was born on December 31, 1858. Emanuel's wife gave birth to Bertha around the same time. The loss of Monika heralded a spate of separations. Indeed the Freud family could hardly hope to continue life in a situation in which the daughter of their landlord was accused of being a thief. The following spring, when Sigismund was 3, Emanuel, his wife, his children, and Philipp left Freiberg for Manchester, England. A few months later Amalie, Jacob, Sigismund and Anna also departed Freiberg. Their destination was Leipzig.

Later Childhood

We can imagine that the moves were momentous for the whole family. Jacob experienced the loss through separation of his biological children. In wondering why Emanuel's family went one way and Jacob's another, it occurs to us that Emanuel's wife may have had relatives in England. Freud later referred to the English branch of his family. At this point in his life, Jacob's economic prospects began to diminish, and he seems to have depended on his wife Amalie's family connections in his attempt to reestablish himself. After a brief stay in Liepzig, Sigismund's family moved on to Vienna, where Amalie had relatives.

Freud was almost 3½ when he left his birth place. Freud tended to place his age closer to 3 and to make the subsequent move to Vienna seem to have occurred a year later. Yet the Freud family actually moved to Vienna only a few months later, when Freud was 4. Rosa, Freud's next and reportedly favorite sister, was born within a few months of their arrival in Vienna. Three more sisters were born before Alexander, his last sibling, was born when Freud was 10. If we assume that Freud's mother gave birth at approximately 18-month intervals, and the appearance of the children in pictures gives this impression, then Mitzi was born when Freud was 6, Dolfi when he was 7½, Paula when he was 9, and Alexander when he was 10½.

After the move, the Freud family maintained its relationship with a Fluss family in Freiberg. *Fluss*, meaning *river*, came to have the significance of a tie to the past for Freud. That significance linked the Flusses to Freud's extended family in England. Among the children in the Fluss family, one son, Emil, became a favorite correspondent in Freud's adolescence. Although he was just Sigismund's age, Freud tended to defer to him as if he were John's age. Gisella Fluss, who was about 18 months younger than Sigismund, became Sigismund's image of adolescent love. His feelings for her encompassed feelings he once had for Pauline and Julius.

The Vienna to which Freud moved was a cradle of political ferment according to Schorske (1980). An aristocratic concern for culture permeated the middle classes. Aesthetic and intellectual concerns were vital to the age. It was in this cultural context that Freud entered the Leopoldstadter Gymnasium—a year earlier than most of his peers. By the time he began school he had already read many of the German classics and the works of Shakespeare. The Bible and various military histories made up his favorite early reading. Books and learning were the essential pleasures of his latency and adolescence.

When Freud was 10 years old, his family moved into a new apartment in the Kaiser Joseph Strasse section of Vienna. Freud was given a long narrow room of his own, which he filled with books. Although the girls had to share rooms lighted only by candles, Freud had an oil lamp to himself. Freud inhabited the long room between the ages of 10 and 27. There for 17 years Freud burned the midnight oil. He could not bear any interruption in his studies. When his sister's practicing the piano was felt to be a terrible interruption, the piano lessons had to be abandoned. Jacob Freud encouraged his son's studies and indulged Sigismund's habit of buying books. This, Freud's main indulgence, had a symptomatic intensity.

A brilliant student in the gymnasium, Freud developed intense, intellectual friendships during his adolescence. According to Eissler (1978), for example, Freud was friendly with Heinrich Braun, a classmate two years older than Freud. Braun was to become a lawyer and politician. Freud himself believed that he was to become a lawyer until he opted for medicine when he was 16 years old. Braun was the first in a series of richer, well-spoken friends who helped Freud enlarge his scope. Braun made available to Freud his family's extensive library. Clearly identifying knowledge with power and intellectual control, Freud used his immersion in books to defend himself against the intense and primitive imagery of the passion that threatened to break through during his adolescence. Trips away from home came to have great emotional significance as periods of liberated excitement.

Both of these themes were at work in Freud's adolescent relationship with Edward Silberstein. When he was 13 years old, Freud formed a secret Spanish Academy with Silberstein. Their relationship centered with their learning a new language, Spanish, and on reading the works of the great Cervantes. They used

Cervantes's imagery as a code of their own secret organization. Freud appears to have had no barrier to acquiring new languages as he was also completely fluent in English, and knew Italian, French, Latin, Greek, and Hebrew. When he was graduated from the gymnasium with honors at the age of 17, his German prose style was recognized as showing unusual merit.

When he was 14 years old, Freud took a trip to Freiberg with his friend Silberstein. Silberstein and Freud saw Gisella Fluss and her brother Emil on the visit. Freud's adolescent passion for Gisella did not flower, however, until the age of 16 when he again visited Freiberg and stayed for some time with the Fluss family. His brief passion for Gisella changed Freud's self-perception and was a determining factor in the efflorescence of his prose style, as his letters to Emil Fluss in the aftermath of the visit show. Freud's awareness of his passion and his interest in the sources of it in his own mind came to counterbalance the rigorousness of his study. Freud began to wonder at the themes of Hamlet and Oedipus as his love for Gisella lingered in his mind. All this was to condense in a decision at the age of 17 to study medicine at the University of Vienna.

Freud's father rewarded him for his excellence in study by giving him a trip to England when Freud was 19. That trip, reviving the reality of Freud's early childhood and infancy, helped Freud relinquish his childhood. It must also have consoled him after the loss of his strong fantasy attachment to Gisella Fluss due to her impending marriage.

Freud's interest in the natural sciences attained new sublimatory focus in his investigation of the determinants of evolution. Thus, when he was 20, he received a fellowship from Carl Clauss, a well-known zoologist, to go to Trieste and conduct research on the gonadal constitution of the eel. Taking him away from the protection of room and family, Freud's trip to this southern shore stimulated his sexual feelings. He retreated from Clauss's enthusiastic, easily sexualized researches, however, and entered Brucke's more staid Physiological Laboratory when he was 20 years old.

Freud continued to work in this laboratory for the next seven years. A new acquaintance, Fleischl, who already worked at the laboratory, became another upper-class benefactor to Freud. Paneth, who also worked in the laboratory, was also upper class, and helped Freud financially. Brucke, whom Freud admired above all other men, became a father figure to him. Brucke was extremely well read, articulate, and steadfast in his research. He set Freud the task of discovering the origin of a particular kind of nerve cell, important in studies then being conducted on evolution. Freud spent years doing microscopic histologic work, first on dead fixed specimens and then on live tissue. Thus Freud's stay at the Physiological Institute reinforced his strong latency fixation on study. Freud used his reverence for Brucke to close the door on his adolescent yearnings.

Freud was 26 when he met his future wife, Martha Bernays. She was a friend of his sisters; he met her in the family parlor. At the end of this period Freud developed a friendship with Joseph Breuer, whom he met at the Physiological Institute. This friendship gave Freud the courage and the means to leave the protective umbrage of Brucke. At that point Freud reentered the mainstream of his emotional life.

2

Reconstruction of Freud's Infancy

Freud's creative life was fixated to the thought process of the transitional era. The fixation, which originated in the birth and death of Freud's younger brother, Julius, is apparent in all Freud's work and also in relationships with the intimates with whom Freud shared his creative life. Freud cathected his writings and his literary friendships as he had cathected his brother Julius. Thus, the writings and these friendships all underwent a process of libidinization followed by a period of sharply aggressive cathexis. This pattern is especially obvious in the letters to Wilhelm Fliess that surround the *Non vixit* dream and in the dream itself, for the *Non vixit* dream expressed Freud's wish to understand the nature of his creative relationship to his friend, Fliess. Freud needed to analyze his illusion that Fliess was the necessary instrumentality in his writing of *The Interpretation of Dreams*. The *Non vixit* dream shows that Freud's relationship with Fleiss recapitulated Freud's transitional relationship to his brother Julius. The dream focused on the earlier libidinal and the later, more aggressive aspects of Freud's transitional relationship to Fliess-Julius. For all these reasons, Freud was devoted to the transitional era.

As Winnicott (1953) understood it, the infantile form of thinking (transitional thinking) consists of a particular kind of illusion-making. The infant feels that the object in reality is a product of his own gestural effort. Thus, the object in reality, which can be any object including the mother or the self, is felt to exist through the mediation of a special subjective effort. This is a wishful form of thinking which establishes the links between the visual-objective world and the subjective-kinaesthetic world. This kind of reality construction is the prototype of all later creative thinking, and it evolves into the mental world of the imagination. Thus, every creator becomes devoted to a re-creation of transitional thinking.

As noted in Chapter 1, infantile thinking of the transitional kind is shattered by the primal scene. The infant experiences the failure of his wishful effort to force images into reality. This shattering of infancy normally occurs when the child is between 18 months and 2 years old.

The beginning of the end of Freud's infancy was occasioned by Julius's birth when Freud was 19 months old. The end of his infancy was triggered by Julius's death when Freud was 25 months. Julius's life coincided with the period in which Freud was naturally most sensitive to the primal scene, and Freud condensed the conditions of Julius's life with his primal scene experience. Julius's death occurred when Freud was attempting to resolve his devotion to transitional thinking, and must have facilitated Freud's contact with the bedrock imagery of the periods, forming a deep stratum of Freud's unconscious life.

One striking image in many of Freud's dreams is the image of the eye. The eye is an image of the creation and destruction of life natural to the period of transitional illusion-making, in which one has but to open an eye to create life and to close it to cease creating. This basic image is related to the turning on of consciousness by wakefulness and its turning off by sleep.

Now the image of the eye had a natural place in *The Interpretation of Dreams*. Freud was investigating the nature of the visual phenomena, dreams, and their role in the sleeper's mental life. Wishes force dreams into being, just as they produce the illusion of creating reality in infantile life. In order for Freud to penetrate to the beginning of his own consciousness, he had to recognize and resolve some infantile and childhood conflicts: Freud had to understand the nature of his death wish to Julius in order to free his creativity and to allow himself to produce *The Interpretation of Dreams* in its entirety.

Freud's relationship with his friend Wilhelm Fliess recreated his relationship to his brother Julius. This is to say Freud experienced Fliess transitionally, as an extension of his own mind. A biological theory of the periodicity of life and death cycles that Fliess had invented corresponded to Freud's transitional illusion of creating and destroying Julius. In other words Freud treated Fliess as if Fliess were the creative force within his own mind—Freud entered completely into Fliess's biological theories about the creation and destruction of life.

Biographers of Freud have wondered how Freud could believe Fliess's blatant irrationality. The answer is that Freud wanted Fliess to be the spokesman for unspeakable transitional experiences of his own infancy. These Freud needed to understand so that he could free himself from a primal anxiety attached to them. Because Julius really did die, Freud's normal death wish for the sibling who seemed to have taken away the infant's satisfactions with his mother developed into a fixation to a primal scene construct containing images of Julius's death. To free himself of the anxiety attached to this primal scene construct Freud needed to analyze his fear of Julius's return and dispense with Fliess's irrationality.

By October of 1898 Freud began to sever his primary process ties with Fliess in order to objectify and to complete *The Interpretation of Dreams*. This motive produced the *Non vixit* dream, which is an example of Freud's transitional-era thinking. The *Non vixit* dream strongly evokes Freud's transitional relationship with Julius, and it shows Fliess to be a revenant of Julius essential to Freud's creative process.

Schur (1972) described some of the factors precipitating the *Non vixit* dream. The dream occurred before October 30th, a few days after Fliess's 40th birthday, which he celebrated on October 24, 1898. Birthdays were important in the Fliess-Freud numerology. According to this numerology the first of several critical periods for Freud would take place when Freud was 41 or 42 years old. Thus, Fliess's birthday seemed an unwelcome reminder to Freud of his own possible death. Since we know that Julius died on April 15, we know that he was also born six months earlier in October. Fliess's decade birthday indicated a period of vulnerability for Fliess. Insofar as Fliess was a replica of Julius, his birthday precipitated Freud into a re-creation of the trauma of Julius's life and death.

What is more, Fliess was sick at the time of Freud's *Non vixit* dream. Fliess was about to undergo an operation that was to be performed in secret. Freud was not supposed to reveal this secret to anyone. The shrouded nature of Fliess's operation evoked Julius's illness and death in Freud's mind.

Another anniversary motif pointed out by Schur is that Freud's father had died on October 26, 1896. Moreover, on October 16, 1898, Freud had gone to the unveiling of a memorial to his friend Fleischl. An attempt of Freud's to treat Fleischl's addiction to morphine with cocaine appears to have contributed to Fleischl's death, for which Freud felt responsible. That sense of guilt added to the magnitude of conflict over his death wish for Fliess.

A friend of Freud's who had worked with him at a physiological institute run by the famous Brucke had also died. This friend, Paneth, had wanted to get ahead in the institute, just as Freud had wanted to. Like Fliess, Paneth was also younger than Freud, a year younger, but Paneth was a more innocuous figure in Freud's mind, for the simple reason that Freud did not feel implicated in his death. In the *Non vixit* dream Paneth plays an intermediate role, standing in for Fliess.

In the letters to Fliess preceding the *Non vixit* dream, Freud had begun to see Fliess as a deterrent to his completing *The Interpretation of Dreams*, for Fliess had forbade Freud to use a particular "big" dream that Freud had analyzed and felt was essential to the structure of *The Interpretation of Dreams*. Thus, in the letter #99 of October 23, 1898, in which Freud wishes Fliess a happy birthday he adds a reference to *The Interpretation of Dreams:*

The dream book is irremediably at a standstill. I lack any incentive to prepare it for publication, and the gap in the psychology, and the other gap left by the thoroughly analyzed example, are both obstacles to finishing it that I cannot overcome yet (Kris 1954, p. 269).

The *Non vixit* dream was both a restitution and a retaliation on the part of Freud. It replaced the dream that Fliess would not allow him to use with another dream centered on a death wish to Fliess.

Another factor concerning the circumstances of the *Non vixit* dream is that Freud was himself developing a physical affliction. Schur (1972) points out that Freud falsely used a painful boil as an excuse for not being able to go visit Fliess when Fliess had his operation, since the boil became a problem only after the operation. Indeed, Freud's rationalization for his refusal to visit Fliess was that he could not afford to worry about his colleague when his own health and sustenance was in jeopardy.

The Non vixit *Dream*

I had a very clear dream. I had gone to Brucke's laboratory at night, and, in response to a gentle knock on the door, I opened it to (the late) Professor Fleischl, who came in with a number of strangers and, after exchanging a few words, sat down at his table.

This was followed by a second dream. My friend Fliess had come to Vienna unobtrusively in July. I met him in the street in conversation with my (deceased) friend Paneth, and went with him to some place where they sat opposite each other as though they were at a small table. I sat in front at its narrow end. Fliess spoke about his sister and said that in three-quarters of an hour she was dead, and added some such words as that was the threshold. As Paneth failed to understand him Fliess turned to me and asked me how much I had told Paneth about his affairs. Whereupon, overcome by strange emotions, I tried to explain to Fliess that Paneth (could not understand anything at all, of course, because he) was not alive. But what I actually said—and I myself noticed the mistake—was *Non vixit*. I then gave Paneth a piercing look. Under my gaze he turned pale; his form grew indistinct and his eyes a sickly blue—and finally he melted away. I was highly delighted at this, and I now realized that Ernest Fleischl, too, had been no more than an apparition, a revenant, and it seemed to me quite possible that people of that kind only existed as long as one liked, and could be got rid of if someone else wished it (*Standard Edition*, vol. V, p. 421).

ASSOCIATIONS TO THE *NON VIXIT* DREAM

In explaining the slip in his associations to the dream, Freud wrote that he meant to say *Non vivit* (he is not alive) rather than *Non vixit* (he did not live). The fact that just this slip is central to the dream is significant, for Freud had just begun analyzing his slips during the previous two months.

In letter #94 to Fliess, dated August 26, 1898, Freud makes his first reference to slips. The reference, which he does not use in *The Psychopathology of Everyday Life*, is, nevertheless, the harbinger of an inciting image for that book. That first analyzed slip, and the *Non vixit* slip are intimately related.

I have at last understood a little thing that I have long suspected. You know how you can forget a name and substitute part of another for it, to which you could swear, though it invariably turns out to be wrong. That happened to me not long ago over the name of the poet who wrote *Andreas Hofer*. . . . I felt it must be something ending in -au, Lindau, Feldau, or the like. Actually, of course, the poet's name was Julius Mosen; the "Julius" had not slipped my memory. I was able to prove (i) that I had repressed the name Mosen because of certain associations; (ii) that material from my infancy played a part in the repression; and (iii) that the substitute names that occurred to me arose, just like a symptom, from both groups of material. The analysis resolved the thing completely; unfortunately, I cannot make it public anymore than my big dream . . .

Best regards. How long shall we have to wait for little Pauline's arrival (Kris 1954, pp. 261–262).

Substituting other persons for a "Julius" is as relevant to an understanding of the *Non vixit* dream, as it is to understanding the impulse behind *The Psychopathology of Everyday Life*. Freud often substituted the names of new arrivals for lost or forgotten ones. The tendency originated in his transitional relationship to Julius. The same compensatory tendency motivated many of the elements in the construction of the *Non vixit* dream. *He did not live*, applied to Julius, is an element of wishful transitional thinking. The illusion that one can create and cease creating (forget), as one can create and stop creating images in a dream, is a central wishful element in the

Non vixit dream. (Conceivably "Mosen" refers to Moses, Freud's family romance fantasy identity. Freud used the artifice imposed on his birth circumstances to provide himself with a self-created identity as bearer of the truth.)

That Julius and Fliess both become the ghosts of Freud's *Psychopathology of Everyday Life* can be seen in a late letter in the correspondence (letter #145 of August 7, 1901): Freud announces that the relationship has all but come to an end. Here, one sees in the context of Fliess's complaint about Freud, to which Freud refers, that Fliess was aware of the way in which Freud used him as an object of primary identification.

> . . . you take sides against me and tell me that "the thought-reader merely reads his own thoughts into other people," which deprives my work of all its value.
>
> If I am such a one, throw my Everyday Life unread into the waste-paper basket. It is full of reference to you: obvious ones, where you supplied the material, and concealed ones, where the motivation derives from you. Also you supplied the motto. Apart from any permanent value that its content may have, you can take it as a testimonial to the role you have hitherto played in my life . . . (Kris 1954, p. 334).

The dedication motto makes Fliess into another ghost of Freud's past, as Freud excludes him from his creative life:

> Nun ist die Luft von solchem Spuk so voll,
> Dass niemand weiss, wie er ihn meiden soll.
> *Faust*, Part II, Act V, Scene 5
>
> Now fills the air so many a haunting shape,
> That no one knows how best he may escape.
> (*Standard Edition*, vol. VI, p. vii)

The reference in letter #94 to the "big" dream that is left out is followed by three dots, indicating an elision in the text of the letter. One wonders both about the nature of the exclusion from the letter and about the nature of the dream which Fliess censored. In this case conjecture is warranted. It is known that references to Breuer were screened out of the correspondence between Fliess and Freud before publication. Breuer was always in the background of the Freud–Fliess relationship. He was certainly as important to that relationship as Brucke was to the relationship between Freud and his colleagues Fleischl and Paneth at the Physiological Institute. Breuer introduced Fliess to Freud and had a role in mediating simmering ill feelings between Fliess's wife and Freud. Moreover, the intimate revelations of *The Interpretation of Dreams* delved into the same kind of material as that which ended Freud's collaboration with Breuer. Probably Freud was afraid that Breuer would criticize him severely for his indiscretions in *The Interpretation of Dreams*. For all these reasons it seems not unlikely that Fliess censored a dream of Freud's concerning Joseph Breuer.

Although Freud was ambivalent about Fliess's act of censorship, Fliess remained a necessary ally against a powerful father figure, much as did the half-brother, John, in Freud's early childhood. For in the *Non vixit* dream, Fliess comes in for transference from the relationship with John as well as with Julius. In his associations to the dream, Freud says that another Joseph had reproached him for indiscretion when he was at the Physiological Institute and, as the editors of the *Standard Edition* surmise, this must be Joseph Breuer, whom Freud first met at the Physiological Institute. In the dream then, we can see Brucke representing the more immediate figure of Breuer. As Freud noted, the whole male family constellation of the dream—Brucke (Father), Fleischl (John) and Paneth (Julius)—no longer lived:

. . . during the ceremonial unveiling of the memorial, I had reflected thus: "What a number of valued friends I have lost, some through death, some through breach of friendship! How fortunate that I have found a substitute for them and that I have gained one who means more to me than ever the others could, and that, at a time of life when new friendships cannot easily be formed, I shall never lose his!" My satisfaction at having found a substitute for these lost friends could be allowed to enter the dream without interference; but there slipped in, along with it, the hostile satisfaction derived from the infantile source. It is no doubt true that infantile affection served to reinforce my contemporary and justified affection. But infantile hatred, too, succeeded in getting itself represented (*Standard Edition*, vol. V, p. 486).

Freud used Fliess to offset the loss of Julius to death and of John through separation. Fliess thus compensated for losses incurred early in Freud's life, as well as for Freud's loss of the Physiological Institute family. Freud denied his death wish toward Fliess, expressed in another portion of his associations to this dream—by consoling himself with the thought that Fliess was the very person who made good Freud's earlier losses. He identified with Fliess so far as to say that though they shared losses they did have each other and needed each other only. This regression to the mode of transitional thinking is an example of Freud's including Julius in his own symbiosis with his mother.

Freud associates *Non vixit* with the inscription on the Kaiser Joseph memorial: "Saluti Patriae vixit no diu sed totus," translated: "For the well-being of his country he lived not long but wholly." This is a fine memorial inscription for Julius. Freud associates a series of names with Kaiser Joseph: Kaiser becomes Caesar, which becomes Julius Caesar. From Julius, Freud associates to July, which he then associates to the last time he had seen Fliess. Freud refers the Joseph to Joseph Paneth (mentioned earlier), who in the dream acts to screen out, and thus represent Julius.

Freud mentions his anxiety about Fliess, who was about to undergo an operation in another city. Schur (1972) points out that Freud is dissimulating when he uses his own painful boil as a reason why he cannot journey to his friend's side. Schur indicates that Freud added the association about his boils in 1899, a year after the dream. It was Freud's practice to add some associations to his dreams at a much later date, which gives a certain creative latitude to his associations.

Seeking to console himself for the sense of loss involved in his death wishes for Fliess, Freud produces a mélange of transitional thoughts: Fliess has lost a sibling early in life; it is possible to make up for the loss through a later substitute; identical names evocatively repair the loss of the person whose name is lost; phonetic similarity resubstantiates an identity. In the end, Freud consoles himself with the thought that one's children are the only path to immortality (*Standard Edition*, vol. V, p. 486). Thus Freud continues:

In addition to this, however, the dream contained a clear allusion to another train of thought which could legitimately lead to satisfaction. A short time before, after long expectation, a daughter had been born to my friend. I was aware of how deeply he had mourned the sister he had so early lost, and I wrote and told him I was sure he would transfer the love he felt for her onto the child, and that the baby girl would allow him at last to forget his irreparable loss . . . my friend's baby daughter had the same name as the little girl I used to play with as a child, who was of my age and the sister of my earliest friend and opponent. It gave me great satisfaction when I heard that the baby was to be called "Pauline." I had replaced one Joseph with another in the dream and found it impossible to suppress the similarity between the opening letters of the names "Fleischl" and "Fliess" (*Standard Edition*, vol. V, p. 486).

But Freud also shows a more hostile "survivor" attitude in reaction to his musing about Fliess's dying. He tells an anecdote about a married couple, one of whom says, "If one of us dies, I shall move to Paris." A little research shows that this anecdote is intimately related to Freud's transitionally fixated feelings about Fliess, and by extension related to the original alter ego, Julius. For Freud also cites this anecdote in *Thoughts for the Time on War and Death*:

These loved ones are, on the one hand, an inner possession, components of our own ego; but on the other hand they are partly strangers, even enemies. With the exception of only a very few situations, there adheres to the tenderest and most intimate of our love relations a small portion of hostility which can incite an unconscious death wish (*Standard Edition*, vol. XIV, p. 298).

THE FORM OF THE MANIFEST DREAM

The meaning, sequence, and organization of mental events recapitulates the process of transitional thinking in which reality yields to the wishes of the infant. Freud's sense of delight in the dream comes about through a restoration of the illusion of its yielding. He is able to create or cease creating images of reality by willing to do so. Here the strength of the wish to have the ability to create and destroy Julius is stimulated, not only by Fliess's illness, but by Freud's pride in learning more about dreams. He is discovering how wish fulfillment works in dreams by experiencing wish fulfillment in the dream and remarking on it. Thus the record of the manifest dream is in part a description of Freud's transitional experience with Julius. To paraphrase that element in the dream record:

I see Julius, he is dead. He only lived a short while. His image is my dream. I can't talk to him. He never really lived. I can make him disappear with my eyes, as all my dreams disappear when I open my eyes.

Insofar as it is a representation of Freud's creative relationship with Fliess, the record of the manifest dream might be paraphrased as follows:

I see Fliess. He is dead. He only lived a short while. His image is my dream book. I can't talk to him. He never really lived. I can make him disappear by finishing my dream book.

End of the Transitional Era (*Age 25 Months*)

The discussion of Freud's infancy up to this point has emphasized the transitional thinking of the 19-month-old. By exerting special effort Sigismund could make images come to consciousness and disappear. With the intervention of the primal scene, however, a large measure of frustration and aggression was brought under the organization of thought processes. As Sigismund passed the age of 2, at which time it became neuropsychologically necessary to yield to the aggression inherent in parent's commands, Julius died.

Just as Julius's birth fixated Sigismund on the transitional act of creation, his death fixated Sigismund on the transitional act of destruction. Around the age of 2 the primal scene shatters belief in the transitional thinking of infancy. The mobile, visual cathexes that characterize infant thought are superceded by verbal order.

Neuropsychologically, the new organization of consciousness is swept along by a large measure of new anal aggression. The experience of reality is mediated by the aggressive cathexis of words. Words are equated concretely with objects in reality.

Julius's death imparted an urgency to Freud's age-appropriate need to be on fluent verbal terms with his environment. The coincidence of Sigismund's transitional disappearance-wish for Julius and his actual death stimulated young Sigismund to the formation of verbal forms of magical thinking. If Julius could be destroyed through Sigismund's formulations of aggressive language, then Sigismund was liable to destruction through his parents' intonations. It was important for the young child to learn verbal ways of defending himself, using whatever notions of causality were available in his 2-year-old's lexicon.

It is tempting to think that Freud's ease in learning languages grew out of a late transitional fixation occasioned by Julius's death. The importance of names to Freud and the magical importance of naming have already been noted. Freud's associations were over-determined by puns, slips, and other kinds of verbal similarity. The *Non vixit-Non vivit* equation evinces fixation to the era when aggression was still loosely applied to the use and formation of language.

FURTHER ASSOCIATIONS TO THE *NON VIXIT* DREAM

Freud noticed a familiar cadence in his associations about Paneth:

As he had deserved well of science I built him a memorial; but as he was guilty of an evil wish I annihilated him.

The cadence and the content made Freud into Brutus saying,

As Caesar loved me, I weep for him; as he was fortunate I rejoice at it; as he was valiant, I honour him; but, as he was ambitious, I slew him.

In connection with this association Freud recalled that at the age of 14 he had played the part of Brutus in *Julius Caesar* to his nephew John's Julius Caesar during a visit John had made to Vienna. He then recalled the crucial infantile memory of this reconstruction. "Why are you hitting John," asked his father:

"My reply—I was not two years old at the time—was "I hit him 'cos he hit me." It must have been this scene from my childhood which diverted *Non vivit* into *Non vixit*, for in the language of later childhood the word for 'to hit' is *'wichsen'*" (*Standard Edition*, vol. V, p. 425).

As Freud was 2 years old at the time of Julius's death, we can take this remembered question and reply as an allusion to Julius's death and as representative of Freud's defense against wishing for it. The defense was that it was not Julius he had hit (hurt or "killed"), but John. Sigismund felt justified in hitting John, for by hitting John, not Julius, 2-year-old Freud deflected his aggression onto another target. *Non wichsen* is a verbal memory indicating the crossover of aggression from Julius to John: "I didn't kill Julius, I hit John." Thus, the cadence of language in Freud's mind as he thought of Paneth's death marked the return of early neuro-psychological rhythms of aggression as Freud associated to his dream, while "Julius" replaced "Caesar" in the allusion to the Brutus speech. Similarly, as Freud substituted John for Julius, he substituted Fleischl for Paneth. Freud knew that he was innocent of Paneth's death, and he knew that he tried to save Fleischl. The equation broke down, however, because Freud felt real guilt over Fleischl's death, and this guilt began to shade into a later, oedipal vicissitude of aggression against older and stronger rivals. In the present context, however, the oedipal theme was more comfortable to Freud than the theme of causing Julius-Fliess's death by magically and aggressively wishing it.

Of course the father is the one who is ultimately in charge of mediating all aggression, just as Brucke in the dream, with his steely blue eyes, has all the power to destroy character and defenses with his piercing certainty. In this sense Freud's association to Brucke is a later recapitulation of the 2-year-old's childhood scene:

It came to Brucke's ears that I sometimes reached the student's laboratory late. One morning he turned up punctually at the hour of opening and awaited my arrival. His words were brief and to the point. But it was not they that mattered. What overwhelmed me were the terrible blue eyes with which he looked at me and by which I was reduced to nothing—just as Paneth was in the dream, where, to my relief, the roles were reversed. No one who can remember the great man's eyes, which retained their striking beauty even in his old age, and who has ever seen him in anger, will find it difficult to picture the young sinner's emotions (*Standard Edition*, vol. V, p. 422).

This is an image of young Sigismund's fear that his father might annihilate him as he himself had annihilated Julius or as his father might have done. Thus, the father figure's piercing, objectifying eyes become the bedrock image of aggression, transforming the earlier bedrock theme of subjectifying eyes that create or destroy with the infant's effort. Comparing the way he had melted Paneth with his eyes to the way Brucke had once fixed him with his gaze, Freud refers to himself as "the young sinner," thus linking his experience with Brucke to his earlier, 2-year-old's experience with his father.

Based in late transitional denial, especially toward the end of their friendship, Freud's treatment of Fliess was modeled on his struggle to substitute John for Julius. For Freud never treated Fliess as a younger colleague. He paid him instead the kind of deference due a slightly older colleague. Treating Fliess's works and ideas as if they were far more valuable than they were, buttressing and bolstering Fliess's image, Freud defended himself against death wishes toward Fliess.

This reversal of sibling relationships is demonstrated in Freud's own reconstruction of his childhood relationship with John and Julius. In a letter to Fliess (#70), dated October 3, 1897, Freud says:

. . . I welcomed my one-year younger brother (who died within a few months) with ill-wishes and real infantile jealousy, and . . . his death left the germ of guilt in me. I have long known that my companion in crime between the ages of one and two was a nephew of mine who is a year older than I am and now lives in Manchester (Kris 1954, p. 219).

A good deal can be reconstructed from the incidental imagery of this passage. The key words are "ill" and "germ." Julius died of dysentery, and the knowledge of the cause of the death enjoys a kind of cryptoexistence within the image of Freud's omnipotent belief in having caused the event by wishing it. In the peculiar and irrational second sentence of this passage, Freud lessens his own culpability for "murdering" Julius in the second year of his life by implicating John in the proceedings. Thus Freud characteristically and repeatedly deployed sibling rivalry and oedipal conflict to defend himself against the murderous implications of his late infantile fixation to the destruction of Julius. The fixation left Freud with a source of relatively unbound aggression. Freud is known to have fainted when this aggression emerged suddenly as a death wish for an intimate friend. Usually, however, this fund of unbound aggression was rechannelled to produce intense feelings of sibling rivalry or oedipal rivalry. Freud's creativity offered the best mechanism for neutralizing this residual aggression.

Creatively, Freud used the aggression that was fixed on a death wish to Julius to structure his works. Many of his works are organized along the lines of taking a rival, letting the rival stand for a position that Freud is attacking, then asserting his own belief, and finally finding some compromise position that emphasizes the priority of his own truth. Lurking inside this structure, however, is the more primitive one in which the rival is totally demolished, is shown, in fact, not to have lived at all intellectually. What is more, Freud's concern for priority and his peculiar insistence that he lacks priority where it is in fact his, also point to the transitional relationship with Julius and Freud's subsequent defenses against it. Even beyond this, Freud's insistence on the priority of his truth over his father's dramatizes that his real birth was prior to the social artifact his father fabricated.

Julius's Death and Funeral

Freud's *Riding on a Horse* dream yields further information about the older boy's response to his brother's death. The major processes of this dream are the construction of an identity between Freud and Fliess and the substitution of Fliess for Julius in the creation of this identity. Dreamt shortly after the *Non vixit* dream and giving rise to many of the same associations, Freud's dream of riding on a high horse was presented originally to Fliess as an excuse for not visiting Fliess in the critical aftermath of an operation Fliess had undergone. Rather than visit Fliess, Freud untruthfully excused himself from the anticipated visit on the grounds that he was also under a doctor's care. Committed to his claim of illness, Freud tacitly refused to alter the chronology of the operation/boil episode in the 1899 manuscript of the dream book, even though Fliess pointed out to him in 1899 that his own operation preceded Freud's boil (Schur 1972). The posture of sympathetic identification was too heavily cathected to be altered in the light of facts. For in this dream Freud also meets Paneth, who again acts as a surrogate for Julius and Fliess. Again Freud tries to refer his relationship to Paneth to his earlier relationship with John, and even recalls the same episode of hitting John. Reviving Freud's late transitional defenses, this dream refers also to the death of Julius, and perhaps to his funeral and the feelings that developed in the aftermath of his death as well.

The Riding on a Horse *Dream*

I was riding on a grey horse, timidly and awkwardly to begin with, as though I were only reclining upon it. I met one of my colleagues, P., who was sitting high on a horse, dressed in a tweed suit, and who drew my attention to something (probably to my bad seat). I now began to find myself sitting more and more firmly and comfortably on my highly intelligent horse, and noticed that I was feeling quite at home up there. My saddle was a kind of bolster, which completely filled the space between its neck and crupper. In this way I rode straight in between two vans. After riding some distance up the street, I turned around and tried to dismount, first in front of a small open chapel that stood in the street frontage. Then I actually did dismount in front of another chapel that stood near it. My hotel was in the same street; I might have let the horse go to it on its own, but I preferred to lead it there. It was as though I should have felt ashamed to arrive at it on horseback. A hotel "boots" was standing in front of the hotel; he showed me a note of mine that had been found, and laughed at me over it. In the note was written, doubly underlined: "No food," and then another remark (indistinct) such as "No work," together with a vague idea that I was in a strange town in which I was doing no work (*Standard Edition*, vol. IV, pp. 229–230).

ASSOCIATIONS TO THE *RIDING ON A HORSE* DREAM

. . . for some days before I had been suffering from boils, which made every movement a torture; and finally a boil the size of an apple had risen at the base of my scrotum, which caused me the most unbearable pain with every step I took (*Standard Edition*, vol. IV, p. 230).

Freud's image of the boil as the size of an apple is provocative. Since the doubly underlined message in the dream says "No food," we may take this as a significant image/allusion. Freud has an exaggerated, pathological food source near his anus. He makes another allusion to food in his associations:

I was riding on a grey horse, whose color corresponded precisely to the *pepper-and-salt* color of the suit my colleague P. was wearing when I had last met him in the country. The cause of my boils had been ascribed to my eating *highly-spiced* food—an etiology that was at least preferable to the *sugar* [diabetes] which might also occur to one in connection with boils (*Standard Edition*, vol. IV, p. 231).

The pepper-and-salt color (grey) is a synesthesia (of color and taste), an overdetermined condensation indicating highly charged material. Paneth's suit refers to Julius's dysentery. Julius had intractable diarrhea—the doctor would naturally first ascribe the etiology to the wrong food, to food that was too highly spiced. His prescription, underlined twice, would be "No food!"

At the time of dreaming Freud wondered whether the boils indicated an illness that would kill him. As a matter of fact, the question of the etiology of spice or sugar (diabetes) occurs in some of Freud's other dreams. Conceivably there is a historical referent in this overdetermined reference to a sugar etiology. One imagines the parents asking the doctor, "If he can't have any food, what can he have?" The doctor would reply, "Just water, with sugar in it."

In his letters to Fliess, Freud ascribed the basis of his neurosis and of his travel phobia to an infantile feeling of a poverty of food. This he associated with greedy feelings brought on by the presence of Julius. If Julius died of the wrong kind of food, and if Julius was forbidden food, then the infant Sigismund would be thrown into conflict over his own food. He would be gratified that Julius could take no more of the sustenance he wanted all for himself. At the same time he would feel that the same sustenance and greedy wish for it could kill him as well.

There is another set of associations to this dream that lend themselves extremely well to reconstructing the family's reaction to the loss of Julius:

But the dream was not content with "suggesting away" my boil by obstinately insisting upon an idea that was inconsistent with it and so behaving like the hallucinatory delusion of the mother who had lost her child or the merchant whose losses had robbed him of his fortune (*Standard Edition*, vol. IV, p. 230).

Each member of the family lost what was dearest and most sustaining. First we see the reaction of Freud's mother and father to their loss of Julius. Second, Freud's associations to Paneth in this dream indicate infant Sigismund's feelings about Julius in relation to the mother they shared. Freud writes that Paneth had ridden the high horse over him by replacing him as the physician to a woman patient who was able to pay a high fee. Freud felt he had had priority, and that in spite of it he had been replaced in the affection and bounty of the woman patient. Freud used this feeling as a personal excuse to justify his failure to travel to see Fliess. He, Freud, had to work hard in order to make enough money to feed his family. "No work," "no food," Freud reiterated with justification. But what is essential here is that Freud is angry about being replaced by a younger sibling who deprives him of work and food and whom he himself would like to depose. As in the *Non vixit* dream, this impulse is defended against by the transference of anger from a younger to an older rival. In the aftermath of remembering the patient's loss Freud alludes to the 2-year-old *wichsen* episode of hitting the older boy, John, in connection with a memory of the last time he had seen his colleague Paneth. Apparently, Freud had hostile feelings toward Paneth before Paneth's death. He felt that Paneth had taken the bread out of his mouth. The next time Freud saw Paneth was at the latter's funeral. In Freud's unconscious, Paneth had committed Julius's crime and suffered Julius's death. Naturally enough, an underlying theme of memorials and funerals is connected to this dream by way of the *Non vixit* associations: after Julius died he must have been buried.

In the dream Freud is riding between two vans. They stop in front of a chapel. It must be the funeral chapel, and Freud is in the procession. Freud is sitting on something soft, which gives him comfort. It must be his mother's lap. Freud associates the horse with a woman, a woman about whom he is in competition for food and comfort with Paneth-Julius: "Thus the horse acquired the meaning of a woman patient" (*Standard Edition*, vol. IV, p. 231). He must be sitting on his mother's lap in the funeral procession for Julius. It is the establishment of a memorial for Julius. Freud's mother is depressed. She does not want to acknowledge that she has really lost a child. She holds Sigismund to her. But, given the complete comfort of mother again, Sigismund feels vulnerable. It could happen to him; he could go into a coffin and be buried in the earth. Therefore, Freud must make amends. He must give up the notion that he can make Julius appear and disappear. He must make the transition to anal orderliness. If he wants to eat, he must learn to work, to give up his illusions.

Freud makes one last punning association to this dream. The association evokes Freud's phobia of travel, his current reluctance to visit Fliess, and his consuming wish to spend one congress with Fliess in Rome:

. . . I recalled the meaning which references to Italy seem to have in the dreams of a woman patient who had never visited that lovely country: "*gen Italien* [to Italy]"—"*Genitalien* [genitals]"; and this was connected, too, with the house in which I had preceded my friend P. as physician, as well as with the situation of my boil (*Standard Edition*, vol. IV, p. 232).

The references to intercourse in the riding of the horse and the *Genitalien* association are the first hints of Freud's fantasy of Julius's ultimate fate. The female box is equated with a coffin, an eternal bed. In association to the *Count Thun* dream, a dream we shall analyze later, Freud mentions he was told that when he was 2 years old he offered to buy his father a new red bed to replace the one he had soiled. The 2-year-old is said to have offered to purchase the bed in N., a large town near Freiberg. For our reconstruction, the implication is that the 2-year-old recalled an earlier trip to N. Possibly, Julius's burial ceremony required the purchase of a coffin in N. The journey to another—'Italian'—locale in the end of the dream refers ultimately to Catholic symbolism associated with Julius's fate. The one-eyed doctor and the nurse must have also attended the funeral.

3

Reconstructing Anal Origins of Freud's Creativity

During his anal period (ages 2 to 3), Sigismund had to encompass the trauma of Julius's death as well as the normal neuropsychological dilemmas that face a child of that age. His creator's syndrome enlarged its scope as a large quota of energy was invested in bedrock, anal age fantasies. In this chapter, focal events in Freud's 2 to 3-year age period are presented in a context of considering how the creator's fixation affected and determined Freud's response to these events.

Sigismund equated the burial of Julius with Julius's return to the inside of their mother's body. There is evidence that the major organizer of Freud's unconscious mental life at this time was the bedrock fantasy that Julius had been digested, decayed and then reconstituted in the process of the mother's growing pregnancy, finally to be born again as a revenant child. This prototypical anal fantasy synthesized with primal scene imagery as Freud had experienced it before the age of 2. In this synthesis, his father's role was that of the irresistible intruder who enters the anal or oral orifice with his powerful, penetrating organ. In the context of Freud's anality, his father's organ was imaged as an irresistible aggressive force, responsible for the damage to Julius and for his disappearance into a cavity of the earth. Julius had been "boxed up" by his father, only to be brought forth later by his mother.

Notions of causality are present only randomly in this scenario. The vagueness of causality is relevant to an understanding of the nature of young Freud's creator's defense against a resolution of the age-appropriate anal conflicts because the age of 2 or 3 is the time when denotative relationships between words and concrete objects are worked out. This period produces intense aggression which is normally bound into words to delineate objects in reality, for the anal age is an age of sorting and organizing. In Freud's case, however, ego organization through sorting was unusually affected by the presence of the diffuse bedrock fantasy of Julius's fate. Indeed the traumatically induced bedrock fantasy about Julius's interment was to generate copious derivatives throughout Freud's life.

The particular shape of this fantasy was Freud's variant on the common creator's theme of the crucible which constantly molds new forms of life. As a result, during his anal period, rather than allocate the power to effect reality to his parents, Freud maintained a system of fluid identifications with aggressors. Like a rebellious child, he refused to concede authority. Unlike a rebellious child, he avoided investing any one figure with too much controlling aggression by parcelling the aggression out among several figures. Thus at this stage of his life, Freud the creator began to maintain an affinity to certain primary process modes, although not in a maladaptive way. Freud maintained his allegiance to his transitional beliefs in making and shaping reality by devoting himself to omnipotent thinking during the anal period. Refusing to accept his father as the main arbiter of reality, Freud continued to believe in his own omnipotent possibilities.

As mentioned, one mechanism young Freud used to maintain his own sense of omnipotence was the division of authority into alternative figures of aggression. His father, Emanuel, Philipp, the family physician (Doctor Pur), his nurse, his nurse's God, all became awesome figures of power, but manipulatable ones because they were so many. An alternative mechanism Freud relied on to maintain omnipotence was to invest an older child with mutable power. Unlike these semi-inviolable figures, John, Freud's older nephew, was seen as an available source of power. Young Sigismund felt more powerful around John. Moreover, John figured in a reaction formation in which Freud was no longer the destroyer of the weak, young Julius, but rather in need of defense himself against the powerful John; in addition Freud could fight alongside John against their common adversaries. With John, he felt omnipotent. This mechanism is similar to the transitional holding of Julius as an extension of himself Freud used during the preceding period of his life.

In later years these derivatives entered into the position Freud maintained with his friend Fliess in relation to the powerful Dr. Breuer. Not only Freud's relationships but his creativity and his writing were influenced by these derivatives. As we shall see, the course of Freud's adult creativity made it necessary for him to try to reconstruct these anal-period derived elements of his history.

Freud's 2 to 3-year-old creative defense shows up both in the content of his early theories of psychoanalysis and in the sense and the style of what he wrote to Fliess about his self-analysis. For instance, his theory that neurosis is caused by the seduction of a child by a father expresses this anal theme of the father being an omnipotent, damaging figure. In his attempts at reconstructing his own 2 to 3-year-old period, Freud is very diffuse in his thinking. One person stands for another, concepts are not delimited, time sequences flow in and out of logical order. Thus Freud's important reconstructive letters to Fliess revive the young creator at work on the facts of his life, but they do not accurately depict him. The young creator saw life, death, separation, all the inevitable events of life as both mutable and potentially susceptible to magical sequelae of his thought.

Some Reconstructions from Freud's Self-Analysis

Freud submerged himself in his self-analysis during the late summer of 1897, with the purpose of reconstructing the significant events of his anal period. In his August 15, 1897 letter to Fliess

(#67), Freud wrote: "The chief patient I am busy with is myself. My little hysteria, which was much intensified by work, has yielded one stage farther" (Kris 1954, p. 213). Then in letter #69 Freud announced that his belief in his theory of hysteria and in his understanding of neurosis in general had collapsed. Heretofore Freud had believed that the cause of neurosis was seduction by the father during childhood, that the cause of hysteria was seduction during infancy and that his own hysteria exhibited this etiology.

This inexact theory collapsed as he progressed into his self-analysis:

Let me tell you straight away the great secret which has been slowly dawning on me in recent months. I no longer believe in my neurotica. . . . Then there was the astonishing thing that in every case . . . [elision by editors of *Standard Edition*] blame was laid on perverse acts by the father, and realization of the unexpected frequency of hysteria, in every case of which the same thing applied, though it was hardly credible that perverted acts against children were so general. . . . So far was I influenced by these considerations that I was ready to abandon two things—the complete solution of neurosis and sure reliance of its etiology in infancy (Kris 1954, p. 215).

Central here is the nature of the anal fantasy Freud had at first condensed into his theory of the traumatic origins of neurosis and hysteria. Freud had maintained a strong belief that his father had seduced him during his infancy or early childhood. He conceded only gradually that in some cases the seduction was carried out by an older sibling or some other person. Apparently then, the traumatic theory of the origin of neurosis could not be given up easily. In his own case, indeed, he vacillated about his father's role. This can be attributed in part to Freud's conviction that the seduction theory held the key to the cure of neurosis and his belief that he could make his fortune by curing neurosis. The bedrock fantasy of the desirability of penetration by the father must have been the main cause of Freud's fixation on traumatic etiology for neurosis and hysteria. In the end of letter #69 Freud made an interesting image-allusion to support his contention that he had been relieved of the fantasy that cure of hysteria would bring him wealth, fame, and freedom from financial worry:

Now I can be quiet and modest again and go on worrying and saving, and one of the stories from my collection occurs to me: "Rebecca, you can take off your wedding-gown, you're not a bride any longer!" (Kris 1954, p. 218).

This is evidence of Freud's belief that young Sigismund imagined himself taking the passive feminine position in a sexual scene with his father. This in turn must have been connected with Freud's fantasy that he would achieve wealth and power through the auspices of what his father had given him in his infancy. If Freud did indeed associate Rebecca with Jacob's wife, then putting himself in the place of Jacob's dead wife was equivalent to the anal period wish to succumb completely to the prehistorical, and therefore godly, father's omnipotent power.

In the following letter (#70) to Fliess, Freud showed himself completely immersed in his self-analytical attempt to understand his infantile and childhood past. Treating Fliess as the recipient of his associations, Freud expressed a long, distorted reconstruction of his early childhood. His tasks in his reconstruction were to under-stand the major infantile events that had traumatized him and to discover the mechanisms that he had used as a young child to deal with infantile trauma.

Material in letter #70 helped him and helps us in this task. This is a two-part letter. The first part condenses and reconstructs Freud's early childhood relationships; the second, written the next day, contains a dream stimulated by the important dynamic ques-tions Freud was immersing himself in as he tried to overcome the lingering effects of his belief in seduction by his father. Letter #70 and the succeeding letter, #71, which continues to associate to the dream contained in letter #70, show Freud's 2 to 3-year-old dynamics in their relation to the figures of his nursemaid and the one-eyed doctor whose image pervaded Freud's dreamlife. Between the ages of 2 and 3 Freud had to come to grips with the trauma of Julius's death and burial, as well as the developmental conflicts inherent in the anal era of development.

There is no doubt that the one-eyed doctor was seen as an intruder capable of penetrating any orifice, as a powerful organ capable of creating new life with the potential to destroy old life in the process. This bedrock image, which follows and derives from the transitional images of the eye that builds or denies reality, became the nodal point of Freud's creativity as it derived from his anal period. For the one-eyed doctor was an image of complete, irresistible power.

Shifting the imaged instrument of power from his father to the doctor allowed young Sigismund to have a normal relationship with his father while maintaining a full but split-off belief in the myth of the magic organ. Indeed, in the fantasy life of Freud's anal period, the nurse and the doctor form a bedrock pair who are split off from Freud's normal development and who serve as a basic building block for the family romance themes that were to emerge with greater clarity later in Freud's development.

The Method of Reconstruction

It is fortuitous that Freud's letter #70 was written in two sections, corresponding to two days' thought. On the first day Freud attempted to reconstruct the important events in his childhood. On the second day he reported a dream that he had overnight and that contains strong images of his third year of life. Freud continued to associate to this dream in letter #71. There is a sequence of images and screen memories in letter #71 that corresponds to the chronology of events in Freud's third year. The analysis and reconstruction of these images and screen memories as they pertain to Freud's third year of life constitute the path to reconstructing this period. Freud attempted in letter #70 to dispel the notion that his father had seduced him:

. . . in my case my father played no active role, though I certainly projected on to him an analogy from myself; that my "primary originator" was an ugly, elderly but clever woman who told me a great deal about God and hell, and gave me a high opinion of my own capacities; that later (between the ages of two and two-and-one-half) libido toward *matrem* was aroused; the occasion must have been the journey with her from Leipzig to Vienna, during which we spent a night together and I must have had the opportunity of seeing her *nudam* . . . and that I welcomed my one-year younger brother (who died within a few months) with ill wishes and real infantile jealousy, and that his death left the germ of guilt in me. I have long known that my companion in crime between the age of one and two was a nephew of mine who is a year older than I am and now lives in Manchester. We seem occasionally to have treated my niece, who was a year younger, shockingly. My nephew and younger brother determined, not only the neurotic side of all my friendships, but also their depth. My anxiety over travel you have seen yourself in full bloom.

I still have not got to the scenes which lie at the bottom of all this. If they emerge, and I succeed in resolving my hysteria, I shall have to thank the memory of the old woman who provided me at such an early age with the means for loving and surviving. You see how the old liking breaks through again. I cannot give you any idea of the intellectual beauty of the work (Kris 1954, p. 219).

Freud is clearly immersed in a creative and emotional recapitulation of his early childhood experiences. That night he had a dream stimulated by his wish to recapture the past:

. . . last night's dream produced the following under the most remarkable disguises:

She was my instructress in sexual matters, and chided me for being clumsy and not being able to do anything . . . I saw the skull of a small animal which I thought of as a "pig" in the dream, though it was associated in the dream with your wish of two years ago that I might find a skull on the Lido to enlighten me as Goethe once did. But I did not find it. Thus it was "a little *Schafskopf*" [Sheep's head]. The whole dream was full of the most wounding references to my present uselessness as a therapist. Perhaps the origin of my tendency to believe in the incurability of hysteria should be sought here. Also she washed me in reddish water in which she had previously washed herself (not very difficult to interpret: I find nothing in my chain of memories, and so I take it for a genuine rediscovery); and she encouraged me to steal "Zehners" (ten-Kreuzer pieces) to give to her. A long chain of associations connects these first silver Zehners to the heap of paper ten-florin notes which I saw in the dream as Martha's housekeeping money. The dream can be summed up as "bad treatment." Just as the old woman got money from me for her bad treatment of me, so do I now get money for the bad treatment of my patients; a special role in it was played by Q, who conveyed through you a suggestion that I ought not to take money from her as the wife of a colleague . . . (Kris 1954, p. 220).

Freud's persona in the dream fluctuates from adult-doctor to that of a child with his nursemaid.

Freud presents many of his associations to this dream in the following letter (#71), which he sent to Fliess some 11 days after the dream. The dream and its associations launched Freud on an extensive investigation of his childhood.

The skull of the little animal is a reference to Julius, for Freud is exploring his early history. In the dream Freud cannot find the location of the skull, which means he cannot understand what happened to Julius. This detail is associated with Freud's inability to understand what is at the bottom of his hysteria. Significantly, Julius's disappearance is connected with Freud's hysteria and sense of impotence; one aspect of the dream deals with Freud's feeling useless as a therapist because he cannot handle women—he cannot penetrate to the heart of their difficulties.

The futile search is succeeded by the detail of being washed in the reddish water in which his nurse has already bathed. The detail is overdetermined and hard for Freud to fathom: although he knows the red water to be bloodied by menstruation or birth, he is uncertain of its origin. Thus, at the end of letter #70 he remarked that this detail was alien both to his knowledge and his experience. Reconstructing, Sigismund's alternative affiliation with the alien Christian couple leads him to feel inculcated with the sense of Julius's life and death in terms of the flesh and blood of the communion. Stealing life and feelings of greed are hardly differentiated in his experience of the Christian church imagery.

Thus, the first two visual images of the dream (the skull and the water) point to Julius's death and birth. Christian imagery—the little lamb's head—familiar to Freud through his having been taken to church, reminds one of baptism and of being washed in the blood of the lamb. The line of association takes on added significance when it is added to the fact that Freud's nursemaid was always linked in his mind with the Christian world. In this context, moreover, the little lamb's head, becoming also a pig's head, refers to something greedy and unkosher, brought into the house by the nurse. These trends, reinforced by the symbolism of coming out of the bloody water, point to imagery concerned with Julius's birth and Freud's fantasy of the nurse's role in it. It is not at all unlikely that the nurse would have played the role of midwife in Julius's birth and that Dr. Pur would have been the attending doctor.

Freud's conflict about receiving payment for bad treatment of a woman patient is a major theme in many of Freud's dreams. It derives from rivalry with a younger sibling for the gratification and supplies that a mother can provide only one of them. The theme of Freud's primitive guilt over Julius's death is present through its derivative in the day residue of the dream. It is also present in the dream episode where young Sigismund steals money from his mother.

Freud further associated to the dream in letter #71:

I asked my mother whether she remembered my nurse. "Of course," she said, "an elderly woman, very shrewd indeed. She was always taking you to church. When you came home you used to preach, and tell us all about how God conducted his affairs. At the time I was in bed when Anna was being born she [the nursemaid] turned out to be a thief, and all the shiny Kreuzers and Zehners and toys that had been given you were found among her things. Your brother Philipp went himself to fetch the policeman, and she got ten months." Now see how that confirms the conclusion from my dream interpretation. I have easily been able to explain the one possible mistake. I wrote to you that she got me to steal Zehners and give them to her. The dream really means that she stole them herself. For the dream-picture was a memory that I took money from a doctor's mother, *i.e.*, wrongfully. The real meaning is that the old woman stood for me, and that the doctor's mother was my mother (Kris 1954, p. 221).

In exonerating himself Freud denied his own infantile greed and the attendant death wish for Julius. The nurse is made to bear the brunt of the crime.

Here Freud added another element to the manifest content of the dream: that he had stolen Zehners from a doctor's mother.

Thus, Freud's next association in letter #71 is also connected with the dream. There, Freud says that he had also had a dream about the doctor the family had in Freiberg. This new dream, or dream fragment, Freud added to the material he had excavated in his attempt at reconstruction:

I also asked about the doctor we had in Freiberg, because I had a dream full of animosity about him. In analyzing the dream personage behind whom he was hidden I remembered a Professor von K., my history master, who did not seem to fit in, as I had no particular feelings about him and indeed got on with him quite well. My mother told me that the doctor of my infancy only had one eye, and among all my masters Professor K. was the only one with the same disability! (Kris 1954, p. 222)

The one-eyed doctor is such a comprehensive basal image theme in Freud's mental life that its presence can be seen to signal a major identity conflict. Most of Freud's dreams refer imagistically to this figure, and many of those that do not, refer to him associationally. Here animosity towards Doctor Pur implicates him in the events that surrounded Julius's life. It also adds evidence to the reconstruction that the nurse and the doctor constituted an alternative parental pair in Freud's dream life.

The Scar (Age 2 Years, 8 Months)

In reconstructing Freud's childhood, the next focal or organizing episode after Julius's death and the ceremonial travel to his burial place is the incident of 2-year-old Sigismund's fall from a stool while trying to reach into a 'store cupboard' to get something. The fall gashed his chin, and the one-eyed doctor was called to sew up the laceration. This incident was to center a screen-memory linking Julius's death with Anna's birth. Animosity was focused on the doctor's intrusion into young Sigismund's body occasioned by the fall and injury.

In his letter to Fliess, Freud mentioned neither the scar nor the deeply foreboding image of the doctor. These aspects of the memory of the doctor are revealed elsewhere:

I had a dream of someone who I knew in my dream was the doctor in my native town. His face was indistinct, but was confused with a picture of one of the masters of my secondary school, whom I still meet occasionally. When I woke up I could not discover what connection there was between these two men. I made some inquiries from my mother, however, about this doctor who dated back to the earliest years of my childhood, and learned that he only had one eye. The schoolmaster whose figure had covered that of the doctor in the dream, was also one-eyed. It was thirty-eight years since I had seen the doctor, and so far as I know I had never thought of him in my waking life, though a scar on my chin might have reminded me of his attentions (*Standard Edition*, vol. IV, p. 17).

In "Lecture XIII" of his *Introductory Lectures*, Freud describes the one-eyed doctor as proof that dreams retain the essence of infantile events:

. . . he was one-eyed, short, stout and with his head sunk deep into his shoulders (*Standard Edition*, vol. XV, p. 201).

This rendering of the doctor as the image of the male organ leaves little doubt that Freud's animosity contained a strong measure of fear that the doctor could intrude into his body. This anxiety and the image of the doctor as an aggressive intruder are highlighted in a dream of punishment.

The News from the Front *Dream*

Twenty years after the writing of *The Interpretation of Dreams*, Freud had a dream that sheds further light on the connection the 2½-year-old Freud made between his fall, the gash on the chin, the doctor's ministrations, his mother's new pregnancy, and Julius's death. The *News from the Front* dream, which was introduced into *The Interpretation of Dreams* in the 1919 Edition, was occasioned by Freud's concern for his son, who was then fighting in the first World War. At the time Freud lacked patients and so was experiencing serious financial difficulties. Freud's concern for his son revived earlier experiences with Julius. What's more, Freud's 18-month-old grandson was also on his mind, reviving his sense of his own infantile past and stimulating the interest he showed in repetition compulsion in *Beyond the Pleasure Principle.* In his conclusion to the dream's analysis, Freud stated that the dream concerned the envy of those who have grown old for those who are young. This theme is a latter day version of the infant Freud's envy of the still younger infant Julius. The 2-year-old Freud's past returns to the 61-year-old Freud in the full regalia of his early thematic imagery. Examination of the manifest content of the dream shows the similarity to Freud's *Zehner* dream of his nurse:

Indistinct beginning. I said to my wife that I had a piece of news for her, something quite special. She was alarmed and refused to listen. I assured her that on the contrary it was something that she would be very glad to hear, and began to tell her that our son's officers' mess had sent a sum of money (5000 Kronen?) . . . something about distinction . . . distribution. . . . Meanwhile I had gone with her into a small room, like a storeroom, to look for something. Suddenly I saw my son appear. He was not in uniform but in tight-fitting sports clothes (like a seal?), with a little cap. He climbed up onto a basket that was standing beside a cupboard, as though he wanted to put something on the cupboard. I called out to him: no reply. It seemed to me that his face or forehead was bandaged. He was adjusting something in his mouth, pushing something into it. And his hair was flecked with grey. I thought, "Could he be as exhausted as all that? And has he got false teeth?" Before I could call out again I woke up feeling no anxiety, but with my heart beating rapidly. My bedside clock showed it was two-thirty" (*Standard Edition*, vol. V, pp. 558–559).

ASSOCIATIONS TO THE
NEWS FROM THE FRONT DREAM

The last statement, indicating that it was two-thirty, a seemingly trivial detail, can be used to date Freud's belief that his age in the dream scene was 2½. Similarly the denial of evident anxiety can be attributed both to the dreamer's attempt to deny anxiety over his son's fate and young Freud's attempt to deny his anxiety as he climbs up to the storecupboard. Surely, this is a scene in which young Freud seeks to steal something from the mother, Kronen or Zehners. The dreamer, reverting to the self-centered state of the 2-year-old, wishes that his son would die, as Julius died, so that there would be more for him. "Distinction" refers to the son's wished death; "distribution" refers to the acquisition of his belongings after his death; and the "officers' mess" refers to the nature of the oral supplies the young Freud seeks from his mother. In this dream, as in the *Zehner* dream, the money refers to something Freud would share with his wife. Freud said he had just had a financially agreeable occurrence in his medical practice. Martha's household money in the earlier dream was equated with the supplies that young Freud could better get from his mother with the younger rival out of the way.

In his associations to the dream Freud discussed these matters and then turned to the portion of the dream in which the memory is located. He indicated that the change or locale in the dream showed the operation of threshold symbolism. The dreamer passed a threshold and entered into the imaged storecupboard of his past.

The locality in a store-closet and the cupboard from which he wanted to take something . . . these allusions reminded me unmistakably of an accident of my own which I had brought on myself when I was between two and three years old. I had climbed up on to a stool in the store-closet to get something nice that was lying on a cupboard or table. The stool had tipped over and its corner had struck me behind my lower jaw; I might easily, I reflected, have knocked out all my teeth. The recollection was accompanied by an admonitory thought: "that serves you right" (*Standard Edition*, vol. V, p. 560).

A seal moves from element to element. That Freud's son is dressed as a seal in the dream is an allusion to birth and to movement between locales as death and life, unconsciousness and consciousness. In the context of the present reconstruction, the little cap refers primarily to the "lucky caul" with which Freud was born.

The son gains more prominence as an alter-ego figure when Freud mentions his son's proficiency in mountain climbing. Freud took pride in his own mountaineering—almost his only physical proficiency. The memory of a fall his son took while skiing in the mountains leads Freud to his own memory of his fall from the cupboard. Thus the *News from the Front* dream condenses the image of a child being born with the image of young Freud trying to climb back into the womb to get his gratification and to destroy the coming baby. Freud's mother was visibly pregnant with Anna when Freud fell from the stool while scaling the cupboard.

Freud cited this as an example of a punishment dream. From this one may reconstruct that the fall was not accidental. At the age of 2½, justice is swift. In young Sigismund's mind the doctor arrived to mete out punishment. In the dream something is being pushed into the youngster's mouth. This element, beside representing the desired food, and beside alluding to the older Freud's mouth, which at the time of the dream was actively precancerous, is meaningful for this reconstruction. When the doctor was summoned, he must have pushed something into the boy's mouth, possibly to see if there was any bleeding on the inside of the mouth as well as from the chin. Perhaps Freud had seen the doctor force something into Julius's mouth when the latter was sick.

The 2-year-old Sigismund was trapped in the crucible of his own imagery. He desperately wanted to reenter his mother in order to recreate or redestroy the new image of Julius that was growing there. Julius had been put into a box by some powerful aggressor— either his father or Emanuel or Philipp—all imaged as the one-eyed doctor who was bigger than life. Freud wanted to usurp the role of the aggressor to create and destroy life through some magical means. For the efforts represented by his attempt to climb into the cupboard, young Sigismund received a punishing blow to his bodily integrity, imaged as protocastration and as the organ-doctor intruding into his mouth. After the fall young Sigismund must have feared that he, like Julius, had been infected by the doctor with the seeds of destruction.

In the weeks after letter #71, Freud continued to associate intensely in his self-analysis to the reconstructive *Zehner* dream. The storecupboard began to take on a metaphoric significance. The image of searching was itself a sign that Freud had not yet fully reconstructed the dynamics of this period. In letter #73, dated October 31, 1897, just two weeks after #71, Freud wrote:

My own analysis is still going on, and it remains my chief interest. Everything is still dark, including even the nature of the problems, but at the same time I have a reassuring feeling that one only has to put one's hand in one's own store-cupboard to be able to extract—in its own good time—what one needs (Kris 1954, p. 227).

Freud still groped in the dark of his mother's insides. At the same time he reexperienced the fearful malady that ended Julius's life. For Freud continued in letter #73 to associate first to his daughter Anna's stomach upset, and then to his own:

Little Anna, aged one-and-one-half, had to fast for a day at Aussee, because she had been sick in the morning, which was attributed to eating strawberries. During the night she called out a whole menu in her sleep: "Stwawbewwies, wild stwawbewwies, omblet, pudden!" I may perhaps already have told you this.
    Under the influence of the analysis, my heart-trouble is now often replaced by stomach-trouble (Kris 1954, pp. 227–228).

We know that Freud hunted wild strawberries and mushrooms together (Balmary 1982). One can easily imagine Freud's anxiety that the mushrooms were the one-eyed variety capable of ending an infant's life.

Crying at the Cupboard
(2 Years, 10 Months)

A month or two after the fall, another focal incident occured that involved, and was no doubt partly condensed with, the fall Freud sustained while searching in the storecupboard. The incident is described in letter #71 to Fliess and also in *The Psychopathology of Everyday Life*: this incident is a screen memory. An association to Freud's *Zehner* dream, the screen memory emerges just after Freud mentions the dream full of animosity to the one-eyed doctor. The incident that gave rise to the screen memory occurred just after the dismissal of Freud's nursemaid.

Then a scene occurred to me which for the last 29 years has been turning up from time to time in my conscious memory without my understanding it. I was crying my heart out, because my mother was nowhere to be found. My brother Philipp (who is 20 years older than I) opened a cupboard for me, and when I found that mother was not there either I cried still more, until she came through the door, looking slim and beautiful. What can that mean? Why should my brother open the cupboard for me when he knew that my mother was not inside it and that opening it therefore could not quieten me? Now I suddenly understand. I must have begged him to open the cupboard. When I could not find my mother, I feared she must have vanished, like my nurse not long before. I must have heard that the old woman had been locked, or rather "boxed" up, because my brother Philipp, who is now 63, was fond of such humorous expressions, and still is to the present day (Kris 1954, p. 222).

Freud's emphasis on ages is symptomatic and distorted in this recollection. According to Eissler (1976), Philipp was born in 1838, so Philipp was just 18 years old. It is Emanuel who would have been 63 at the time of writing, since Freud was then 41.

Since Freud refers to Emanuel's age, the memory probably alludes to Emanuel as well as to Philipp. Indeed Freud probably obscures a reference to Emanuel, whose wife gave birth to a little girl, Bertha, when Freud's mother was about to give birth to Anna. Thus it may have been Emanuel who unlocked the mystery of pregnancy to the little boy by telling him that the baby grows inside the mother. At the time of writing this letter to Fliess, Freud was still under the influence of the misconception that the storecupboard referred to a place where the nurse had been locked up when she had been sent to prison. It is not until the 1924 edition of *The Psychopathology of Everyday Life* that Freud shows that he understood that the imagery of this scene referred to his mother's pregnancy. Thus Freud had a powerful motive to obscure the information that his new sister had come out of his mother's insides.

The distortion of dates is very telling in reconstructing the meaning of the episode. Freud must have realized the discrepancy connected with ascribing the episode to Philipp, for he tried to push his own age farther up when he recounted this episode in *The Psychopathology of Everyday Life*. There he says that he was in his

43rd year when he remembered the incident. If Philipp was indeed 20 years older, then Philipp's age would be closer to 63 if Freud really had been in his 43rd year. A possible explanation for the distortion of ages is that by averaging Emanuel and Philipp's ages, and by so condensing their persons, Freud pushed his own age upward by two years. Freud wrote in *Psychopathology of Everyday Life* that this memory had been recurring to him for 29 years. That he was so positive about the number means that he had calculated it. If Freud is pushing his age forward by two years, then instead of being 12 at the time the memory first occurred to him he would have been 10. This is what one would expect, for the screen memory of his mother giving birth to a sibling who represented the return of Julius would certainly recur with the birth of Freud's brother Alexander when Freud was 10. Alexander was the first "true" revenant of Julius, since he was the first boy born after Julius's death.

Pursuing the thread of reconstruction, Freud's mother became pregnant just as Julius became deathly ill, for Julius died on April 15, 1858, and Anna was born on December 31, 1858. During the ensuing months Freud viewed his mother's swelling pregnancy, and feared and hoped that a revenant of Julius was growing there. If this were to be a return of Julius, then Freud would be free of his transitionally determined belief that he had caused Julius to disappear. Yet, the return of Julius would deprive Freud once again of the vital supplies he still longed to steal from his mother.

We must conclude on the basis of this combined evidence that the scene Freud remembered of himself standing in front of the cupboard crying is a screen memory for the episode of his mother's giving birth to Anna. As Freud wrote in his paper, "Screen Memories" (*Standard Edition*, vol. III, pp. 301–322), the hallmark of a screen memory is the presence of the self objectified in the memory. In this case Freud saw himself crying in front of the cupboard. Thus his mother's giving birth to Anna constituted another trauma to Freud. Not the least part of the trauma was the fact that his nursemaid disappeared at that time. Her disappearance was encapsulated in the single punning association given to Freud by his half-brother Philipp, that she had been "boxed up" for stealing. Thus, we see that Freud condensed the episode of his

mother's giving birth to Anna and the explanation for that which
Emanuel provided with the episode of the nurse's disappearance,
which was explained by Philipp. "She's boxed up" must have meant
to Freud that the nurse was put into a coffin as Julius had been put
into a coffin. If Monika Zajic was felt by the Freud family to have
stolen life, her punishment would be death. However, Monika was
still in her forties and she might indeed have become pregnant
(Balmary 1982).

It must have been at this time, moreover, that the anal child
first experienced the efficacy of words to focus a whole melange of
visual associations and trends of thought. Thus Freud would have
condensed the whole frightening episode under the simple phrase
"she's boxed up" to defend himself against the traumatic significance of events through working over the phrase. In *The Psychopathology of Everyday Life*, Freud's emphasis is on his brother's pun
of explanation for the mother's and the nurse's disappearance. For
the young Freud, verbal distortion (as much as the distortion of
dates) became a way of condensing and screening the emergence of
painful affects. The boxing-up pun shows verbal material taking
precedence over visual-plastic material in the formation of new
imagery. Thus, Freud was actually standing in front of his mother's
wardrobe when be began to cry for her, but a focal word connected
the incident to his earlier episode of falling from the storecupboard.

I saw myself standing in front of a cupboard ["Kasten"] demanding
something and screaming, while my half-brother, my senior by 20 years,
held it open. Then suddenly my mother, looking beautiful and slim, walked
into the room, as if she had come in from the street. These were the words
in which I described the scene, *of which I had a plastic picture* [author's
italics] . . . in my first translation of the picture I called it a "wardrobe"
(*Standard Edition*, vol. VI, pp. 49–50).

It can be assumed that it was a wardrobe but that it condensed
with the earlier memory in connection with Philipp's pun.

I learned a variety of details, among them that this clever but dishonest
person had carried out considerable thefts in the house during my
mother's confinement and had been taken to court on a charge preferred

by my half-brother. . . . The sudden disappearance of the nurse had not been a matter of indifference to me: the reason why I had turned in particular to this brother, and had asked him where she was, was probably because I had noticed that he played a part in her disappearance; and he had answered in the elusive and punning fashion that was characteristic of him: "She's 'boxed up' [*eingekastelt*]" (*Standard Edition*, vol. VI, p. 51).

In this recounting Freud added the detail that the nurse's thefts had occurred during the period of his mother's confinement. Thus, the screen memory concerned the wish to steal away the life of the new baby from the moment of its birth. The *Zehner* dream is a wishful variant of this screen memory. In the screen memory the mother had given birth and was restored completely to the young Sigismund. Somehow, the new baby had been disposed of. In the dream the stolen Zehners condensed with the imagery of giving birth and with the imagery of a dead baby. Freud was overwhelmed with his anal-age wish to magically destroy the new baby who had been growing inside of the *tomb* of his mother. As his nurse was his accomplice in the first crime of killing Julius, she was to be his accomplice in the new crime. But the nurse had now been boxed up herself. Young Sigismund feared that would be his fate too.

In his 1924 addendum to this section in *The Psychopathology of Everyday Life*, Freud comes to some approximations of these conclusions:

Anyone who is interested in the mental life of these years of childhood will find it easy to guess the deeper determinant of the demand made on the big brother. The child of not yet three had understood that the little sister who had recently arrived had grown inside his mother. He was very far from approving of this addition to the family, and was full of mistrust and anxiety that his mother's inside might conceal still more children. The wardrobe or cupboard was a symbol for him of his mother's inside. So he insisted on looking into this cupboard, and turned for this to his big brother, who (as is clear from other material) had taken his father's place as the child's rival. Besides the well-founded suspicion that this brother had had the lost nurse "boxed up," there was a further suspicion against him—namely that he had in some way introduced the recently born baby into the mother's inside (*Standard Edition*, vol. VI, p. 50).

"Boxed-up" and "store-cupboard" give anal and verbal bed-rock imagery to the anal child's identity. Precisely these word images solidified Sigismund's mental structure in identification-with-the-aggressor.

Ending of the Anal Phase

The birth of Anna stimulated young Sigismund to consolidate a more normal anal-age resolution of his aggressive strivings. At the same time, his exposure to the genitals of his new sister stimulated another advance and fixation in Freud's psychosexual drive development. His screen memory of the empty cupboard concealed more than just Freud's awareness that a new baby had grown inside his mother; it also screened his horror. Neither his mother nor the new baby had evidence of an external genital. We recall Freud's mention to Fliess in letter #70 that he had seen his mother naked when he was between the ages of two and three.

After Anna was born Freud developed a more satisfying sibling relationship with John. Anna's birth allayed fears connected with Julius's death, but evoked images of castration. The focus shifted from a relatively more intense preoedipal conflict to a less intense early-oedipal dynamic. This is evinced by the fact that Freud thought the fantasy of Philipp's having made his mother pregnant to be the most significant dynamic explanation of the screen memory of the episode of the wardrobe and his mother's reappearance. In letter #71, immediately after Freud recounted the same episode of screaming by the cupboard, he shifted to an overly generalized oedipal explanation of all these childhood difficulties.

It appears that just before he was 3 Freud began to experience an early onset of oedipal conflicts. Any exploration of the resolution of Freud's anal period, and the concomitant introduction to the oedipal period, should keep in mind that Freud maintained a strong belief in fantasies of anal omnipotence, which left the path open for regression from oedipal conflicts to preoedipal ones.

The castration imagery in his sister's lack of a penis evoked the image of the one-eyed doctor who had operated on him. Freud's response to the sister's penisless state was to produce strong, fetishistic imagery. Flowers and mushrooms became enduring, bedrock, fetishistic images for Freud. In addition to the fetishistic response, Freud developed an image of himself as both castrated and capable of giving birth. Young Sigismund had been stimulated to a strong wish of identification with his mother from early life. The episode of being recipient of the one-eyed doctor's attention had stimulated Freud's anal birth imagery. One response to his mother's pregnancy with Anna, which protected young Sigismund from his wish to destroy the growing baby, was the fantasy that he himself was going to give birth to a fecal-baby. If he could produce a well-formed fecal-baby, then he would not succumb to the disease of unformed fecal productions that had killed Julius. This passive repository of anal omnipotence remained one of the unconscious determinants of Freud's creative life.

Mushrooms were to become the image-container of this tendency. Mushrooms became an anal stage protosymbol of life and death, dangerous germs which could be passed along with the fecal column, causing death, or could remain within the body growing into a baby. In the transition to his phallic era Freud's mushrooms could be aesthetically cleansed and transformed into the fetish imagery of flowers. That this was in Freud's mind during the early stages of his self-analysis can be seen in this quote from Draft L. on May 2, 1897: "There was a girl last summer who was afraid to pick a flower or *even* a mushroom, because it was against the will of God; for He forbids the destruction of any germs of life" (Kris 1954, p. 98).

In his 1895 letters to Fliess about *Project for a Scientific Psychology* Freud used birth imagery to account for his production of the new psychology over such a sustained period of time as constitutive of a pseudocyesis. It is notable that the 1895 creativity corresponded to his wife's pregnancy with their daughter Anna. Thus his daughter was a revenant of Freud's wishful identification with his mother during her pregnancy with Freud's sister Anna.

On a day-to-day level, the birth of Freud's sister Anna allowed him to remain detached from the death wishes toward the revenant, and also to detach himself from his identification with his pregnant mother. The birth ushered in Freud's period of real sibling rivalry. Bertha and Anna, the two new siblings of John and Sigismund, prompted the two boys to form an alliance in which they were superior to the girls, who were so poorly endowed by nature. In their play, the boys took Pauline as an available target for the feelings they harbored about the new siblings. Anna and Bertha were objects of envy as well as derision.

The Screen Memory *(2 Years, 11 Months)*

Thus, younger girls were heir to the creative and destructive imagery that had been spent on Julius. A baby's helplessness became concentrated in the quality of being a girl, which to the young Freud's mind was equated with having no penis. As revenant then, sister Anna showed that Julius was not completely destroyed—only his genitals had been destroyed. Thus in the "Screen Memories" paper (*Standard Edition*, vol. III) about to be discussed, snatching the flowers away from Pauline, deflowering her, was equated with seeing the young girl as having no genitalia, and as therefore helpless against the stronger boys. It was precisely her helplessness, however, that gained her access to the nurse and mother figures of the screen memory.

It is significant that the screen memory arose in Freud's mind when he was 16 years old and visiting the Fluss family. There Emil, whom Freud treated as an older sibling, was Freud's age; Gisella was two years younger. The friends corresponded to John and Pauline-Anna. Freud's adolescent, idealizing, masturbatory wish to deflower Gisella, whose image is intermingled with that of her strong brother, corresponds in the screen memory with the young Freud's pairing up with John, his accomplice in crime, to snatch Pauline's flowers away. The screen memory follows:

I see a rectangular, rather steeply sloping piece of meadow-land, green and thickly grown; in the green there are a great number of yellow flowers— evidently common dandelions. At the top end of the meadow there is a cottage and in front of the cottage door two women are chatting busily, a peasant-woman with a handkerchief on her head and a children's nurse. Three children are playing in the grass. One of them is myself (between the age of two and three); the two others are my boy cousin, who is a year older than me, and his sister who is almost exactly the same age as I am. We are picking the yellow flowers and each of us is holding a bunch of flowers we have already picked. The little girl has the best bunch; and, as though by mutual agreement, we—the two boys—fall on her and snatch away her flowers. She runs up the meadow in tears, and as a consolation the peasant- woman gives her a big piece of black bread. Hardly have we seen this than we throw the flowers away, hurry to the cottage and ask to be given some bread too. And we are in fact given some; the peasant woman cuts the loaf with a long knife. In my memory the bread tastes quite delicious—and at that point the scene breaks off (*Standard Edition*, vol. III, p. 311).

Freud characteristically wrote in an associative way, so that commentary coming before and after a dream or memory referred to Freud's sense of meaning. After noting the intensity of the yellow flowers and the almost hallucinatory taste of the bread, Freud was reminded of a visual image from a burlesque exhibition he had seen in which portions of a lady's anatomy were built up in three dimensions. This is certainly a reference to the breasts; so that the deli- cious taste makes the bread a breast-milk image to which the younger girl had more immediate access. In fact this must be the reason for the intense envy. The building up of the woman's anatomy from nothing has another referent as well. The intense, blinding yellow screens out a perceived absence; for in this case deflowering refers to taking something away from the young girl. It must be her genitalia that is taken away. The imagery of the long knife is the signature of castration anxiety. In the context it may also represent a fear of female retaliation for the crime of deflowering, taking away the female genitalia. The black bread also makes a fecal-baby im- age—transformed in the female oven the image becomes a recom- pense for being deflowered.

Thus the screen memory is a window into Freud's daily life as it transpired shortly before his third birthday. The original scene covered by the screen can be calculated fairly accurately. John and Pauline left at some point in the springtime around Freud's third birthday. As the presence of the flowers made this a spring-like memory, the memory must be a flare of imagery designed to maintain the bond with John and Pauline against the loss of these sibling figures. Surely the children all played together and were watched during the long days as their mothers worked. They were watched by local nurses or peasant women, Monika Zajic having departed. The castration imagery is contained in the fetishistic bundle of flowers. The imagery serves to demarcate the end of the anal era of development. With the departure of his half-family, the window shut on Freud's early childhood. At the age of 3 Freud suddenly had no friends. Instead he was thrown into more prolonged contact with his parents as his immediate family prepared to move.

Departures, Separations, and Losses (Age 3)

The losses of John and the rest of Sigismund's half-family set the 3-year-old some hard emotional tasks. The young boy was challenged by the necessity of understanding that the separation from his half-family was different from the separation from Julius, and also different from his separation from his nurse. Still, though the losses were different in kind, they evoked the same pain of emptiness. Because the variety of losses challenged the young boy's capacity to bind them separately, it was necessary to produce some simple explanation for them all. Another emotional problem for the young boy was the difficulty in consolidating his sense of identity: Julius and John had been experienced as self-extensions; the loss of John exposed Sigismund to renewed feelings of weakness.

The explanation for the losses young Sigismund must have proposed to himself was that the Christians were responsible for them all. For, without words to express his sorrow, young Sigismund resorted to a form of repression in order to shore up his sense of identity. Thus, while the child consciously blamed Christianity for his losses, his conscious affirmation of Judaism covered a repressed wish to be a Christian. If his family had been a Christian family, they would not have had to endure separation and loss. Still, he set out with his parents to make a new Jewish life. With the aid of pressure from his family, the Christian world was made the simple antithesis of the Jewish one. All the losses, separations, and migrations were due to the Freuds' being Jews.

The Dream of My Son the Myops

In the aftermath of John's and Pauline's departure, Freud developed a set of feelings which can be reconstructed from the letters which mark the closing phase of the Freud-Fliess relationship and from a dream Freud called *My Son the Myops*. It became necessary at this time that Sigismund proceed through the world without his self-extension, John, and that he make an emotional life which would necessarily leave the Freiberg ties, associations, and losses in the past. The emotional work Sigismund did as his family departed from Freiberg was to have powerful ramifications in his future life.

We can reconstruct 3-year-old Sigismund's response to leaving Freiberg through analyzing Freud's associations to the *My Son the Myops* dream. These associations treat Fliess as an object of transference, recapitulating Freud's earlier relationship and separation from John and also his relationship with Julius, who entered into the repressed, infantile, alternative world of Freud's unconscious where the one-eyed doctor and the nursemaid reigned eternally. The repression of this world, until it finally became a buried city of the mind, was reinforced by the emigration of the Freud family.

A key element in Freud's transference to Fliess consisted of shared imagery, ambiguous enough to refer each to his own unconscious strivings while maintaining the illusion of shared identity. Fliess believed that bilaterality was directly and even proportionally related to bisexuality: the dominant side was masculine and the non-dominant, feminine. In this code, reference by Freud to a left-sided migraine headache with a corresponding difficulty in writing was a message to Fliess that meant Freud was bothered by a repression in the feminine side of his bisexual nature, determined by a "period" in Freud's feminine cycle. In renouncing Fliess, Freud would declare that he no longer needed to be in touch with the "weaker," irrational side of his own nature, the feminine side as it were, which was also identified with Julius, who had succumbed to the one-eyed doctor. But in giving up this part of Fliess, Freud would also have to give up his buddy, who like John helped Freud feel omnipotent.

A further effect of Freud's departure from his native place and of his perception of his Jewishness as being its cause, was a sharply repressed, compensatory wish that he had been born a Christian. An understanding of the fate of the imagery of the Christian world of associations which Sigismund repressed is necessary to understanding many of Freud's dreams and crucial to the understanding of the *My Son the Myops* dream. This dream provides insights into the psychic effects of the Freud family's diaspora on their first son. In the world of Freud's unconscious, Rome was to become a pictorial reference to an early past with which Freud's mature creativity would need to be in contact. In *Civilization and its Discontents* he wrote:

Now let us, by a flight of the imagination, suppose that Rome is not a human habitation but a psychical entity with a similarly long and copious past—an entity, that is to say, in which nothing that has come into existence will have passed away and all the earlier phases of development continue to exist alongside the latest one (*Standard Edition*, vol. XXI, p. 70).

Rome, as we will see, was to become the locale of Freud's oedipally determined family romance. It was to be the place where his nurse and the one-eyed doctor reigned eternally. Cathected as heavily as the repressed desire to be a Christian, the Easter-Passover season resurrected Julius's image and the Freud family's migration.

While the imaginatively cathected world of Rome was powerfully connected with Freud's "alternate" identity as creator, and while the Easter-Passover season was a strong reviver of the family's removal from Freiberg, in the *Myops* dream, as elsewhere, Freud's children were to become suitable vehicles for representing Freud's own childhood condition in his adult dreams. In the *Myops* dream, Freud's oldest son, Martin, stands for himself as he did in the previously discussed dream of *News From the Front.*

On page 269 I reported a short dream to the effect that Professor M. said: *"My son, the Myops . . ."*, and I explained that the dream was only an introductory one, preliminary to another in which I *did* play a part. Here is the missing main dream, which introduces an absurd and unintelligible verbal form which requires an explanation.

On account of certain events which had occurred in the city of Rome it had become necessary to remove the children to safety, and this was done. The scene was then in front of a gateway, double doors in the ancient style (the "Porta Romana" at Sienna, as I was aware during the dream itself). I was sitting on the edge of a fountain and was greatly depressed and almost in tears. A female figure—an attendant or nun—brought two boys and handed them over to their father, who was not myself. The elder of the two was clearly my eldest son; I did not see the other one's face. The woman who brought out the boy asked him to kiss her good-bye. She was noticeable for having a red nose. The boy refused to kiss her, but holding out his hand in farewell, said "Auf Geseres" to her, and then "Auf Ungeseres" to the two of us (or to one of us). I had a notion that this last phrase denoted a preference (Standard Edition, vol. V, pp. 441–442).

ASSOCIATIONS TO *MY SON THE MYOPS*

The final association, in a footnote, tied the dream firmly to the departure of Freud's half-family:

Incidentally, the situation in the dream of my removing my children to safety from the city of Rome was distorted by being related back to an analagous event that occurred in my own childhood: I was envying some relatives who, many years earlier, had had an opportunity of removing their children to another country (*Standard Edition*, vol. V, p. 444).

Thus we can see that Rome is a symbol of the original city that Freud connected with his infancy and early childhood.

The dream was constructed on a tangle of thoughts provoked by a play which I had seen called *Das neue Ghetto* (*The New Ghetto*). The Jewish problem, concern about the future of one's children, to whom one cannot give a country of their own, concern about educating them in such a way that they can move freely across frontiers—all of this was easily recognizable among the relevant dream thoughts (*Standard Edition*, vol. V, p. 442).

The thoughts originated in the migrations of Freud's own childhood.

The crux of Freud's feelings of split identity, as well as of his separation anxiety, is represented in the verbal dichotomy *Geseres–Ungeseres*. This is an example of Freud's concern with the antithetical meaning of primal words. The outstanding example of his treatment of primal words is his analysis of *heimlich–unheimlich* (homelike–unhomelike) in his essay, "The Uncanny" (or "The Unfamiliar") (*Standard Edition*, vol. XVII, pp. 219–252). The dichotomy contained in the words *Geseres–Ungeseres* is the nub of an associational network. The fact that Freud expressed himself in terms of an antithesis is an indication of the genetic origin of Freud's concern with Jewish–unJewish. The formulation of identity in antithetical terms allowed an immature mechanism of repression to exert itself against feelings of loss.

Freud wrote that *Geseres* was a Hebrew word referring to weeping and wailing. Freud then referred to the Jews' bewailing their lost homeland during the Babylonian captivity. Associating in Hebrew and replacing the German "*Auf Wiedersehen*" with the Hebrew "*Auf Ungeseres*", Freud thus identified himself as a Jew. The dynamic significance of the switch is that the young boy refused to say goodbye, either to his nurse or to the rest of his family: the family sense of being a Jew was meant to protect Freud from goodbyes.

Then *Geseres* alludes to oral supplies as well as to separation. The reference turns on the German for salted and unsalted: *gesalzen–ungesalzen*. Freud intimated that his sister-in-law, to whom he thought he would entrust his children if anything happened to him, preferred the aristocratic, unsalted variety of caviar. This was said ironically in light of Freud's fear of starvation.

The idea of entrusting his children to her reminded him of his children's nurse, who is depicted as a nun in the dream. Of course, Freud's nursemaid was Catholic, so that the personal childhood referent is to Freud's childhood nurse. In the dream the young boy refuses to say goodbye to his nurse, whose face is contorted with the crying of her own sorrow at the separation. Indeed Freud did refuse to say goodbye; he maintained revenants for every person he had ever lost. Here, we see his sister-in-law, who became part of the Freud household, had become a stand-in for Freud's beloved nurse.

The next association to *Geseres* continued the theme of Jewishness and separation. For, according to Freud, *Geseres* was an allusion to leavened (and unleavened) bread. In their flight from Egypt the Jews did not have time to put a rising agent in their bread. This harks back to the fear of oral deprivation, which was the reason (as the child understood it) for the Freud family leaving Leipzig. Thinking of Passover, Freud remembered a trip to Breslau he had undertaken the previous Easter with Fliess. The memory of that trip contains strong, allegorical allusions to Freud's early childhood:

. . . during the previous Easter, my Berlin friend and I had been walking through the streets of Breslau, a town in which we were strangers (*Standard Edition*, vol. V, p. 443).

But Freud was not a complete stranger to Breslau, for in letter #77 to Fliess on December 12, 1897, when he was making arrangements to meet Fliess the following spring in Breslau, Freud said:

Breslau plays a part in my childhood memories. At the age of three I passed through the station when we moved from Freiberg to Leipzig, and the gas jets, which were the first I had seen, reminded me of souls burning in hell. I know something of the context here. The anxiety about travel which I have had to overcome is also bound up with it (Kris 1954, p. 237).

The gaslights derived from the Christian hell of his nurse, and were thus a locale in his unconscious from which he was trying to extricate himself. Freud continued his allegorical story of the previous Easter, with an episode that expresses the same dynamics as those characterizing the two big boys picking on a smaller girl:

A little girl asked me the way to a particular street, and I was obliged to confess that I did not know; and I remarked to my friend: "It is to be hoped that when she grows up that little girl will show more discrimination in her choice of the people whom she gets to direct her" (*Standard Edition*, vol. V, p. 443).

Freud was strongly under the influence of unconscious determinants: the one-eyed doctor surfaces in the midst of his story:

Shortly afterwards, I caught sight of a door-plate bearing the words "Dr. Herodes. Consulting hours: . . ." "Let up hope," I remarked, "that our colleague does not happen to be a children's doctor." At this same time my friend had been telling me his views on the biological significance of *bilateral symmetry* and had begun a sentence with the words "If we had an eye in the middle of our foreheads like a Cyclops . . ." (*Standard Edition*, vol. V, p. 443).

The simultaneous appearance of the doctor's sign and the remark about the cyclops makes Dr. Herodes—whose name evokes the Jewish sect in Rome who opposed Jesus—into a murderer: Dr. Herodes is imaged as the terrible child killer who obtained the blood of Christians for Passover matzos.

The association to the one-eyed doctor led to a reference to the ever-threatening fate of Julius:

This led to the professor's remarks in the introductory dream, *My son the Myops* . . . and I now had been led to the principal source of *"Geseres."* Many years before, when this son of Professor M.'s, today an independent thinker, was still sitting at his school desk, he was attacked by a disease of the eyes which, the doctor declared, gave cause for anxiety. He explained that as long as it remained *on one side*, it was of no importance, but that if it passed over to the *other eye* it would be a serious matter. The affection cleared up completely in one eye; but shortly afterwards signs in fact appeared of the other one being affected. The boy's mother, terrified, at once sent for the doctor to the remote spot in the country where they were staying. The doctor however, now went over *to the other side.* "Why are you making such a 'Geseres?'" he shouted at the mother, "if *one* side has got well so will the other" (*Standard Edition*, vol. V, p. 443).

The story is restitutional. It is meant to undo (*Ungeseres*) the loss of Julius. If Julius, one side, had been lost, then the infant Freud, the other side, could also be lost. Freud is reassuring himself about his losses. He is a survivor. As a matter of fact, one side of the family, the side that moved to England, recovered, and so would the other side, the side that moved to Vienna.

Freud continued the restitutional theme with the hope that his children would not turn out to be short-sighted, one-sided thinkers. Freud was concerned about the reception of his dream book. In this context he takes *Ungeseres* as an example of the logic that lies behind the apparent absurdity of dreams. The absurdity is a defense against speaking a truth that may lead to the speaker's total social and professional isolation, and Freud was anxious that what he had to say about dreams would not be taken for absurdity. Though he spoke with authority, he wondered if an audience of peers would accept his statements. He demonstrated this aspect of the meaning of *Ungeseres* through an identification with Hamlet:

Dreams, then, are often most profound when they seem most crazy. In every epoch of history those who have had something to say but could not say it without peril have eagerly assumed a fool's cap. The audience at whom their forbidden speech was aimed tolerated it more easily if they could at the same time laugh and flatter themselves with the reflection that the unwelcome words were clearly nonsensical. The Prince in the play, who had to disguise himself as a madman, was behaving just as dreams do in reality; so that we can say of dreams what Hamlet said of himself, concealing the true circumstances under a cloak of wit and unintelligibility: "I am but made north-north-west: when the wind is southerly, I know a hawk from a handsaw!" (*Standard Edition*, vol. V, p. 444)

4

The Primal Scene: Revisited and Oedipally Revised

In his oedipal period Freud created an alternative world. That world of "collective alternates" (Greenacre 1971) allowed Freud to evade, in a way that is characteristic of creators, a full resolution of oedipal conflicts. Freud used the bisexual role-playing available to the oedipal child to expand the scope of his fantasy life to an unusual degree. Moreover, he avoided the necessity of giving up his oedipal fantasies by further extending the preoedipal splitting of his father image. The aggressive aspects of his father were assigned to Christian figures. He saw his own father as indulgent and ordinary. By assigning the aggressive aspects of the oedipal father to various fantasy figures, Freud evaded castration anxiety. This neutralized his father's image and allowed him to extend his fantasy world to an unusual degree, but at the cost of populating that world with avenging chimeras.

Freud's lack of oedipal closure was also determined by his transitional fixation to creation and destruction. Freud's greatest fear was a revival of the extinguishing forces of his primal period. The nature of his castration anxiety was determined by his earlier anxiety of losing consciousness and becoming entirely vulnerable as Julius had. The terrors of his primal period led Freud to welcome the opportunity to restructure his world in the oedipal period.

Thus, Freud characteristically favored oedipal explanations.

For example, in letter #71 to Fliess he turned away from the infantile scenes as he evoked Oedipus. In that letter the sequence of Freud's associations about important events in his childhood leads from the incident of crying in front of the cupboard, through Philipp's pun, to the general explanation of the role of oedipal conflicts in the mental life of mankind.

Only one idea of general value has occurred to me. I have found love of the mother and jealousy of the father in my own case too, and now believe it to be a general phenomenon of early childhood, even if it does not always occur so early as in children who have been made hysterics (Kris 1954, p. 223).

The various objects of aggression in Freud's preoedipal experience form a composite of a generalized father figure:

. . . the Greek myth seizes on a compulsion which everyone recognizes because he has felt traces of it in himself. Every member of the audience was once a budding Oedipus in phantasy, and this dream-fulfillment played out in reality causes everyone to recoil in horror, with the full measure of repression which separates his infantile from his present state (Kris 1954, pp. 223–224).

While the anal development verbalizes the primary identity and the sense of reality that emerge from the primal scene, the oedipal development transforms them. Freud used his positive and negative oedipal fantasies to recast and reconstruct his primal scene experiences. He revised and repressed his preoedipal conflicts in two stages, each of which corresponded to an event in his childhood. The first primal scene revision was triggered by the family's move from Freiberg to Leipzig when Sigismund was about 3 years and 10 months old, a revision that continued to include strong anal components. The second, more positive revision of the primal scene was triggered by the trip from Leipzig to Vienna when Freud had passed his fourth birthday. That second revision further revised the first primal scene revision.

Neuropsychological advances around the age of 4 produce a reorganization of mental process. The development of an oedipal fantasy at a bedrock level requires the onset of such mental advances as:

1. A new experience of anxiety grounded in prolonged anticipation
2. A newly elaborated, finely discriminating repression acting on verbal and affective derivatives of conflict-arousing impulses
3. A shift to a pre-eminence of pleasurable sensations in the phallic, as opposed to the oral and anal zones
4. A less sensation-oriented, more representational kind of thinking, which supports the natural formation of the capacity for metaphor and symbol
5. A capacity for continuous self-observation
6. A distinct ego-state of fantasizing

The last of these ego functions is of most interest. At age 4 the creator adopts a particular and characteristic relationship to the portion of his identity invested in the fantasy state, as opposed to the reality-involved ego states. As shown in *The Roots of Artifice* (Harris and Harris 1981), when the creator is in the fantasy state, an open channel is maintained to the forms of thinking that prevailed before the 4-year-old advances. We must assume from what we know about creators that their fantasy lives contain more sensation, more concrete experience, more directly revived memory from pre-oedipal eras, and more unbound sexual and aggressive themes available as animation of the fantasy life than is usual.

The Trip from Freiburg to Leipzig: Freud's First Oedipal Revision

Freud's progress in his own reconstruction is mirrored in the letters to Fliess that follow letter #71. The movement demonstrated in letters going on into the late fall of 1897 recreates the emotional experiences that Freud had at the time of his trip from Freiburg to Leipzig. The embarkation point for following Freud on the simultaneous journeys of his own analytic reconstruction and the progress of his childhood is Freud's letter #75 (Kris 1954).

Letter #75 is full of pregnancy and birth imagery. The content of the letter is connected with all the ideas about childhood sexuality that culminated in his *Three Essays on Sexuality*. A mention of the left-sided headache was Freud's signal to Fliess that he thought the ideas came out of his female nature during a period critical to his feminine production: this reinforced his identity as one who gives birth. In the context of investigating his childhood, the birth imagery recapitulated childhood fantasies.

It was November 12th, 1897; the sun was in the eastern quarter, and Mercury and Venus in conjunction—no, birth announcements do not begin like that anymore. It was on November 12th, a day under the influence of a left-sided migraine, on the afternoon of which Martin sat down to write a new poem[1] and on the evening of which Oli lost his second tooth,[2] when, after the terrible pangs of the last few weeks, a new piece of knowledge was born to me. Truth to tell, it was not entirely new; it had repeatedly shown and then withdrawn itself again; but this time it remained and saw the light of day (Kris 1954, pp. 229–230).

In order to follow Freud's imagery closely for its value to this reconstruction, two of the footnotes that Freud added to this birth announcement must be considered: (1) "I was not supposed to know this; his poetic tonsils seem to have been cut out." (2) "The first was extracted by his nurse on the evening of November 9th, otherwise it might perhaps have lasted to the 10th." In these footnotes Freud's jocularity is strongly marked by an oralized castration imagery. The mouth and throat imagery—the birthing of the poem, the aura of harmless castration as it can only be imagined by the preoedipal child—forecast Freud's theory of childhood sexuality. Freud went on to note how his self-analysis had led him to startling conclusions about the childhood development of sexuality:

. . . I wrote to you once during the summer that I was about to find the source of normal sexual repression (morality, shame, etc.), and then for a long time I did not find it. Before the holidays I mentioned that my most important patient was myself, and after my holiday trip my self-analysis, of which previously there had been no trace, began. A few weeks ago I mentioned that I wanted to get behind repression to the essential that lies behind it, and that is what I am writing to you about now. . . . Now, the zones which no longer produce a release of sexuality in normal and mature human beings must be the region of the anus and the mouth and throat. This is to be understood in two senses: first, that the appearance and idea of these zones no longer produce any exciting effect, and secondly, that the internal sensations arising from them no longer make any contribution to the libido like the sexual organ proper (Kris 1954, p. 231).

Later in the letter, as Freud wrote about the genesis of repression, he indicated what he thought about the development of his own neurosis:

And now for the neuroses. Experiences in childhood which merely affect the genital never produce neurosis in males (or masculine females) but only complusive masturbation and libido. But since as a rule experiences in childhood also affect the two other sexual zones, the possibility remains open for males also that libido awakened by deferred action may lead to repression and neurosis. In so far as a memory refers to an experience connected with the genitals, what it produces by deferred action will be libido. But in so far as it refers to the anus, mouth, etc., it will produce internal disgust; and the final result of this will be that a certain amount of libido will be unable to make its way through, as it normally would, to action or to translation into psychical terms, but will be obliged to proceed in a *regressive* direction (as happens in dreams). Libido and disgust would here seem to be associatively linked (Kris 1954, p. 233).

The argument tied Freud's fantasy of seduction by his father to his oral and anal zones. Then Freud came to a conclusion that began to separate him from Fliess's ideas:

. . . I have also given up the idea of explaining libido as the masculine factor and repression as the feminine one (Kris 1954, p. 234).

At the end of the letter Freud returned to his self-analysis.

My self-analysis is still interrupted. I have now seen why. I can only analyze myself with objectively acquired knowledge (as if I were a stranger); self-analysis is really impossible, otherwise there would be no illness. As I have come across some puzzles in my own case, it is bound to hold up the self-analysis (Kris 1954, pp. 234–235).

However, in letter #77, two weeks later, Freud appears to have applied his new knowledge of preoedipal sexuality to his own case. In this letter Freud was concerned with the actual event that triggered his fantasies about the nature of sexuality when he was a child. A new idea is mentioned:

. . . the idea which occurred to me during my euphoria withdrew again, I no longer liked it, and it must wait to be born again. . . . I have to wait until things move inside me and I experience them (Kris 1954, pp. 235–236).

In the letter Freud moved gradually toward bringing Fliess into the center of a childhood scene. The movement in the letter refers to themes that are familar to us from the analysis of the *My Son the Myops* dream. Freud was concerned that antisemitism would ruin his communion with Fliess in Breslau as it did the year before in Prague:

All this is only introductory to the subject of our meeting—in Breslau as Ida (Fliess' wife) suggested, if the train connections suit you. You know that what happened in Prague proved that I was right. When we decided on Prague last time, dreams played a big part. You did not want to come to Prague, and you know why, and at the same time I dreamt I was in Rome . . . Thus the dream had fulfilled my wish to meet you in Rome rather than in Prague (Kris 1954, p. 236).

Since the dream mentioned is treated in *The Interpretation of Dreams* we know that Freud connected Prague, Czechoslovokia with his childhood nurse. Freud wanted to enter the Rome of his unconscious, but he balked at telling Fliess everything:

Since I have started studying the unconscious I have become so interesting to myself. It is a pity that one always keeps one's mouth shut about the most intimate things.

Das beste, was Du wissen kannst,
Darfst Du den Buben doch nicht sagen.

Breslau plays a part in my childhood memories. At the age of three I passed through the station when we moved from Freiberg to Leipzig, and the gas jets, which were the first I had seen, reminded me of souls burning in hell. I know something of the context here. The anxiety about travel which I have had to overcome is also bound up with it. I am good for nothing to-day . . . (Kris 1954, p. 236).

The quote, "The best that you know you must not tell to boys," from Goethe's *Faust* was a favorite of Freud's. In the context he is reiterating that he knows something intimate and sexual from his past that he cannot divulge. The retraction at the end shows the child's fantasy of giving birth retreating from the consciousness of the man. Though the man knows the mysterious facts of life, the child only imagines.

The nature of these secrets must have been stirred up in the 3-year-and-10-month-old Sigismund's mind as he travelled away from his birthplace, never to see his beloved nurse again. During the night trip, he was in a compartment with his family: father, mother, Anna, and the unborn new sibling who was already visible in the mother's pregnant body. Young Sigismund dreamed of his nurse, boxed up, buried, pregnant—all images of the past merging with the present as the young boy had his own vision of pregnancy. Images of actual primal scenes involving his parents and fantasies of his participation must have recurred to him as he tried to go to sleep in intimate proximity to his father and pregnant mother.

The intimate secret of the little boy must have been that he imagined impregnation occuring through fellatio and birth through the anus. This construction allowed the boy to imagine himself as a recipient of the father's love and, by extension, to be so close to his mother that he produced the baby. According to Jones (1953), Rosa, Freud's next born sibling, was his favorite. This revised, more object-related primal scene held less terror for the boy than the underlying one where the one-eyed doctor and the Christian nurse coupled in a way which destroyed the infant who was embroiled in the middle of the hellish scene.

The Trip to Vienna (Age 4)

While the first move from Freiberg to Leipzig initiated Freud's passive revision of the primal scene, the second move from Leipzig to Vienna triggered the active revision of the scene. On that trip, Freud declared that his libido was aroused toward his mother after having seen her naked.

Soon after writing the description of passing through Breslau as a child, Freud wrote another letter to Fliess. Letter #79 was about masturbation. Thus, the sequence of childhood development continued to be recapitulated in the sequence of the Freud-Fliess letters. The present letter was confessional, both in the context of his adult life and his child life. There is an indication that Freud had been renouncing his active sexual life, for this letter appears to indicate that in this period, at least, Freud was masturbating. How else could he explore the childhood masturbation that was at the root of the Oedipus complex?

It has occurred to me that masturbation is the one great habit that is a "primary addiction," and that the other addictions, for alcohol, morphine, tobacco, etc., only enter into life as a substitute and replacement for it. Its part in hysteria is prodigious, and perhaps my great outstanding obstacle is, wholly or in part, to be found in it. The doubt of course arises whether such an addiction is curable, or whether analysis and therapy must stop short at this point and remain content with transforming a hysteria into a neurasthenia (Kris 1954, pp. 238–239).

Besides its physically addictive sensations, masturbation's other addictive quality is its creation of a fantasy state. In the oedipal period, the experience of parental embraces triggers intense oedipal fantasies that revise the primal scene in all its previous development. In a similar way castration imagery becomes a preeminent signal of intense anxiety, including within its scope all earlier forms of anxiety. In the bedrock, oedipal fantasy that organizes childhood masturbation, simple aggressive and libidinal themes include and reorganize all of the preceding, preoedipal, libidinal and aggressive developments while oedipal imagery includes and preempts earlier preoedipal images. Refusing to fully resolve his Oedipus complex, the child developing a creator's syndrome spends more time than usual enmeshed in the fantasy state that comprises the mental side of masturbation. Strongly gripped by the family romance aspect of the oedipal myth, Freud was fascinated with the Oedipus legend throughout his life.

Freud's Attachment to Oedipus

There is much about the Oedipus myth that gives insight into Freud's fantasy life. For example, he mentioned its power to affect his mood in a letter to Emil Fluss when he was only 17 years old:

I have a good deal of reading to do on my own account from the Greek and Latin classics, among them Sophocles' *Oedipus Rex*. You deprive yourself of much that is edifying if you can't read all these, but on the other hand, you retain that cheerfulness which is so comforting about your letters (E. Freud 1969, p. 423).

Freud's letter #71 to Fliess—in which the myth is interpreted as representing a general, early childhood condition of loving the mother and jealousy of the father—is interrupted by a parenthetical discovery that can be read as personally applicable to Freud:

I have found love of the mother and jealousy of the father in my case too, and now believe it to be a general phenomemon of early childhood . . . (similarly with the "romanticization of origins" in the case of paranoiacs ——heroes, founders of religion) (Kris 1954, p. 223).

This interpolation may be taken as a piece of self-knowledge. For Freud, his own mother and father were the equivalent of

Polybus and Periboea, Oedipus's stepparents, who, although they were a king and queen, were more in the manner of ordinary people, while Freud's one-eyed doctor and nurse reigned in the Thebes of Freud's alternative world as his Laius and Jocasta. Just as Oedipus was attacked as an infant and almost destroyed, so the infant Sigismund felt the one-eyed doctor had almost killed him. In Sigismund's imagination the one-eyed doctor resembled Laius in another detail, for Laius had consummated a child killing, sacrificing the boy Chrisippus as a surrogate for himself to insure the continuation of his own reign, while the one-eyed doctor was seen as Julius's murderer.

Hence, the Oedipus myth corresponds to the bedrock themes of Freud's oedipal period. The sphinx represents the essence of fantasy life. Given its power by the Muses, the sphinx was composited of raw sexual and aggressive drives of a bisexual character. The face and the breasts of a woman promise satisfaction; the lion's body and the tail of a serpent reveal the destructive force; the wings of the eagle show the power of the imagination. Oedipus mastered this bisexual composite creature by understanding its relationship to the life of man.

The bisexual composite creature represents the oedipal child's creative, alternative solution to a resolution of the oedipal complex. Among other things the sphinx represents the life of the imagination in the 4-year-old child. The sphinx's riddle focuses on the mysteries of man's life. Oedipus's ability to answer the riddle, "What being, with only one voice, has sometimes two feet, sometimes three, sometimes four, and is weakest when it has the most?" comes in part from Oedipus's mastery of his weakness of the feet. Laius had driven a nail through the feet of Oedipus when he was an infant. Oedipus means "swollen foot," and, in the symbolic language that Freud decoded, Oedipus means swollen penis, an erection. Of course this is the accompaniment of the state of fantasying, or dreaming. The child must first learn this connection in the 4-year-old stage of life when fantasy comes to be accompanied by erection. The castration theme is thus fully implicit in the riddle's defeat of ordinary expectations that when man has most (when he exhibits an erection) he is most powerful.

The themes of Oedipus's blindness and the equation of blind-ness with castration were permanently significant to Freud. Blind Tiresias, like the return of the repressed to Oedipus, is a harbinger of mortality and brings the one-eyed doctor theme back to Freud. There is no escape from fate. An understanding of the roots of fantasy can inform one's life experience but cannot permanently transform it. These were themes Freud was struggling with as he tried to fathom the roots of his Oedipus complex and of the family-romance fantasy that contained the Oedipus fantasy within it.

These themes can be brought to life by sampling some of the imagery which Freud presents in his paper, "The Uncanny." Freud's treatment of the familiar and the unfamiliar, the return of the repressed, the loss of distinction between what is fantasy and reality, all add to the sense that the themes in "The Uncanny" relate Freud's own oedipal conflicts. For example, Freud's long retelling of Hoffman's oedipal, Sand-Man story suggests that Freud felt bound to explicate a story that must have had uncanny overtones for him, reanimating his frightening primal parents (the nurse and the one-eyed doctor) and the parents of his oedipal period:

This fantastic tale opens with the childhood recollections of the student Nathaniel. In spite of his present happiness, he cannot banish the memories associated with the mysterious and terrifying death of his beloved father. On certain evenings his mother used to send the children to bed early, warning them that "the Sand-Man was coming"; and, sure enough, Nathaniel would not fail to hear the heavy tread of a visitor, with whom his father would then be occupied for the evening. When questioned about the Sand-Man, his mother, it is true, denied that such a person existed except as a figure of speech; but his nurse could give him more definite information: "He's a wicked man who comes when children won't go to bed, and throws handfuls of sand in their eyes so that they jump out of their heads all bleeding. Then he puts the eyes in a sack and carries them off to the half-moon to feed his children" (*Standard Edition*, vol. XVII, p. 227).

Freud associated the Sand-Man's sack of eyes with the self-blinding of Oedipus:

The self-blinding of the mythical criminal, Oedipus, was simply a mitigated form of the punishment of castration—the only punishment that was adequate for him by the *lex talionis*. We may try on rationalistic grounds to deny that fears about the eye are derived from the fear of castration, and may argue that it is very natural that so precious an organ as the eye should be guarded by a proportionate dread. Indeed, we might go further and say that the fear of castration itself contains no other significance and no deeper secret than a justifiable dread of this rational kind. But this view does not account adequately for the substitutive relation between the eye and the male organ which is seen to exist in dreams and myths and fantasies (*Standard Edition*, vol. XVII, p. 231).

Thus, in his oedipal period Freud remade the primal image of the penetrating one-eyed doctor into an image of pure castration threat.

By the time he wrote "The Uncanny," Freud had internalized and assimilated into his own mature image many of the aspects of the one-eyed doctor. The tightly bearded, compact Dr. Freud had unconsciously developed a one-eyed, penetrating squint. His one-eyed gaze and the single phallic flame of his cigar, nearly duplicated the fearsome mien of the one-eyed doctor of old. An interesting allusion to his reduplication enlivens "The Uncanny" itself. Freud, who was obsessed by the idea of a double as he got older, wrote in "The Uncanny" about the meaning of a double as a defense against death and castration and as a herald of death and castration. The anecdote shows his denial of the theme arising in what was for Freud a super-charged atmosphere, the inside of a railway compartment:

I was sitting alone in my wagon-lit compartment when a more than usually violent jolt of the train swung back the door of the adjoining washing-cabinet, and an elderly gentleman in a dressing gown and a travelling cap came in. I assumed that in leaving the washing-cabinet, which lay between the two compartments, he had taken the wrong direction and come into my compartment by mistake. Jumping up with the intention of putting him right, I at once realized to my dismay that the intruder was nothing but my own reflection in the looking-glass on the open door. I can still recollect that I thoroughly disliked his appearance. Instead, therefore, of being *frightened* by our "doubles," both Mach and I simply failed to recognize them as such. Is it not possible, though, that our dislike of them was a vestigial trace of the archaic reaction which feels the "double" to be something uncanny? (*Standard Edition*, vol. XVII, p. 248)

Symptoms of Oedipal Origin

Freud's oedipal conflicts produced symptoms and sublimations in his adult life. The symptoms included a phobia of travel, feelings of anxiety and claustrophobia, sexual inhibitions, and inhibitions of his creativity. These symptoms emerged out of a common ground in childhood, and they are related. The preoedipal roots of these symptoms anastomose under the ground. An examination of these neuroses will lead to a reconstruction of his oedipally revised primal scene.

The most obvious symptom was Freud's phobia of train travel. It invaded every aspect of his ambition. The evidence of Freud's letters, dreams, and papers is that the phobia originated in Freud's oedipal period and that the symptomatology converged central, conflictual material from Freud's preoedipal life. The phobia entered into Freud's work as a creator in important ways.

The train first appeared in Freud's life as a physical entity and became a bedrock symbol at two critical periods in Freud's childhood. The first was the actual trip away from the scene of his infancy and early childhood; the second was his trip to Vienna, the scene of his life for the next 22 years. The phallic train, with its sexually arousing motion and its close intimate compartments, stimulated Freud to excitement. Because events on the train aroused his castration anxiety as well as his sexual being, Freud hardly ever undertook a trip without expressing concern over the nature of his ticket. Did he have a whole ticket, a half ticket, or no ticket at all? Nor was he ever sure of his right to be a passenger in the sexual night scene he unconsciously associated with trains.

Freud's general phobia of travel included a specific claustrophobia within the train compartment. The elements in Freud's claustrophobia included (1) an anxiety about separation from loved ones, with an attendant feeling of oral deprivation; (2) a primal scene feeling of there being no space for him within the primal parent's physical embrace, attended by a fear of loss of consciousness or death; (3) an anxiety that he might relax into the motion of the train, which was accompanied by a fear of losing his bodily integrity; and (4) an anxiety that he would be so lost in ambitious fantasy on the train as to compromise his urethral control.

As is true of all symptoms, each level of conflict also contained intense, excited wishes for gratification. Throughout his life, Freud's gratificatory travel themes were connected with Rome. The themes of gratification at Rome all contained complete-multileveled, well sublimated and less sublimated wishes. Much of Freud's reading and his interest in art and archeology retained intense and clear connections to the theme of traveling to Rome. Freud wished to possess all the information that a realization of the meaning of a trip into his earliest past could provide for him. His frequent mention of "trains of thought" was connected concretely to his habit of associating creatively while traveling. Freud created many of his works on actual train rides. Many of his most complete dreams, the ones he reported in *The Interpretation of Dreams*, Freud had before, during, or immediately after train trips. Freud's ungratified wish to travel to Rome for a final congress with Fliess enters almost all of his letters to his friend. The wishes that Freud attached to Fliess in connection with travel pervaded every layer of Freud's mental life during the writing of *The Interpretation of Dreams*. Fliess was literally the travel companion in Freud's self-analysis.

The mechanism that inhibited Freud's ability to travel to congresses interrupted the associations to his self-analysis. Complaints about an inability to associate were in many of Freud's letters to Fliess. One wonders if the phobia was not a necessary restraint. If Freud had traveled too far, too fast, the journey would hardly be worth describing.

In letter #67, August 14, 1897, written at the beginning of his most intense self-analysis, Freud complained that his free association was not free enough:

The chief patient I am busy with is myself. My little hysteria, which was much intensified by work, has yielded one stage further. The rest still sticks. That is the first reason for my mood. This analysis is harder than any other. It is also the thing that paralyses the power of writing down and communicating what so far I have learned. But I believe it has got to be done and is a necessary stage in my work (Kris 1954, pp. 213–214).

The next letter, written four days later, shows the connection between Freud's little hysteria and his little travel phobia:

Martha is looking forward to the journey, though the daily reports of train accidents do not make the father and mother of a family look forward to travelling with any pleasure. You will laugh—and rightly—but I must confess to new anxieties which come and go but last for half a day at a time. Fear of a railway accident deserted me half an hour ago when it occurred to me that Wilhelm and Ida were also on their way. That ended the idiocy. This must remain strictly between us (Kris 1954, p. 214).

The important words in this passage are "confess" and "deserted." Freud feels guilty, and he is afraid he will be deserted. On the surface of things, he feels guilty about taking a trip away from his children for his pleasure. The pleasure theme—moving toward a possession of Rome and the things for which it stands—follows characteristically in Freud's next remark in the letter:

This time I hope to go rather more deeply into Italian art. I begin to see your point of view, which looks, not for what is of cultural-historical interest, but for absolute beauty clothed in forms and ideas and in fundamentally pleasing sensations of space and colour (Kris 1954, p. 214).

The fact is, Freud's train phobia was a symptomatic equivalent of the oedipally revised primal scene which pointed to an unresolved, oedipal fantasy that long ago replicated and reordered the whole structure of Freud's preoedipal life. Freud investigated the meaning of the sensation of inhibited movement in a dream. This was significant to Freud himself because of the claustrophobic feeling of paralysis and entrapment Freud felt on trains:

What is the meaning of the sensation of inhibited movement which appears so commonly in dreams and verges so closely upon anxiety? One tries to move forward but finds oneself glued to the spot, or one tries to reach something but is held up by a series of obstacles. A train is on the point of departure but one is unable to catch it (*Standard Edition*, vol. IV, pp. 335–336).

Freud's answer:

It is also easy to see, on my explanation of anxiety, why the sensation of an inhibition of will approximates so closely to anxiety and is so often linked with it in dreams. Anxiety is a libidinal impulse which has its origin in the unconscious and is inhibited by the preconscious. When, therefore, the sensation of inhibition is linked with anxiety in a dream, it must be a question of an act of volition which was at one time capable of generating libido—that is, it must be a question of sexual impulse (*Standard Edition*, vol. IV, pp. 337–338).

Freud later rescinded the part of this theory that equated anxiety with transformed libido; but the material does explain Freud's symptomatic experiences on trains. The claustrophobia begins with a sexual impulse. Missing a train means missing the train of excitement.

Dreams of Travel to Rome

On several occasions Freud referred to a series of travel dreams to Rome. These dreams point to the genetic roots of the travel fear.

. . . though the wish which had instigated the dream was a present-day one, it had received powerful reinforcement from memories that stretched far back into childhood. What I have in mind is a series of dreams which are based on a longing to visit Rome. For a long time to come, no doubt, I shall have to continue to satisfy that longing in my dreams: for at the season of the year when it is possible for me to travel, residence in Rome must be avoided for reasons of health (*Standard Edition*, vol. IV, pp. 193–194).

In this statement Freud showed his symptomatic inhibition, and suggested a reason for the inhibition: the possibility of contracting a disease during the time of year when he could visit Rome. Alluding to death in Rome, Freud alluded to Julius's death and to the fear that he also could become a casualty.

In subsequent editions of *The Interpretation of Dreams* Freud added a footnote at this point:

I discovered long since that it only needs a little courage to fulfill wishes which till then have been regarded as unattainable; and thereafter became a constant pilgrim to Rome.

In fact, when he had completed *The Interpretation of Dreams*, Freud had completed a symbolic journey. The accomplishment completely freed Freud of his Roman travel inhibition and his inhibition about exploring his infantile past.

One sees the longing for these accomplishments in a series of Rome travel dreams in *The Interpretation of Dreams*. In the first he sees Rome from a train but never sets foot in it. In the second someone shows him Rome half-shrouded in mist from a hilltop:

. . . the theme of "the promised land seen from afar" was obvious in it (*Standard Edition*, vol. IV, p. 194).

Freud detailed one of his Rome dreams:

In a third dream I had at last got to Rome, as the dream itself informed me; but I was disappointed to find that the scenery was far from being of an urban character. *There was a narrow stream of dark water; on one side of it were black cliffs, and on the other meadows with big white flowers. I noticed a Herr Zucker* (whom I knew slightly) *and determined to ask him the way to the city* (*Standard Edition*, vol. IV, p. 194).

ASSOCIATIONS TO THE DREAMS OF
TRAVEL TO ROME

This dream and its associations exhibit the structure of Freud's neurosis. *Zücker* means sugar, and it refers to diabetes. The implication of illness refers to the danger of going to Rome. In the *Riding on a Horse* dream, in the associations to which Freud expressed his fear of traveling to meet Fliess, Freud wondered whether eating sugar, which he associated with diabetes, or some highly spiced food, was the cause of the boils. Sugar alluded to Julius's death and especially to the feeling of infantile fault for having taken something sweet that he did not deserve and that belonged to the baby. On the occasion of the present dream Freud had wanted to meet Fliess to discuss constitutional defects.

Freud's most telling association to this dream was an anecdote about Karlsbad, the spa:

> An impecunious Jew had stowed himself away without a ticket in the fast train to *Karlsbad*. He was caught, and each time tickets were inspected he was taken out of the train and treated more and more severely. At one of the stations on his *via dolorosa* he met an acquaintance, who asked him where he was travelling to. "To Karlsbad," was his reply, "if my constitution can stand it" (*Standard Edition*, vol. IV, p. 195).

The deeper humor of the anecdote lies in the fact that the mineral waters taken at spas are cathartic. Thus, "if my constitution can stand it" refers to Julius's death from dysentery. The thought of entering a train without a ticket, which occurs in Freud's associations to train dreams with great regularity, refers to a young boy's image of castration anxiety. Here, the castration theme has expanded to a threat to the whole bodily integrity. This threat rebounds upon the child who repeatedly tries to steal pleasure while concealing his identity. The association refers also to the trip from Freiberg to Leipzig. One recalls that the Freuds were poor Jews, traveling to a foreign country. This is the reality that surrounded the young boy on his train trip as he fantasized intruding into a sexual scene between his parents. Perhaps he had no ticket. Perhaps his parents had not bought him one. Perhaps he did not have the right to travel.

Ticketlessness corresponds to the fantasy of stealing gratification. In the associations to the Rome dream the deeper Freud penetrated into his interior travel scene, the further he went without a ticket, the more severe his punishment would be. Freud's association to "the way to the city" was the phrase "all roads lead to Rome," which suggests that the wish to get to Rome was over-determined. Freud associated the flowers in the dreams with some water lilies he had recently found in Ravenna, which once super-ceded Rome as the capital of Italy. The water lilies were unexpectedly difficult to pick. Freud's memory of the lilies alludes to an unexpected difficulty in finding masturbatory pleasure. In the screen memory paper, taking flowers had referred to stealing sexual gratification; breaking off branches referred to masturbation. Indeed these Rome dream flowers reminded Freud of narcissi (self-pleasure).

All of the associations lead to Rome, to the wish for a complete and forbidden gratification. The dark cliffs, like the dark unyielding water, represent the danger to the constitution if one tries to penetrate as far as Rome. If one steals from Julius, or deflowers Anna-Pauline, or enters the primal scene, one will be in danger of losing everything, being deserted, losing consciousness, becoming castrated. Thus, the flowers on one side and the dark cliffs on the other are a very symbolic and allusive analogue to Freud's Rome conflict. The water represents a major current in Freud's emotional life, with gratification and danger lined up on either side.

The Rome travel dreams are the prototypes of Freud's neurosis:

A fourth dream, which occurred soon after the last one, took me to Rome once more. I saw a street-corner before me and was surprised to find so many posters in German stuck up there. I had written to my friend with prophetic foresight the day before to say that I thought Prague might not be an agreeable place for a German to walk about in. Thus, the dream expressed at the same time a wish to meet him in Rome instead of in a Bohemian town, and a desire, probably dating back to my student days, that the German language might be better tolerated in Prague. Incidentally, I must have understood Czech in my earliest childhood, for I was born in a small town in Moravia which has a Slav population. A Czech nursery rhyme, which I heard in my seventeenth year, printed itself on my memory so easily that I can repeat it to this day, though I have no notion of what it means. Thus, there was no lack of connections with my early childhood in these dreams either (*Standard Edition*, vol. IV, pp. 195–196).

The Revised Primal Scene
in Freud's Childhood

Freud revealed the structure of his own childhood dynamics in his paper analyzing a childhood recollection of Goethe's. This paper is one of several instances in his writing in which Freud brought a death wish for a younger sibling and the primal scene into juxtaposition.

Freud analyzed Goethe's 4-year-old's recollection of throwing all the toy crockery, then all of the real crockery out of the window to see what a fine shatter it made. Freud wrote that he had come to an understanding of the incident by way of analyzing a patient of his who had done the same thing. When this patient was 4 he had attacked his infant brother in the cradle:

Now this patient related that, at about the time of the attack on the baby he so much hated, he had thrown all the crockery he could lay hands on out of the window of their country house into the road—the very same thing Goethe relates of his childhood in *Dichtung und Wahrheit*! (*Standard Edition*, vol. XVII, p. 150)

Freud's own resistance to this data becomes apparent in his assessment of Goethe's relationships to his sibling:

Goethe's next youngest sister . . . was born . . . when he was fifteen months old. This slight difference in age almost excludes the possibility of her having been an object of jealousy. It is known that, when their passions awake, children never develop such violent reactions against the brothers and sisters they already find in existence, but direct their hostility against the newcomers (*Standard Edition*, vol. XVII, p. 151).

Although this conclusion is wrong, it points to the amount of passion Freud invested in the death wish toward the sibling he identified with his parents' love-making at a time when love-making had taken on an oedipal significance. For Freud attributed Goethe's death wish to the sibling who was born when Goethe was 3 years and 3 months and who died when Goethe was nearly 10. Goethe shed no tears over this death and appeared irritated that the death affected and moved his parents. Freud said he could go no farther with the Goethe case than his conclusion that the crockery smashing was a symbolic act of getting rid of the unwanted sibling.

Freud put his paper on Goethe away for a long time, unable to connect the child's passion with the death wish toward an unwanted sibling. Then—significantly, it was during a train trip—further connections occurred to Freud in association to another patient of his. Freud still did not quite link his memory of the primal scene with the act of conception; it is the parents' connection in love-making that results in the conception of the new sibling that the child wants to shatter:

Then, one day I had a patient who began his analysis with the following remarks, which I set down word for word: "I am the eldest of a family of eight or nine children. One of my earliest recollections is of my father sitting on the bed in his night-shirt, and telling me laughingly that I had a new brother. I was then three and three-quarters years old; that is the difference in age between me and my next younger brother. I know, too, that a short time after (or was it a year before?) I threw a lot of things, brushes—or was it only one brush?—shoes and other things, out of the window into the street. I have still an earlier recollection. When I was two years old, I spent a night with my parents in a hotel bedroom at Linz on the way to the Salzkammergut. I was so restless in the night and made such a noise that my father had to beat me" (*Standard Edition*, vol. XVII, p. 153).

Freud first connected the symbolic act of throwing the articles out of the window with throwing the sibling out of the window and then showed the intense anger of the child witnessing the primal scene. The primal scene and the hatred for the new sibling are juxtaposed, but Freud does not bring the two dynamics together:

Evidently the two-year-old child was so restless because he could not bear his parents being in bed together. On the journey it was no doubt impossible to avoid the child being a witness of this. The feelings which were aroused at that time in the jealous little boy left him with an embitterment against women which persisted and permanently interfered with the development of his capacity for love (*Standard Edition*, vol XVII, pp. 153–154).

Freud's own unresolved oedipal conflicts made it impossible for him to conclude that the primal scene as it is revised at the oedipal period includes the realization that in love-making the parents may conceive a new child. This child of the parents' love is anathema to the older child whose oedipal wishes have been stimulated and frustrated by the current experience of the primal scene.

Freud's failure to make this connection is explained by his feeling of identity with Goethe:

I have, however, already remarked elsewhere that if a man has been his mother's undisputed darling he retains throughout life the triumphant feeling, the confidence in success, which not seldom brings actual success along with it. And Goethe might well have given some such heading to his autobiography as: "My strength has its roots in my relation to my mother" (*Standard Edition*, vol. XVII, p. 156).

Thus, 4-year-old Sigismund's oedipal revision of the primal scene took the following form: penetrating the mother so as to kill the father; destroying preexisting concepti—the "proofs" of earlier parental encounters—and producing a new conceptus, the child of the boy's love for his mother. Thus, oedipal fantasy sexualized the transitional experience of creation and destruction during the original primal scene.

In letter #126, December 21, 1899, to Fliess, just over the threshold of his publication of *The Interpretation of Dreams*, Freud provided evidence for this reconstruction:

Another line of best wishes for Christmas—which used to be one of our congress-times. I am not without *one* happy prospect. You remember (among the absurd dreams) my dream which so daringly promised an end of E.'s treatment, and you can imagine how important this one continuing patient has become to me. Well, the dream now seems to be coming true. I say cautiously "seems" so, but I am pretty confident about it. Buried deep beneath all his phantasies we found a scene from his primal period (before twenty-two months) which meets all requirements and into which all the surviving puzzles flow. It is everything at the same time—sexual, innocent, natural, etc. I can hardly bring myself to believe it yet. It is as if Schliemann had dug up another Troy which had hitherto been believed to be mythical. Also the fellow is feeling shamelessly well. He has demonstrated the truth of my theories in my own person, for with a surprising turn . . . he provided me with the solution of my own railway phobia (which I had overlooked) (Kris 1954, pp. 305–306).

At this point there is a deletion in the letter. It picks up again with the following:

My phobia, if you please, was a poverty, or rather a hunger phobia, arising out of my infantile gluttony (Kris 1954, p. 306).

5

Three Oedipal Dreams

1898

While Freud's adult neurosis centered on the fixations that developed from oedipal revisions of the primal scene, the plasticity of Freud's imagination also originated in oedipal revisions of the scene.

By 1898 Freud had entered a new phase in his writing of the dream book. Intense self-analysis, the exploration of his own dreams, and the reconstruction of his early childhood provided Freud with the book's basic materials while anchoring dream interpretation in the context of his general psychology. What remained was for Freud to make explicit connections between psychological development and its representation in dreams.

Recognizing an analogy between symptom formation and dream formation, and believing that an understanding of symptom formation would lead him to the discovery of a treatment modality for neurosis that would make him rich and famous, in 1898 Freud set out to describe the relationship between the dynamic structure of dream formation and symptom formation in the context of his general psychology. The need for mastery evoked oedipal and ambitious currents that are evident in the dreams, correspondence and writings of the period. Organizing the ensemble of infantile and childhood dynamics he had unearthed earlier required Freud to reanimate the kind of fantasy formation that accompanied his oedipal period masturbation. These forces and the wish to become a professor are clearly present in letter #83, written to Fliess on February 9, 1898:

. . . I am exceedingly cheerful, entirely without cause, and have found my interest in life. I am deep in the dream book, writing fluently and smiling at all the matter for "headshaking" it contains in the way of indiscretions and audacities. . . . Self-analysis has been dropped in favor of the dream book. The hysterical cases are doing rather badly . . . I shall not finish any this year either: next year I shall have no patients to work on. . . .

There is a rumor that we are to be invested with the title of Professor at the Emperor's jubilee on December 2nd. I do not believe it, but I had a fascinating dream on the subject; unfortunately it is unpublishable, because its background, its deeper meaning, shuttles to and fro between my nurse (my mother) and my wife. . . . Well, the best that you know, etc. (Kris 1954, p. 245).

Freud's oedipal dream of ambition must have pointed back to his early past, making his nurse, the mother figure in his family romance, into a sexual object, for, as we shall see, during the period of his putting the dream book together Freud looked back into his past to make his early family history comprehensible to himself and to his proposed audience.

During this period of his creative cycle, Freud's relationship to Fliess changed. His inspiration complete, Freud no longer found it necessary to hold Fliess as an alter ego, a Julius-John figure. If Fliess were to be shown manuscript, he must be both as appreciative as an ideal audience and as critical as a demanding one. Thus in 1898 Fliess became more of a superego figure for Freud, representing to him the ego-ideal and moral qualities of a generalized father figure. This change in Fliess's role became apparent as Freud renounced the bisexuality-bilateralism that was the code for their fusion of identity and purpose. Now, more logical links were essential.

In the process of revising his manuscript, Freud became more of a critic himself. He learned to read his dreams as literature. From the reading of dreams as literature, it must have been a short step to the reading of literature as dreams. In 1898 Freud began analyzing novels as if they were themselves dreams that could be analyzed according to the same principles he used in understanding the meaning of dreams. As a result his day-residues and associations were often literary. Like an oedipal child lost in fantasy, Freud immersed himself in his reading in an unusually complete way. Continually negotiating the boundary between oedipal fantasy and scientific description, Freud became preoccupied with the telling of stories. He discovered that stories, like dreams and symptoms, had a manifest content screening underlying, latent connections with real experience. It remained for him to establish that oedipal fantasies contained latent connections with earlier dynamics and experience.

These creative oedipal trends are apparent in Freud's 1898 letters to Fliess. During this period Fliess introduced Freud to the novelist Conrad Ferdinand Meyer. Reading Meyer became an enjoyable pastime for Freud. He did his first literary analysis on *Die Richterin* (*The Female Judge*) by Meyer. Freud wrote about this in his June 20, 1898 letter #91 to Fliess:

There is no doubt that this is a defense against the writer's memory of an affair with his sister. The only remarkable thing is that this happens exactly as it does in neurosis. All neurotics create a so-called family romance (which becomes conscious in paranoia); on the one hand it serves the need for self-aggrandizement and on the other as a defense against incest (Kris 1954, p. 256).

Freud went on to write that overt or disguised literary tales of incest arise out of fantasies the oedipal child directed toward his mother. These the child—and later the adult writer—transforms into narratives of family romance. The agent of transformation is a story of incest or seduction told to the child, often by a female servant. Thus:

In all analyses one comes upon the same story twice; the first time as a phantasy relating to the mother, and the second time as a real memory of the servant (Kris 1954, p. 256).

In analyzing *Die Richterin* Freud generalized about repetition. The oedipally derived story corresponds to an underlying experience or fantasy of experience from a genetically earlier phase. Thus like dreams, *Die Richterin* and all such oedipal tales and fantasies possess both manifest and latent contents. Similarly, the oedipal child's fantasy of incest as it accompanies masturbation evokes and revises earlier primal scene experiences.

At the end of the letter Freud's difficulty in linking his psychology with his dreams is apparent:

The psychology is going curiously; it is nearly finished, was written as if in a dream, and certainly is not in a form fit for publication—or, as the style shows, intended for it. I feel very hesitant about it. All its themes come from the work on the neurosis, not from that on dreams. I shall not finish any more before the holidays (Kris 1954, p. 256).

Thus Freud set a very formidable task for himself. He had to understand enough about his own neurosis to be able to link his dreams with his neurosis and hence with his theoretical psychology. In order to do this he needed to understand more about his family romance, his incestuous feelings and fantasies, the underlying primal scene, and the anal and urethral material that related to his oedipal period.

In his next letter to Fliess (#92, July 7, 1898), Freud included another chapter of his dream book for Fliess's perusal. The letter shows that Freud was still concerned with the manner in which oedipal fantasies revise the past, especially in Conrad Meyer's literary work. His preoccupation with oedipal revision is indicative of the area in which Freud had to make further connections in order to understand psychological theory sufficiently to finish and revise the dream book:

Here it is. I found it very difficult to make up my mind to let it out of my hands. Personal intimacy would have been an insufficient justification for letting you have it, but our intellectual honesty to each other required it. It was all written by the unconscious, on the well-known principle of Itzig, the Sunday horseman. "Itzig, where are you going?" "Don't ask me, ask the horse!" At the beginning of a paragraph I never knew where I should end up. It was not written to be read, of course—any attempt at style was abandoned after the first two pages. In spite of all that I of course believe in the results. I have not the slightest idea yet what form the contents will finally take (Kris 1954, pp. 257-258).

Although this portion of the creative work resembled fantasy formation in its open-endedness, it was meant to produce convincing statements about the experience of mental life. Notice that Freud was ambivalent about submitting his manuscript and himself to Fliess's judgment.

The letter goes on to show Freud's interest in revision of the past:

Our author's [Meyer's] best novel and that furthest removed from infantile scenes, seems to be *Die Hochzeit des Monchs* (*The Monk's Wedding*), which illustrates magnificently how in the process of phantasy formation in later years the imagination seizes on a new experience and projects it into the past, so that the new figures are a continuation of the old and provide patterns for them (Kris 1954, p. 258).

The Positive Oedipal Revision of the Primal Scene

Freud ended his letter to Fliess on July 7, 1898 with the following conclusion about the novel by Meyer:

"The monk is a *frate*, a brother. It is as if he constructed a phantasy before his wedding, meaning: A brother like me should not marry, or my infantile love affair will be revenged on my wife" (Kris, 1954, pp. 258-259).

Thus on the night of July 18, 1898, Freud was still concerned with the theme of revision of the past through a projection of fantasy onto personal, historical material of dynamic importance, for Freud's *Hollthurn* dream of July 18 originates in a fantasy of wreaking revenge on a couple Freud imagined copulating in the train compartment they were forced to share for the night. In his dream transformation of the fantasy, the couple is turned into a brother and sister. Because the incestuous basis of this fantasy, like that in the Meyer novel, concerns Freud's relationship with sibling figures as well as with his parents, deductions based on Freud's analysis of the dream will contribute much to a reconstruction of family dynamics of positive oedipal revision of the primal scene. While the *Hollthurn* dream itself is described in *The Interpretation of Dreams*, Freud's concluding analysis of the *Hollthurn* is found in *The Psychopathology of Everyday Life*:

Anyone who reads through the dream analyses on p. 266 [*Standard Edition*, 455 ff.] will in part find undisguisedly, and will in part be able to guess from hints, that I have broken off at thoughts which contained an unfriendly criticism of my father. In the continuation of this train of thoughts and memories there in fact lies an annoying story in which books play a part, and a business friend of my father's who bears the name of *Marburg*— the same name that woke me when it was called out at Marburg station on the *Südbahn*. In the analysis I tried to suppress this Herr Marburg from myself and from my readers: he took his revenge by intruding where he did not belong . . . (*Standard Edition*, vol. VI, p. 219).

It should come as no surprise to the reader who is aware of Freud's revealing imagery that the dream makes the primal scene imagined into an oedipal scene of intrusion and revenge. An analysis of the *Hollthurn* dream shows Freud reviving his 4-year-old oedipal revision of the primal scene, for the dream refers to a masturbatory fantasy disguised by a family romance theme, blocked by claustrophobic anxiety, and transformed by an ego state that harks back to the unreality that surrounded the experience of the original primal scene. The *Hollthurn* dream, moreover, shows Freud revising his sense of identity as a mature creator. It recapitulates, in dream form, the process of identity change and revision that began with the oedipal revision of the primal scene. The first part of the manifest form shows a regressive sequence of scenes that are based on experiences from the earlier parts of Freud's life. In these scenes the dynamics become increasingly raw and primitive. The second portion of the dream shows a progressive movement that returns the dreamer to his present moment. At the end of the dream Freud reassures himself that he is becoming a successful writer. The regression and progression manifested in the dream is determined by an oedipal revision of a primal scene fantasy ar i exists effectively as the prototype for the creative process.

The Hollthurn *Dream*

I was travelling along the *Südbahn* railway line during the night of July 18th-19th, and in my sleep I heard: *"Hollthurn, ten minutes" being called out. I at once thought of Holothurians [sea-slugs] —of a natural history museum—that this was the spot at which valiant men had fought in vain against the superior power of the ruler of their country—yes, the Counter Revolution in Austria—it was as though it were a place in Styria or the Tyrol. I then saw indistinctly a small museum, in which the relics or belongings of these men were preserved. I should have liked to get out, but hesitated to do so. There were women with fruit on the platform. They were crouching on the ground and holding up their baskets invitingly. I hesitated because I was not sure there was time, but we were still not moving. I was suddenly in another compartment, in which the upholstery and seats were so narrow that one's back pressed directly against the back of the carriage. I was surprised by this, but I reflected that* I MIGHT HAVE CHANGED CARRIAGES WHILE I WAS IN A SLEEPING STATE. *There were several people, including an English brother and sister; a row of books were distinctly visible on a shelf on the wall. I saw "The Wealth of Nations" and "Matter and Motion" (by Clerk-Maxwell), a thick volume and bound in brown cloth. The man asked his sister about a book by Schiller, whether she had forgotten it. It seemed as though the books were sometimes mine and sometimes theirs. I felt inclined at that point to intervene in the conversation in a confirmatory or substantiating sense. . . .* I woke up perspiring all over, because all the windows were shut. The train was drawn up at Marburg (in Styria).

While I was writing the dream down a new piece of it occurred to me, which my memory had tried to pass over. *I said* [in English] *to the brother and sister, referring to a particular work: "It is from. . . ," but corrected myself: "It is by . . ." "Yes," the man commented to his sister, "he said that right"* (Standard Edition, vol. V, p. 455).

ASSOCIATIONS TO THE *HOLLTHURN* DREAM

In its manifest content the dream is composed of two scenes, both transformations of the railway travel that Freud was undergoing as he dreamed. In the first scene the dreamer sees a museum from the train window and on the platform women offer—metaphorically—their sexual fruits. In the second scene Freud changes compartments. Here,

. . . the second scene of the dream ended in a somewhat extravagant fantasy that my two elderly travelling companions had treated me in such a stand-offish way because my arrival had prevented the affectionate exchanges which they had planned for the night. This fantasy went back, however, to a scene of early childhood in which the child, probably driven by sexual curiosity, had forced his way into his parent's bedroom and been turned out of it by his father's orders (*Standard Edition*, vol. V, pp. 458–459).

Thus a revived primal scene fantasy, which Freud must have had as he was attempting to fall asleep in a hot, stuffy compartment stimulated the dream. Most likely, the scene Freud consciously refers to here is one in which he went as a latency-age child into his parents' bedroom to use the chamber pot to urinate, for that intrusion was germane to two oedipal reconstruction dreams that Freud had during this period.

Because the dream itself begins as a hypnagogic illusion, gradually merges into a sleeping dream, and then gradually turns into a hypnopompic illusion as Freud wakes, we read this dream as an incomplete transformation of the actual situation of riding in a train. Throughout Freud was vaguely aware of the couple's conversation as he was attempting to fall asleep; he was stimulated by snatches of that conversation and by the guard's calling out the name of the station. Significant here is that in the dream he transformed the couple into a brother and sister. The associations to the dream, and the reference to an English brother and sister in the dream, leave little doubt that the screening couple is Emanuel and his wife—one of Freud's family romance couples. At one time Freud had believed that this pair might be his parents. There is auxiliary but strong confirming evidence for this view in *The Psychopathology of Everyday Life* in material that follows a reference to the *Hollthurn* dream. There, discussing the substitution of Hannibal's brother's name for that of the father, Freud remarked,

I could have gone on to tell how my relationship with my father was changed by a visit to England, which resulted in my getting to know my half-brother, the child of my father's first marriage, who lived there. My brother's eldest son is the same age as I am. Thus the relations between our ages would have been no hindrance to my fantasies of how different things would have been if I had been born the son not of my father but of my brother. These suppressed fantasies falsified the text of my book at the place where I broke off the analysis [of his identification with Hannibal] by forcing me to put the brother's name for the father's (*Standard Edition*, vol. VI, pp. 219–220).

This theme of falsification, following the *Hollthurn* dream, must derive from it. The theme of screening, or substituting, transformation has an inherent significance in the *Hollthurn* dream. Freud's claustrophobia led him into a complete transformation of self during the course of the dream—for he wrote that his dream persona was identified with a patient of his whose dynamic history illustrated Freud's own dynamic history. The experience of changing carriages while in a sleeping state alludes to the whole process and history of Freud's sense of primal scene transformation. In other words, the *Hollthurn* dream transforms the claustrophobic compartment into Freud's original primal scene revisory experience.

How did I suddenly come to be in another compartment? I had no recollection of having changed. There could be only one explanation: *I must have left the carriage while I was in a sleeping state*—a rare event, of which however, examples are to be found in the experience of a neuropathologist. We know of people who have gone upon railway journeys in a twilight state without betraying their abnormal condition by any signs, till at some point in the journey they have suddenly come to themselves completely and been amazed at the gap in their memory. In the dream itself, accordingly, I was declaring myself to be one of those cases of "automatisme ambulatoire" (*Standard Edition*, vol. VI, p. 457).

It is understandable that Freud would want to transport himself away from the claustrophobic midst of an ongoing primal scene. The prototype for the twilight state, the fugue state, the hypnagogic state that Freud was actually in during the beginning, and perhaps most, of the *Hollthurn* dream may be found in the primal scene experience. There the child's reality sense is so overwhelmed by the complete evocation of his drives that he has recourse to an altered state of consciousness. Freud's hysterical fugue state in the dream allowed him to understand something of the oedipal basis for the symptom, thus correcting earlier views he had held of this phenomenon. If this train trip reminded Freud of the earlier trip to Vienna when he was a 4-year-old—the one in which he had seen his mother naked ("There were women with fruit on the platform. They were crouching on the ground and holding up their baskets invitingly")—then the transport to another carriage might, besides alluding to a primal scene fantasized by the oedipal child, refer to an actual transfer to another train during the course of the trip.

Freud then gives an account of the patient with whom he identified himself during the course of this dream. The patient was a young man who had been forced to confine himself within four walls for fear of killing his father. Even after the patient's father died, the patient feared he might kill someone else. To explain his impulse the patient said, "All men are brothers." In the associations to the *Hollthurn* dream Freud wrote that two factors lay behind the patient's obsessive symptoms. The first factor was the patient's "Cain fantasy," as Freud termed it. Freud himself identified with the motif of killing a father or a brother:

. . . One day the possibility came into his head that *he might have left his house while he was in an unconscious state* and thus been able to commit the murder without knowing anything about it. From that time onwards he locked the front door of the house and gave the key to his old housekeeper with strict instructions never to let it fall into his hands even if he asked for it.

This, then, was the origin of my attempted explanation to the effect that I had changed carriages while I was in an unconscious state; it had been carried over ready-made into the dream from the material of the dream thoughts, and was evidently intended in the dream to serve the purpose of identifying me with the figure of this patient. My recollection of him had been aroused by an easy association. My last night journey, a few weeks earlier, had been made in the company of this very man. He was cured, and was travelling with me into the provinces to visit his relatives, who had sent for me. We had a compartment to ourselves; we left all the windows open all through the night and had a most entertaining time for as long as I stayed awake. I knew that the root of his illness had been hostile impulses against his father, dating from his childhood and involving a sexual situation (*Standard Edition*, vol. V, p. 458).

What follows in Freud's associations is a linking of this material to his own wish to intrude vengefully into the primal scene. It is noteworthy that Freud mentioned this patient on one earlier occasion in *The Interpretation of Dreams*, as an introduction to his explication of the Oedipus complex. The implication of Freud's identification with this oedipal character is that Freud too wished to kill a sibling whom he had connected with the primal scene and that he also detected in himself a wish to kill his father, who was taking all the mother's fruits for himself. Freud must have thought of his arch-oedipal patient as he was in the airless compartment with his two unpleasant travelling companions while trying to fall asleep and feeling claustrophobic. Here the memory of the open window of the earlier journey indicates Freud's wish to avoid claustrophobia and to escape into another compartment.

With this as background, further examination of the dream as it portrays and dramatizes Freud's revision of the primal scene is warranted.

Freud described his companions:

The door was shut immediately, and pointed remarks were exchanged between them on the subject of opening windows. They had probably seen at once that I was longing for some fresh air. It was a hot night and the atmosphere in the completely closed compartment soon became suffocating. My experiences of travelling have taught me that conduct of this ruthless and overbearing kind is a characteristic of people who are travelling on a free or half-price ticket. When the ticket collector came and I showed him the ticket I had bought at such expense, there fell from the lady's mouth, in haughty and almost menacing tones, the words: "My husband has a free pass." She was an imposing figure with discontented features, of an age not far from the time of the decay of feminine beauty; the man uttered not a word but sat there motionless. I attempted to sleep. In my dream I took fearful vengeance on my disagreeable companions; no one could suspect what insults and humiliations lay concealed behind the broken fragments of the first half of the dream. When this need had been satisfied, a second need made itself felt—to change compartments (*Standard Edition*, vol. V, pp. 456–457).

The issue of the free ticket is familiar: Freud is the little Jew, the ticketless child with no sexual access to the mother, the oedipal child without a big penis like the father.

The image of the little boy's penis is present in the beginning of the dream. Holothurians are sea slugs, or sea cucumbers, a phallic image. The penile image takes Freud on a regression into the past. Freud becomes aware of his penis as he begins to get sleepy in the presence of the primal couple. The dream association to holothurians and the waking thought of them take Freud back into the museum of his mind where rebellious youths attempt to defy strong authoritarian forces. As Grinstein (1980) pointed out, many of Schiller's books take up this theme. Thus Freud enters into an oedipal and masturbatory fantasy in the presence of the primal couple.

His associations took Freud to the shore of the Irish Sea, where he collected marine specimens during his trip to England. Marine specimens had a special phallic, bisexual significance for Freud:

. . . a charming little girl came up to me and said: "Is it a starfish? Is it alive?" "Yes," I replied, "he is alive," and at once, embarrassed at my mistake repeated the sentence correctly (*Standard Edition*, vol. V, p. 519).

In this association there is a quality of a young boy exhibiting his genital to a young girl. We know from other remarks that Freud had fantasies that his England trip would result in his being paired off with his niece Pauline as a future marriage partner. Thus the incident may refer to an earlier fantasy or event of Freud's exhibiting himself as a young boy to his niece Pauline. One also wonders if the "he is alive" referred in an unconscious way to Julius as well as to the penis.

Freud's continuing association and his imagery in his associations indicates a sense of guilt and a wish to confess to some crime. The guilt refers to his wish to confess to anal crime in the railroad compartment, and perhaps to the oedipal crime of exhibiting himself as well. Freud referred the gender error to the error concerning the attribution of authorship in the dream: the word *von* in "Das Buch ist von Schiller" should be translated "by" and not "from" (*Standard Edition*, vol. V, p. 519).

. . . the magnificent piece of condensation . . . was made possible by the identity of the sound of the English "from" and the German adjective "fromm" (pious). But how did my blameless memory of the seashore come to be in the dream? It served as the most innocent possible example of my using a word indicating gender or sex in the wrong place—of my bringing in sex (the word "he") where it did not belong. This, incidentally, was one of the keys to the solution of the dream. No one who has heard, furthermore, the origin of the title of Clerk-Maxwell's "*M*atter and *M*otion" will have any difficulty in filling in the gaps: *M*oliere's "Le *M*alade Imaginaire"—La matiere est-elle laudable?—a *m*otion of the bowels (*Standard Edition*, vol. V, pp. 519–520).

Freud did not want us to miss the point. It was a confession. He had much to confess. For Freud's revenge on the family romance pair coupling in his hypnagogic oedipal fantasy was the same revenge that (Freud said) the Wolf Man took as a child regarding the primal scene—anal discharge. Freud must have farted in the railway compartment: "Flavit et dissipati sunt"—he blew and they were scattered. Thus, the question of authorship, from or by, alludes to Freud's overhearing the couple's response to his rebellious intrusion into the hot stuffy compartment. As the train started moving and as the movement was imagined as the family romance pair coupling, Freud felt his back pressed into their midst and he farted. This reconstruction suggests another motive for wanting to change compartments.

In his associations to the second and progressively hypno-pompic portion of the dream, Freud leaves little doubt that he is indeed the author of the thick volume bound in brown cloth. He refers *Matter and Motion* not only to bowels in motion, but makes much of the *M* sounds as well, referring them to Moliere's *Le Malade Imaginaire*. Moliere's play is about a man so obsessed with his bowels that he goes to doctors for enema after enema. At the end of the Moliere play the man decides to become a doctor himself so that he can administer the treatment, which is: "Once the enema's fed/Keep the bleeder in bed/And purge till he's dead" (Grinstein 1980, p. 350). The doctor who kills through anal penetration is one of Freud's familiar image themes. As we shall see it turns up as the nidus of Freud's negative oedipal revision of the primal scene in the other oedipal dreams considered here. In this instance the oedipal revision of the primal scene returns to the theme of Julius being killed during the course of the scene. Of course Freud was reassuring himself during the course of this dream that no brother figure had been killed, since he was screening the experience of being in the closed hot compartment with the earlier experience of the patient who represented Freud's living and cured brother figure. Moreover, Freud was intent on capturing the whole essence of the oedipally revised scene for his dream book. By taking over the primal scene and equating his discharge with the discharge of writing monumental books, Freud reassured himself that he had survived the ordeal.

During the course of the *Hollthurn* dream and the subsequent associations, Freud learned much about his oedipal fantasies and how they had sunk their roots into his primal scene experience. Still, he did not learn enough to solve his own neurosis. Obviously his train phobia was still troubling him at the time of the *Hollthurn* dream. During the next two to three weeks the same themes remained in Freud's mind, and they are evident in the other two oedipal dreams that centered on Freud's negative oedipal revision of the primal scene.

The Negative Oedipal Revision of the Primal Scene

Two consecutive dreams (*The Open Air Closet* and *Count Thun*) that Freud analyzed in *The Interpretation of Dreams* give background information about his state of mind as he was preparing to leave for his vacation to Aussee in early August of 1898. These dreams make possible a genuine reconstruction of the negative oedipal period of Freud's childhood. Freud's associations to the first dream, *The Open Air Closet*, referred to childhood events. The associations to the next dream referred to the same childhood events as mentioned in the associations to the first dream. Thus it is possible to take the second dream, *Count Thun*, as a genuine dream of reconstruction based on the childhood material that had been brought into focus by *The Open Air Closet* dream.

It is fortunate that Grinstein (1980) has explicated and analyzed the manifold literary associations to both of these dreams. Grinstein's feat of tying the dynamics of the books Freud was reading closely to the dynamics Freud expressed in these dreams shows how intensely involved Freud was in the world of his books.

The Dream of The Open Air Closet

A hill, on which there was something like an open air closet: a very long seat with a large hole at the end of it. Its back edge was thickly covered with small heaps of feces of all sizes and degrees of freshness. There were bushes behind the seat. I micturated on the seat; a long stream of urine washed everything clean; the lumps of feces came away easily and fell into the opening. It was as though at the end there was still some left.

Why did I feel no disgust at this dream? (*Standard Edition*, vol. V, p. 468).

The manifest dream is a metaphor for Freud's attempt to clean up the dream book. In his ambition to finish it, he must wash away the deposits of thought, inspiration, and dreaming which would not find a place in the final structure. Although Freud had made some progress in this direction, a great deal of work still remained to be done. His theory of neurosis too needed work and clarification. Drawing its dynamic thrust from the way the 4-year-old's development of urethral ambition supercedes the 3-year-old's anality, the dream told Freud much he needed to realize about psychosexual development. The dream was thus a form of research, the purpose of which was to supply missing links necessary to the completion of Freud's dream book.

ASSOCIATIONS TO THE DREAM OF *THE OPEN AIR CLOSET*

What at once occurred to me in the analysis were the Aegian stables which were cleansed by Hercules. This Hercules was I. The hills and bushes came from Aussee, where my children were stopping at the time. I had discovered the infantile aetiology of the neuroses and had thus saved my children from falling ill (*Standard Edition*, vol. V, p. 469).

Freud referred to Hercules' feat of cleansing the stables by diverting the river Peneus. The feat is, of course, a metaphor for the instinctual reorganization that occurs in the phallic stage of development. Freud's phallic boasting suppresses a strong affective trend toward feeling weak, submissive, and disgruntled about his work. The antithesis in his feelings corresponds to the feelings of a 3-year-old who is trying to subdue passive wishes with the feelings of urinary power that are developing.

The image of Hercules was brought to Freud by a childish admirer who sickened Freud with his sycophantic praise. This admirer expressed exactly the submissive feelings that Freud was trying to suppress in himself:

And now for the true exciting cause of the dream. It had been a hot summer afternoon; and during the evening I had delivered my lecture on the connection between hysteria and the perversions, and everything I had to say displeased me intensely and seemed to me completely devoid of any value. I was tired and felt no trace of enjoyment in my difficult work: I longed to be away from all this grubbing about in human dirt and to be able to join my children and afterwards visit the beauties of Italy. In this mood I went from the lecture room to an open air cafe, where I had a modest snack in the open air, since I had no appetite for food. One of my audience, however, went with me and he begged leave to sit by me while I drank my coffee and choked over my crescent roll. He began to flatter me: telling me how much he had learned from me, how he looked at everything now with fresh eyes, how I had cleansed the Aegean stables of errors and prejudices in my theory of the neuroses (*Standard Edition*, vol. V, pp. 469–470).

Disgusted by the submissiveness of this weak child-man who wanted to see him as a giant, Freud dreamed of himself as Gargantua astride Notre Dame (Our Lady) peeing on the Parisians. Freud also associated to Gulliver extinguishing the great fire in Lilliput with his stream of urine. Freud's compensatory wish of ambitious greatness is seen most clearly in his identification with the Gargantua of Garnier's illustration to Rabelais. Grinstein (1980) astutely points out that the illustration matches the manifest scene of Freud's dream point for point, and the symbolism of this day residue is appropriate in depicting the oedipal urethral wish to possess the mother (Notre Dame).

What is most interesting for the reconstruction of Freud's childhood, though, is the submissive wish that was suppressed through the dream fulfillment of phallic-oedipal wishes. The way into the submissive wish is through Freud's reading of Meyer's short story, "Die Leiden eines Knaben" ("A Boy's Sorrows"). Freud wrote that he read this story before going to bed on the night of the dream. Grinstein's précis of the story shows that the story line conforms to a negative oedipal revision of the primal scene. In the story a young adolescent boy dies because of his love for his father. Julian Boufflers, the boy, is sent to a Jesuit school by his father, the War Marshall. The chief Jesuit, Father Tellier, hates the boy because his father has exposed a piece of Jesuit financial corruption. In one episode Julian is told that a friend who has been a brother to him recently died in the war. This boy had been allowed to enlist by the Marshall, who had refused to let his son do the same. In another episode the innocent Julian allows himself to be set up as the instigator of a derogatory remark about one of the Jesuit fathers.

Hearing of the incident, Father Tellier beats Julian into fever and delirium. His father is called, and the boy is brought to the house in which he had lived until his mother died and in which he could not remain after his father's remarriage to a new wife who did not want him. The story ends with the Marshall's decision:

. . . to help Julian die more easily. Calling him by name, the Marshall told Julian that he would have to interrupt his schooling and go into the army to do his duty as the King had had great losses. The boy enjoyed sharing this fantasy with his father. Then the Marshall said, "There is the British flag, take it." The dying Julian reached into the air, screaming, "vive le Roi!" and fell back dead as if a bullet had killed him" (Grinstein 1980, pp. 439–440).

In the oedipal dynamics of the story the death of the friend and brother figure with whom he is identified inspires Julian to risk death in battle; for the facing of such risks must be the way to achieve the love of a military father. Yet, to enter the war is to enter the dangerous arena of his father's love. Thus battle is equated with the primal scene which, in its turn, is associated with Julian's dead mother. Here the father figure is divided into the good, loving father, and the bad, sadistic, church father. The boy has lost his good father because of competition from a mother figure whom he wishes to get rid of but cannot. In the final episode the boy shows his love for his father through his willingness to die for him. Figuratively, the final scene equates the boy's entering the war with the primal scene—and symbolizes the power of his father's powerful genital by a bullet.

The story thus contains the significant elements in Freud's childhood history: the family romance themes of a dangerous bad father, the death of a helpless sibling, and the splitting of father figures. What is more, Freud readily identified with the symbolism of persecution over financial issues by decidedly Christian figures.

Significant for the purposes of this reconstruction is that in this story the young hero sacrifices himself in a sexualized scene with the father. The story reminded Freud of the following incident from his childhood:

The following scene from my childhood has been described to me, and my memory of the description has taken the place of my memory of the scene itself. It appears that when I was two years old I still occasionally wetted the bed, and when I was reproached for this I consoled my father by promising to buy him a nice new red bed in N., the nearest town of any size. . . . This promise of mine exhibited all the megalomania of child-hood. We have already come across the significant part played in dreams by children's difficulties in connection with micturition (cf. the dream reported on p. 201) (*Standard Edition*, vol. IV, p. 216).

If Meyer's negative oedipal story reminded Freud of this scene, then the scene must have had a negative oedipal significance to Freud. Since Freud offered to buy his father a new bed, it must have been his father's bed that was soiled. What is more, since this incident was revived as part of the associations to *The Open Air Closet* dream, it must be that Sigismund once washed away an anal discharge he had perpetrated on his parent's bed during an interruption of the primal scene. That the original event was a bowel movement is reinforced by what Freud later wrote about the Wolf Man's uni-versal child method of interrupting the primal scene by passing a stool and then screaming. In connection with that case, Freud also provided a clue as to the meaning of the red bed; for he wrote that the Wolf Man identified his mother's affliction, her bleeding, with the blood that was passed in the stools of dysentery. Freud further stated that in that case the infant boy must have felt that his bowel movement was meant as a gift to the father, showing his tender response to the father, and also as a sacrifice of a part of himself to his father.

Freud's identification of his own childhood dynamics with those of the childhood of the Wolf Man and his association of blood with both the primal scene and dysentery are compelling topics in themselves.

Dysentery was evidently his [the Wolf Man's] name for the illness which he had heard his mother lamenting about, and which it was impossible to go on living with; he did not regard his mother's disease as being abdominal but as being intestinal. Under the influence of the primal scene he came to the conclusion that his mother had been made ill by what his father had done to her; and his dread of having blood in his stool, of being as ill as his mother, was his repudiation of being identified with her in this sexual scene—the same repudiation with which he awoke from the dream. But the dream was also a proof that in his later elaboration of the primal scene he had put himself in the mother's place and had envied her this relation with his father. The organ by which his identification with women, his passive homosexual attitude to men, was able to express itself was the anal zone (*Standard Edition*, vol. XVII, p. 78).

Julius had died of dysentery just about the time of this memory. The introduction of the color red in connection with soiling the bed must refer to the presence of blood in the stools. The infant Sigismund feared that his primal scene excitement discharged in this way would make him another casualty. More than that: the color red in this anecdote of Freud's past must also refer to the female genital perceived as a wound, and therefore to castration anxiety; for the patient's dream to which Freud referred the reader (*Standard Edition*, vol. IV, p. 201) was one in which the red flesh of the lower lids of a mother's eyes stand out. Here their redness is equated with an image of the woman's genitals gaping as she bends to micturate. In that dream, the dreamer reassured himself that he had no such wound, no such "proud flesh," by recalling the upright manner in which he had urinated the day before against a fence. Thus the imagery surrounding Freud's childhood memory depicted him as a 2-year-old submitting in the woman's position to the father's penetration and ending up with the same damage that had killed Julius.

Since the anxiety of this negative oedipal revision of the primal scene is so intense, it may be surmised that Freud emphasized his genital intactness and urinary competence in a compensatory way.

Another association of Freud's to Meyer's story is a later ambitious memory of micturating defiantly in his parents' bedroom when he was 7. His father ordered him out of the room, declaring that he would amount to nothing. This scene implies another primal scene awareness during this portion of Freud's life, which has been superimposed on the original. Thus Freud's ambition to possess his mother in a urinary intrusive way preempts the passive homosexual participation in the primal scene in which the young boy would have to equate his genital area with the mother's missing genital.

There are two more associations to *The Open Air Closet* dream that support this reconstruction. The first is an association that turns up differently in its use as an association to the *Count Thun* dream. In *The Open Air Closet* association Freud wrote:

The fact that all the feces disappeared so quickly under the stream recalled the motto: "Afflavit et dissipati sunt," which I intended one day to put at the head of a chapter upon the therapy of hysteria" (*Standard Edition*, vol. V, p. 469).

Here *afflavit* means he urinated; in the *Count Thun* dream the force of blowing comes from flatus, not from urine. "He blew and they were scattered" appears to me to be a reference to the primal scene where the infant has a bowel movement and his parents are scattered. An understanding of this, and Freud's revised roles in the primal scene, would certainly have cured Freud's hysteria.

The second association to *The Open Air Closet* dream concerns a chair that a woman patient had given Freud as a gift. The chair was the toilet seat of the dream:

The seat (except, of course for the hole) was an exact copy of a piece of furniture which had been given to me as a present by a grateful woman patient. It thus reminded me of how much my patients honored me (*Standard Edition*, vol. V, p. 469).

Much as the 2-year-old Sigismund wanted to give his father a gift associated with feces, so Freud feels ambivalently about this gift associated by Freud with feces and "the new red bed." The hole in the bottom of the dream chair is another reference to the infantile perception of female anatomy, from which Freud is trying to distance himself through his disgust for the submissive and the weak and his identification with the great and the powerful.

The Open Air Closet dream was dreamed in Vienna shortly before his vacation. Freud's associations to that dream and the concerns and wishes it revealed constitute day residue for the *Count Thun* dream. The "revolutionary" dream of *Count Thun* was dreamed on the train during Freud's departure in early August from Vienna. According to Jones (1953), Freud was first going to see Fliess and then meet his sister-in-law, Minna, for an excursion to the Alps before joining his family in Aussee.

   The Open Air Closet dream formed a bridge in Freud's mind between the disgust and disappointment associated with an anal submissiveness and an exuberant self-assertiveness associated with urinary competence:

The day time mood of revulsion and disgust persisted into the dream in so far as it was able to provide almost the entire material of its manifest content. But during the night a contrary mood of powerful and even exaggerated self-assertiveness arose and displaced the former one. The content of the dream had to find a form which would enable it to express both the delusions of inferiority and the megalomania in the same material (*Standard Edition*, vol. V, p. 470).

The changed mood most likely continued into the next day and gained fuel in Freud's anticipation of setting off on his vacation trip; for Freud commented on his mood the previous day as he set the tone for his associations to the *Count Thun* dream:

   . . . the analysis of these three episodes of the dream showed that they were impertinent boastings, the issue of an absurd megalomania which had long been suppressed in my waking life and a few of whose ramifications had even made their way into the dream's manifest content (e.g., "I felt I was being very cunning"), and which incidentally accounted for my exuberant spirits during the evening before I had the dream. . . . The first episode of the dream may also be included among the boastings by anyone who will bear in mind the great Rabelais' incomparable account of the life and deeds of Gargantua and his son Pantagruel (*Standard Edition*, vol. IV, p. 215).

This statement links the dynamics of the *Count Thun* dream to those of *The Open Air Closet* dream. Freud went on in the same section to mention the two childhood incidents that had occurred to him in association to *A Boy's Sorrows*. Here he tied the purchase of the new bed for his father to the acquisition of a new trunk for the trip. The fact that the childhood scenes are day residues for the dream rather than fresh associations to the dream indicates that the dream added motive strength through wishes that were attached to the original childhood incidents. Indeed the *Count Thun* dream portrays the childhood dynamics of the negative, oedipally revised primal scene; for this is one aspect of the kind of research Freud was carrying out through the mediation of his dreams. Thus Freud's connection of the purchase of a new violet-brown trunk to the wish to buy his father a new red bed would indicate that the trunk is a female and an anally receptive symbol for the wished for negative oedipal relationship to the father. Indeed that is how it functions in the *Count Thun* dream.

Our knowledge of Freud's basal image themes informs our understanding of how the red bed and violet-brown trunk images function as links to Freud's dynamic unconscious. The red bed of the infant's primal scene shades into the darker night tones of the analyzed sado-masochistic response to the primal scene. For Freud, the trunk, or box, contains the primal repressed imagery of the one-eyed doctor penetrating the nursemaid–infant Julius. For the dreamer, the railroad car coach becomes the primal box containing the dynamic unconscious revised primal scene. Freud takes the toilet seat imagery and expands it to the whole female box. He succeeds in recreating the step in his development where his urinary ambition preempted the sado-masochistic primal scene imagery.

Thus an examination of the *Count Thun* dream must be attentive to the manner in which the dream portrays Freud's negative oedipal dynamic as an oedipal fantasy, or rather as a series of layered fantasies. Examination of the dream shows that it is manifestly structured first, on the surface, as a revolutionary political fantasy, then below the surface as an oedipal fantasy, and finally, the whole may be taken as a masturbatory equivalent in which the dream progresses toward a urethral/urinary discharge. The progress of this masturbatory, negative oedipal fantasy can be followed in a number of ways. First, it may be read for its "functional phenomena," which is to say, its self-description of its progress. Second, it may be read for its projection of Freud's bedrock themes. Third, it may be read for its literary motifs as they mirror the progress of the dream. The copious literary material in Freud's associations to the dream has been researched and summarized by Grinstein (1980).

The Count Thun *Dream*

A crowd of people, a meeting of students.—A count (Thun or Taafe) was speaking. He was challenged to say something about the Germans, and declared with a contemptuous gesture that their favorite flower was colt's foot, and put some sort of dilapidated leaf—or rather the crumpled skeleton of a leaf—into his buttonhole. I fired up—so I fired up, though I was surprised at my taking such an attitude.

(*Then, less distinctly:*) It was as though I was in the Aula; the entrances were cordoned off and we had to escape. I made my way through a series of beautifully furnished rooms, evidently ministerial or public apartments, with furniture upholstered in a colour between brown and violet; at last I came to a corridor, in which a housekeeper was sitting, an elderly stout woman. I avoided speaking to her, but she evidently thought I had a right to pass, for she asked whether she should accompany me with the lamp. I indicated to her, she should accompany me with the lamp. I indicated to her, by word or gesture, that she was to stop on the staircase; and I felt I was being very cunning in thus avoiding inspection at the exit. I got downstairs and found a narrow and steep ascending path, along which I went.

(*Becoming indistinct again:*) . . . It was as though the second problem was to get out of the town, just as the first one had been to get out of the house. I was driving in a cab and ordered the driver to drive me to a station. "I can't drive with you along the railway line itself," I said, after he had raised some objection, as though I had overtired him. It was as if I had already driven with him to some of the distance one normally travels by train. The stations were cordoned off. I wondered whether to go to Krems or Znaim, but reflected that the Court would be in residence there, so I decided in favour of Graz, or some such place. I was now sitting in the compartment, which was like a carriage on the Stadtbahn (*the suburban railway*); and in my buttonhole I had a peculiar plaited, long-shaped object, and beside it some violet-brown violets made of a stiff material. This greatly struck people. (*At this point the scene broke off.*)

Once more I was in front of the station, but this time in the company of an elderly gentleman. I thought of a plan for remaining unrecognized; and then saw that this plan had already been put into effect. It was as though thinking and experiencing were one and the same thing. He appeared to be blind, at all events with one eye, and I handed him a male glass urinal (which we had to buy or had bought in town). So I was a sick-nurse and had to give him the urinal because he was blind. If the ticket-collector were to see us like that, he would be certain to let us get away without noticing us. Here the man's attitude and his micturating penis appeared in plastic form. (*This was the point at which I awoke, feeling a need to micturate*). (*Standard Edition*, vol. IV, pp. 209–211).

ASSOCIATIONS TO THE *COUNT THUN* DREAM

This dream is considered first as a whole political fantasy, and then as four individual episodes.

The dream as a whole gives one the impression of being in the nature of a fantasy in which the dreamer was carried back to the Revolutionary year 1848. Memories of that year had been recalled to me by the Jubilee in 1898 (*Standard Edition*, vol. IV, p. 211).

Of course Freud wasn't alive in 1848. Grinstein (1980) mentions that Freud's mother had shown Freud some of her old pictures in which there were bullet holes from the revolution of 1848. In connection with this Freud constructed a revolutionary fantasy that included an image of his mother in the violent ferment of the time. Family romance primal scene material emerged from this in Freud's further imaging of an affectionate exchange between his half brother Emanuel, and Emanuel's wife 50 years in the past. Freud continued his associations with an image, which, itself overdetermined, was meant to show that the revolutionary fantasy had an understructure:

This revolutionary fantasy, however, which was derived from ideas
aroused in me by seeing Count Thun, was like the facade of an Italian
church in having no organic relation with the structure lying behind it. But
it differed from those facades in being disordered and full of gaps, and in
the fact that portions of the interior construction had forced their way
through into it at many points (*Standard Edition*, vol. IV, p. 211).

The Italian church imagery points to the same inner sanctum Freud
was searching for in his wish to penetrate as far as Rome.

Freud described the scene that gave rise to the dream imagery
in his preamble to the dream:

I had driven to the Western Station to take the train for my summer
holiday at Aussee, but had arrived on the platform while an earlier train,
going to Ischl, was still standing in the station. There I had seen Count
Thun, who was once again travelling to Ischl for an audience with the
Emperor. Though it was raining, he had arrived in an open carriage. He had
walked straight in through the entrance for the Local Trains. The ticket
inspector at the gate had not recognized him and had tried to take his ticket,
but he had waved the man aside with a curt motion of his hand and without
giving any explanation (*Standard Edition*, vol. IV, p. 208).

This is imagery that is known to have incited primal scene feelings in
Freud. The grand aristocrat entering the luxurious compartment
contrasts with the little Jew who could be overwhelmed for trying to
travel without a ticket. But Freud indicated he was in a revolutionary mood as he set off for Aussee, so he whistled to himself from
Mozart's *Le Noze di Figaro*:

> Se vuol ballare, signor contino,
> Se vuol Ballare, signor contino,
> Il chitarino le suonerò
>
> If my Lord Count is inclined to go dancing,
> If my Lord Count is inclined to go dancing,
> I'll be quite ready to play him a tune . . .
> (*Standard Edition*, vol. IV, p. 208).

This is Freud's announcement that he is ready to enter a sexual and revolutionary scene with the Count. For, as Schorske (1980) points out, Freud had reason to be ambivalent about the Count. Although it is true that the Count replaced the anti-Semitic Lueger as head of the government, still he depreciated German nationalism, which offended Freud. Freud hoped, nevertheless, that the new government, which was not antisemitic, would grant him his professorship. Freud's whole mood was one of provoking authority:

The whole evening I had been in high spirits and in a combative mood. I had chaffed my waiter and my cab-driver. . . . I thought of the phrase about the great gentleman who had taken the trouble to be born, and of the *droit de Seigneur* which Count Almaviva tried to exercise over Susanna (*Standard Edition*, vol. IV, pp. 208–209).

Freud went further in his equation of the Count Thun (which means "to do" in German) with Count Almaviva of *Figaro.* As Grinstein (1980) noted, *Figaro* revolves around patently oedipal themes, as well as around the wish to catch a father figure in the primal act. Figaro is caught in a family romance as he is almost forced, unwittingly, to make love to his mother. Figaro's negative oedipal alternative is Cherubino, who maintains a passive feminine posture. Dressed as a woman for the purposes of the farce, he is always liable to become the object of the Count's love-making, though at one time he is caught with the Count's wife and comes close to being sent off to war.

These familiar themes were present in Freud's mind as he saw a second political figure come on to the platform, getting ready to board the same train Freud was taking:

At this point a gentleman came on to the platform whom I recognized as a Government invagilator at medical examinations, and who by his activities in that capacity had won the flattering nickname of "Government bedfellow." He asked to be given a first-class half-compartment to himself in virtue of his official position, and I heard one railwayman saying to another: "Where are we to put the gentleman with the half first-class ticket?" This, I thought to myself, was a fine example of privilege; after all, I had paid the full first class fare. And I did in fact get a compartment to myself, but not in a corridor coach, so that there would be no lavatory available during the night. I complained to an official without any success; but I got my own back on him by suggesting that he should at all events have a hole made in the floor of the compartment to meet the possible needs of passengers (*Standard Edition*, vol. IV, p. 209).

One sees in this anecdote that Freud had a temporary panic at the thought of being forced to share a compartment with the "government bedfellow." His feeling about sharing a compartment with that sycophantic individual is much the same as his disgust with his admirer of the previous day; which is to say he identified with the position of the submissive man seeking to get something from an authority figure. As he did in the dream of *The Open Air Closet*, Freud renounced this impulse by invoking his urethral ambitions. He joked about cutting a hole in the floor, as he had cut a hole in the chair given to him by his female admirer in the dream the night before, and used the hole to vent his feelings.

Thus the entire revolutionary fantasy is primed to structure the forthcoming dream. Count Thun will be challenged. He will force Freud to submit to his authority, but Freud will have his way. He will expose the Count's selfishness and inherent weakness by his cunning analytic methods, and thus turn the tables on the Count. In the end the Count will be shown to be the one with no right to a ticket, while Freud will become the authority capable of overseeing the affairs of states.

This is the political fantasy. The negative oedipal theme with which it opens is the strain of Freud's teasing and challenging various men. Beneath this is another motive. He wants them to protect him, put him in his place, and take care of him. For underlying this political fantasy is the negative oedipal revision of the primal scene. The provocation unconsciously solicits a sexual response and is destined to lead to Freud's submission to authority. By the last episode of the dream, however, Freud has reversed the roles in this negative oedipal fantasy and achieved a position of strength. This achievement constitutes Freud's reaction to his negative oedipal submissive wishes and his response to the death of his father, which occurred in 1896.

Much has been made of Freud's positive oedipal response to his father's death. For instance, Grinstein (1980) and Schur (1972) concur that Freud's accomplishments, especially *The Interpretation of Dreams*, can be understood as a response to his father's death and as indicative of Freud's ability to understand his own positive oedipal wishes. In this context they agree that guilty feelings about his father's death caused Freud much inhibition and unnecessary suffering until he understood the source of the guilt well enough. This analysis, while true, is incomplete, because it leaves Freud's deeper negative oedipal feelings out of account. By 1898 Freud had not completely analyzed his positive and negative oedipal reactions to his father's death. Many of the 1898 dreams refer to the death. In the *Count Thun* dream Freud expresses submissive wishes to his father. This expression leads him to fear that he himself will be killed through submitting sexually to his father, as he believed Julius had been killed. Reacting to this anxiety, Freud reversed the positions of power in the dream so that his father was liable to being killed in a sexual encounter with him; for at the end of the *Count Thun* dream there is much evidence that Freud saw his father as a weak, paralytic old man, who must be tended gently, but who will inevitably succumb and die.

In this sense then, Freud's increased productivity after his father's death in 1896 can be traced to Freud's reaction against taking on the weak submissive role in homosexual relations himself. The theme of submitting to a man he loves and then turning the tables is a common one in Freud's most intimate friendships.

COUNT THUN, EPISODE ONE

A crowd of people, a meeting of students.—A count (Thun or Taafe) was speaking. He was challenged to say something about the Germans, and declared with a contemptuous gesture that their favorite flower was colt's foot, and then put some sort of dilapidated leaf—or rather the crumpled skeleton of a leaf—into his buttonhole. I fired up—so I fired up, though I was surprised at my taking such an attitude (*Standard Edition*, vol. IV, pp. 209–210).

In this first episode of the dream, the Count challenges Freud's German nationalism. In his associations Freud is reminded of a school episode in which he himself instigated a classroom revolt against a teacher's authority. The scene resembled Julian Bouffant's incurring the wrath of the Jesuit fathers. Freud's own association to the memory is associated to the scene in Shakespeare's *Henry VI* that opens the War of Roses. Shakespeare's action begins as Edmund, young son of the Duke of York (of the White Rose party), is stabbed, sacrificed to the Duke's ambition to wrest King Henry's throne from him immediately. Freud associated white roses with the Vienesse anti-Semites who had taken white roses as their symbol, so that at this point in his associations he is reminded of anti-Semitic provocation he had experienced. Next, the detail of putting flowers into a buttonhole reminds Freud of orchids he had bought a woman friend that day and of the Rose of Jericho, whose "dried fronds unfold under moisture" (*Standard Edition*, vol. IV, p. 212). The train of associations about inviting penetration leads next to another occasion in school when young Freud provoked his older school mate, Victor Adler, who had, by the time of this dream, become the leader of the social democrats, the party represented by red roses. In that provocation Freud took a strong German nationalistic position. Thus in the *Count Thun* dream Freud continued to develop the theme of provoking older and more powerful men, while putting himself in a position of ultimate submission.

A series of associations to the colt's foot leads to various terms of abuse: urinary, fecal, and flatulent. Here a regressive trend materializes as Freud follows a trail of words back to their early, concrete referents. Taking this trail leads Freud to Zola's novel, *Germinal*. In *Germinal*, a novel of social protests, the hero is forced to undergo and to witness degraded acts of primal sexual violence. *Germinal* follows from colt's foot because Freud translates the German for colt's foot into the French *pisse-en-lit*. This French word for dandelion reminds Freud of pissing in bed—a reference, probably, to Freud's primal scene memory of the red bed. Supporting this contention is the fact that Freud proceeds to think about the child in *Germinal* who went out to collect dandelions for supper. Grinstein's précis of *Germinal* referred to the incident in a primal scene context:

One day, after the children finished bathing, the mother, Maheude, told her son Jeanlin to go out to gather dandelions for the evening's salad. This is the request to which Freud refers in his association to his dream.

Maheude told Catherine to stay upstairs while her father was washing and then assisted her husband, Maheu, in his bath. After this the couple had sexual intercourse. Maheude objected that their three-month-old child, Estelle, was watching them and turned the child around.

In the meantime, Jeanlin, who had gone off with a neighbor's daughter and another boy, tried to make love to the little girl in the presence of his boy friend, treating her like his "little wife." The game "playing mama and papa" was modelled after his observations at home. Etienne, who happened to be walking in the vicinity, observed their game as well as other couples on their way to lovemaking (Grinstein 1980, pp. 112–113).

Etienne, who was staying with this family, had fallen in love with the 15-year-old daughter, Catherine. He also witnessed Catherine making love to Chaval, who was Etienne's rival. Etienne wanted to avenge himself on Catherine by killing Chavel. Finally, in the end of the story, during the 1848 revolution, Etienne, Catherine, and Chaval are trapped in a mine shaft together:

Their situation was desperate, and as the days passed, Chaval determined to possess Catherine in Etienne's presence. Etienne insisted that Chaval leave Catherine alone, but as Chaval persisted, they began to fight. In a frenzy of rage, Etienne seized a sheet of slate from the wall and smashed Chaval's skull, killing him instantly. Catherine begged Etienne to kill her too but he refused.

Water from the flood gradually filled their hole. . . . Suddenly Chaval's body floated up to where they were and although they pushed him away, he kept coming toward their legs. . . . As time went on Catherine finally became delirious. She begged Etienne to take her sexually and they finally had relations after which she died (Grinstein 1980, pp. 114–115).

Thus, Freud's dandelion association opens a window to a violent re-enactment of the primal scene.

Freud's next association is to a competition in flatulence described in *La Terre*, another of Zola's novels. As Grinstein points out, Freud mistakenly ascribed this scene to *Germinal*. *La Terre* is a novel yet more brutally oriented toward the primal scene. The father in *La Terre* is savagely robbed of his virility, his power, and his possessions by one of his sons. Another *La Terre* son wins a competition in flatulence. The association to the competition led Freud to associate this dream also to the motto, "He blew and they were scattered."

It will be recalled that at the end of this first dream episode Freud writes, "I fired up" (Ich fahre). As the train of excitement moves off Freud enters his dream world, which consists of an underground place in which as a participant in the primal scene he struggles with dangerous, potentially lethal wishes to submit. Here he regresses to the use of fecal expulsion to try to renounce these dangerous passive wishes. This renunciatory tendency remained active for years after the recording of the *Count Thun* dream and its associations. In 1924 Freud added a footnote to the text at this point. Still chafing against individuals who attempted to force him to submit to their authority, he wrote, "An unsolicited biographer, Dr. Fritz Wittels, has charged me with having omitted the name of Jehovah from the above motto" (*Standard Edition*, vol. IV, p. 214). In the second dream episode, though, Freud is mainly involved in the regressive, submissive, "downward" phase of his wish construction.

COUNT THUN, EPISODE TWO

(*Then less distinctly*): It was as though I was in the Aula; the entrances were cordoned off and we had to escape. I made my way through a series of beautifully furnished rooms, evidently ministerial or public apartments, with furniture upholstered in a color between brown and violet; at last I came to a corridor, in which a housekeeper was sitting, an elderly stout woman. I avoided speaking to her, but she evidently thought I had a right to pass, for she asked whether she should accompany me with the lamp. I indicated to her, by word or gesture, that she was to stop on the staircase; and I felt I was being very cunning in thus avoiding inspection at the exit. I got downstairs and found a narrow and steep ascending path, along which I went (*Standard Edition*, vol. IV, p. 210).

It is as if Freud had crept into the Count's saloon carriage, having glimpsed the inside of it as the Count entered his train. Like the government bedfellow, Freud wanted to sleep with the Count to satisfy his wish to obtain his professorship, for the image Freud had of the atrium or Aula of the university represents Freud's wish for a professorship, his identification with the woman's role in the primal scene imagery of the dreams, and the identification of his body ego with the dream itself. The reference to the university alludes, moreover, to Freud's wish to learn more about dream formation: he watches himself closely in this section of the dream. Even in his sleep he is concerned with the functional phenomenon of dreaming.

The fact that the Aula is cordoned off shows Freud's claustrophobic feeling beginning to intensify. He approaches the role of bed partner to the Count with increasing anxiety. The anxiety is such that even in his associations Freud puts himself in the place of an exalted personage of those revolutionary times who " . . . is said to have suffered from incontinence of the bowels, and so on. I thought to myself that *I should not be justified in passing* the censorship at this point . . ." (*Standard Edition*, vol. IV, p. 211).

Basically though, the association to the bowels indicates Freud's association of the anus and rectum with the receptive female organs. The furniture in the rooms is brown and violet, the fecal colors of Freud's new trunk. The trunk is a female symbol for the current state of Freud's body-ego. (Notice, too, the juxtaposition in symbolism of the male urinal and the female trunk or box.) So, this section of the dream, the trip from the Aula through the beautifully furnished rooms, is both a description of and the expression of a wish for penetration into Freud's body-ego. Freud associated the "rooms," *Zimmer*, with "public women," *Frauenzimmer*, or prostitutes. That the rooms are "ministerial," which is to say used by ministers, indicates Freud's dream wish to be used as a public woman by the Count to get his professorship.

Still watching himself dream, Freud comes to another corridor. The portion of Freud's observing ego that remains awake is identified with the figure of the housekeeper who appears with a lamp. For Freud is tracing his own progress while still dreaming.

In an interesting paper, Siberer (1910) has tried to show from this part of my dream that the dream-work can succeed in reproducing not only the latent dream-thoughts but also the psychical process that takes place during the formation of dreams. (This is what he terms "the functional phenomenon.'') But he is, I think, overlooking the fact that ''the psychical process which takes place during the formation of dreams'' were, like the rest, part of the *material* of my thoughts. In this boastful dream I was evidently proud of having discovered those processes (*Standard Edition*, vol. IV, pp. 214–215).

Thus, in his 1911 footnote, Freud is still so interested in repudiating the submissive wishes expressed in the dream that he would not even allow another man to penetrate into the theoretical concerns expressed in the dream itself.

The significance of the appearance of the housekeeper with a lamp becomes apparent when we understand Freud's footnote as a defensive measure against the anxiety of total physical submission and follow the progress of the dream action using the functional phenomenon as a guide. In order to continue dreaming and to escape his self-observing alarm, which might wake him, in this dream episode Freud the dreamer exerts control over the primal scene fantasy that he has been depicting so intimately in his dream.

In the functional phenomenon of the dream, the light signals shift toward waking consciousness determined by the influence of the observing ego. The light itself may indicate the sleeper's opening his eyes for an instant or his having had a passing light shine in them. Most important is that the anxiety connected with the dreamer's wish to be penetrated like the mother in the primal scene has become so intense, it moves the dreamer toward waking consciousness. The lamp that Freud was offered in the dream shows sexual fulfillment at the end of the tunnel of excitement:

The allusion to the lamp went back to Grillparzer, who introduced a charming episode of a similar kind, which he had actually experienced, into his tragedy about Hero and Leander, *Des Meeres und der Liebe Wellen* (The Waves of the Sea and of Love) (*Standard Edition*, vol. IV, p. 214).

Grinstein recounts this episode. Once when the playwright Grillparzer was about to leave a woman who had treated him rudely all evening, she suddenly put down her lamp, and embraced him from behind. Much taken with this, Grillparzer made her action a motif in his recasting of the Hero and Leander myth. In Grillparzer's tragedy, Hero is pledged to chastity, for she is about to become a priestess. Unluckily, she falls in love with Leander, who has come to witness the ceremony of ordination. That night she leaves a lamp lit in her tower and, drawn to her like a moth to a flame, Leander swims the Hellespont to come to her. Their excitement in Hero's tower is overheard by the guard, who reports it to the priest. The following night Hero lights her lamp again, but the priest has it put out. Leander perishes in the sea, and Hero dies lamenting. Grinstein interprets the two as sibling figures entering an incestuous relationship and hoping to be reunited in the womb of the sea (Grinstein 1980, pp. 126–129).

Thus, in the dream, Freud begins to move on an upward path toward waking consciousness, though his sexual excitement lingers. The presence of the housekeeper recalls his nurse figure. As a superego figure, the housekeeper keeps the dream as clean as possible and protects the dreamer. Yet the image of Freud's nurse-maid, the person who toilet trained him originally, evokes also sexual feeling for the woman who was his 'instructress in sexual matters' and incestuous feelings directed toward a sister figure. Significantly, these ordinarily disturbing wishes here contain the sleep-disturbing tension by helping Freud escape his fear of his homosexual wishes. Before drowning like Leander, Freud needs to achieve a degree of conscious control over the dream process.

COUNT THUN, EPISODE THREE

(*Becoming indistinct again:*) . . . It was as though the second problem was to get out of the town, just as the first one had been to get out of the house. I was driving in a cab and ordered the driver to drive me to a station. "I can't drive with you along the railway line itself," I said after he had raised some objection, as though I had overtired him. It was as if I had already driven with him for some of the distance one normally travels by train. The stations were cordoned off. I wondered whether to go to Krems or Znaim, but reflected that the court would be in residence there so I decided in favor of Graz, or some such place. I was now sitting in the compartment, which was like a carriage on the Stadtbahn; and in my buttonhole I had a peculiar plaited, long-shaped object, and beside it some violet-brown violets made of a stiff material. This greatly struck people. (*At this point the scene broke off.*) (*Standard Edition*, vol. IV, p. 210).

Following the dream's functional phenomena, Freud has begun to alter the nature of the underlying sexual fantasy. He is leaving the body-ego he had imaged as belonging to the cloacally receptive woman of the primal scene. He must get out of that "house" because of the anxiety that he would become a casualty of the primal scene as he believed Julius had been. His problem becomes the maintenance of his excitement—his forward progress as it is represented in the functional phenomenon—while dealing with the anxiety of the negative oedipal revision of the primal scene. His anxiety is thus to evade censorship (the stations are cordoned off) while pursuing the pleasurable current of the dream. Now Freud cannot continue to be driven—carried along sexually—by the father figure of the dream. In his associations Freud writes:

The day before, I had hired a cab to take me to an out of the way street in Dornbach. The driver, however, had not known where the street was and, as these excellent people are apt to do, had driven on and on until at last I had noticed what was happening and told him the right way, adding a few sarcastic comments. A train of thought . . . led from this cab driver to aristocrats . . . Count Thun, indeed, was the driver of the state Coach of Austria. The next sentence in the dream, however, referred to my brother, whom I was thus identifying with the cab-driver. That year I had called off a trip I was going to make with him to Italy. ("I can't drive with you along the railway line itself.") And this cancellation had been a kind of punishment for the complaints he used to make that I was overtiring him on such trips . . . (*Standard Edition,* vol. V, p. 432).

In the ambiguous parenthesis, *"I can't drive with you along the railway line itself,"* the substitution of Alexander for Julius signifies Freud's primal guilt over the death of the first brother. For Julius, of course, could not accompany Freud on the railway journey from Freiberg or along the main line of life itself. It must be recalled also that Freud's father had died recently and was no longer accompanying Freud on his own trip through life. Having both died, Julius and Jacob are equated in a primary process dynamic that made Freud powerful through his nonsubmission to death.

In further associations to the dream Freud recalls next that the metaphor of a journey through life is related to two riddles he was given to solve at a party at the old woman's house. The riddles are like the Sphinx's riddles in that they require an understanding of the stages of life: the progress in this episode of the dream re-capitulates and reconstructs some of Freud's earlier life history. Indeed, the sequence of movements in the episode refers to the original trip of leaving Freiberg, where the first problem was leaving the house and moving the possessions by carriage to the railway station, and the second problem was to leave the town and go to a new town. In that movement, Freud had to leave Julius and his nurse behind him, in his memory. Memory may be represented in the research of the dream as not along the main line.

The day residue for this part of the dream is clear:

. . . One evening, while I was at the house of the hospitable and witty lady who appeared as the housekeeper in one of the other scenes in the same dream, I had heard two riddles which I had been unable to solve. Since they were familiar to the rest of the company, I cut a rather ludicrous figure in my vain attempts to find the answers. They depended upon puns on the words *"Nachkommen"* and *"Vorfahren"* and, I believe, ran as follows:

> 'With the master's request
> The driver complies:
> By all men possessed
> In the graveyard it lies.

The answer is "Vorfahren," ancestors; make precisely predecessors, those who go first. Then,

> 'With the master's request
> The driver complies:
> Not by all men possessed
> In the cradle it lies.

The answer is progeny, or successors (*Standard Edition*, vol. V, pp. 433–434).

When I saw Count Thun *drive up* (fahren) so impressively and when I thereupon fell into the mood of Figaro, with his remarks on the goodness of great gentlemen in having taken the trouble to be born (to become *progeny*), these two riddles were adopted by the dream-work as intermediate thoughts. . . . The dream-thought, however, which was operating behind all this ran as follows: "It is absurd to be proud of one's ancestry; it is better to be an ancestor oneself" (*Standard Edition*, vol. V, p. 434).

Better to be proud of one's own accomplishments than of an ancestor's or of one's progeny. The boast serves to dull Freud's dream anxiety over the possibility of his own death, and it refers to his father (who was not quite an ancestor) and to Julius (who was a younger sibling, of course, and not progeny at all); for Freud's difficulty with the riddles indicates his anxiety over the revised primal scene material he had been working on for several days. In this fantasy, as we have seen, a child died at the culmination of his father's love. It seems inevitable then that in turning around the primal scene fantasy of the *Count Thun* dream so as to get himself out of danger, Freud becomes the powerful person who survives his weaker partners. The movement in this direction begins with the megalomania Freud mentions which expresses itself in evasion of the censorship.

The evasion of the censorship is imaged in his reluctance to alight at Krems and Znaim (both cordoned off) where the affairs of state are going on and where Count Thun will be presiding. Rather than submitting to the count or to censorship, Freud decided—megalomanically, as he wrote—to alight at Graz so that he himself could control the pleasure of the dream:

. . . the mention of Graz went back to the slang phrase "what's the price of Graz?" which expresses the self-satisfaction of a person who feels extremely well off (*Standard Edition*, vol. IV, p. 215).

The introduction of the violets moves the dream in the direction of more satisfaction with less anxiety. The image of the stiff violets appears to represent a dream erection. Transforming the brown and violet color of the female trunk into the pleated brown and violet flowers, Freud contrives to construct an erect male genital in a previously empty buttonhole. His imaginary flower functions in the dream as an intermediary which makes it possible for the negative oedipal fantasy to proceed toward discharge without Freud's being overwhelmed by anxiety; for the stiff violets are a replacement for the anal–genital equation through which Freud had identified himself as a woman in the dream. Reversing the primal scene imagery, Freud becomes the driver, not the driven, the survivor, not the submissive victim. Freud's pride in his imaginary flower fuels the boastful megalomania of surviving a revenant of the primal ordeal Freud's child-mind associates with the annihilation of Julius.

A CREATIVE MECHANISM FOR
ENGENDERING EGO FLEXIBILITY

This section of the dream points to one major source of Freud's adult creativity, for his flowery innovation is a creative and restitutional way of allowing his negative oedipal fantasy to proceed without causing the dreamer to experience intense castration anxiety. The restitution recalls an earlier resolution that allowed him to retain a negative oedipal identification with the mother as a mode of thought. Another way of saying this is that in the dream Freud employs a mechanism from his 4-year-old development to retain omnipotent control over his infantile world. By constructing new fantasy material he controlled the direction of his thought processes. What follows is a detailed exploration of this 4-year-old's restitutional mechanism as it is employed in the third part of the *Count Thun* dream.

The restitution by flowers of the missing genital resembles the fetishist's attachment of an object to the penisless female body. It is significant that Freud adds flowers to his own body image and so alters the depiction of the body-ego that characterized previous portions of the dream. It has already been shown that flowers in the service of the symbolic restoration of missing genitals are a bedrock image for Freud, who added the flowers to Anna's image in the screen memory so that she might represent the missing Julius. Here, the flowers inserted into the buttonhole are an image of re-masculinization.

In his manifest dream imagery Freud placed a peculiar, long, pleated object next to the flowers. This he called a *Mädchenfänger*.

It is a kind of boutonnier, and its name suggests that it attracts women. This duplication of the flower fetish imagery accentuates the exhibitionism inherent in the flower symbolism.

The *Mädchenfänger* becomes a symbol, moreover, for what is new. This fetish symbol for the missing genital encodes the newly acquired oedipal function of fantasying which is a form of thought that accompanies childhood masturbation. In the context of his associations, the newly created *Mädchenfänger* and the brown-violet flowers are both associated with Freud's observation that children believe that "people are struck by anything new" (*Standard Edition*, vol. IV, p. 216). The oedipal child-dreamer is so delighted with his new contrivance imaged in the *Mädchenfänger* that he adds to the dream's manifest content that "it greatly struck people."

The twisted fecal *Mädchenfänger* resembles the anal omnipotent child's delight in his power to produce magical objects. Thus the *Mädchenfänger* is an expression of the productive mental state of which the mature creator can be so proud. The superabundance of the *Count Thun* dream satisfies an anal productive impulse, while it gratifies a childhood masturbatory impulse to produce rich fantasy material capable of overcoming all obstacles to imaginative sexual satisfaction. Freud is proud of producing a fantasy that overcomes the threat of death and castration inherent in the wish to participate in the primal scene as the female partner. His fantasy—and by extension his dream book—proves that he is amounting to something.

In association to the purchase of the new trunk, and to his comment that children are struck by what is new, Freud introduced two childhood memories into the material that surrounds the *Count Thun* dream. The memories are of the offer to buy his father a new red bed and of his having urinated, at a later age, in his parents' bedroom. As we have already surmised in connection with the dream of *The Open Air Closet*, the new red bed memory is an association to the negative oedipal fantasy revising the primal scene, while urinating in the parents' bedroom at a later age is an ambitious compensation for the earlier memory.

The sequence of submission to the father followed by rebellious overcompensation present in these two childhood associations is reproduced in the sequence of the *Count Thun* dream. The fetishistic composition thus presages the dénouement of the dream, for in the last episode of the dream Freud will completely reverse his position with regard to the negative oedipal father. The father, like Julius, will weaken and die, and the young boy-dreamer will complete his negative oedipal fantasy by acquiring the overwhelming penis of his father, which he will use to wash away the last vestige of his own weakness in a urinary discharge—with it he will wash away both his father and Julius.

COUNT THUN, EPISODE FOUR

Once more I was in front of the station, but this time in the company of an elderly gentleman. I thought of a plan for remaining unrecognized; and then saw that this plan had already been put into effect. It was as though thinking and experiencing were one and the same thing. He appeared to be blind, at all events, with one eye, and I handed him a male glass urinal because he was blind. If the ticket-seller were to see us like that, he would be certain to let us get away without noticing us. Here, the man's attitude and his micturating penis appeared in plastic form. (This was the point at which I awoke, feeling a need to micturate.) (*Standard Edition*, vol. IV, pp. 210–211).

In this last episode of the dream, Freud's revolutionary fantasy is fulfilled. He has completely reversed the situation that triggered the dream formation. No longer needing to submit to the powerful Count Thun, Freud has fulfilled the promise of Figaro, he has played the Count a tune, no longer identifying himself as the weak Count "do nothing" (*Nicht Thun*), the holiday-making Freud is now the chief of state. As we shall see, he believes he has solved the riddle of hysteria, and knowing that politics expresses father–son relationships, he believes that he understands politics better than the politicians. Now we can see that the alternative for Count Thun, Count Taafe, who died in 1895, not too long before Freud's father, presaged Freud's oedipal dream-triumph. The stiff, erect violets and fetish represent the triumph of Freud's creativity over the Count's skeletal flower—for in the course of the dream Freud has reduced Count Thun to the status of the dead Count Taafe; he has overcome him in his fantasy.

In his associations to this portion of the dream, Freud tied the
theme of revenge to showing his father, who had come to nothing in
the weakness of his sick old age, that he, the son, had indeed come to
something. The reversal of roles plumbs the negative oedipal
revision of the primal scene so thoroughly that the original scene's
most primal elements are revived in the associations to the dream.
Freud wrote,

The older man (clearly my father, since his blindness in one eye referred to
his unilateral glaucoma) was now micturating in front of me, just as I had
in front of him in my childhood (*Standard Edition*, vol. IV, p. 216).

But there is another interpretation:

He was one-eyed like Odin, the Father-God. *Odins Trost* (Odin's Consolation)—the *consolation* I offered him in the first childhood scene of buying
him a new bed (*Standard Edition*, vol. IV, p. 216).

The theme of consolation refers in part to 2-year-old Sigismund's consolation of his father for having soiled his father's
bed. Thus the theme points to tender and vengeful motifs in Freud's
negative oedipal revision of the primal scene. Like other materials,
the associations to this portion of the *Count Thun* dream indicate yet
again that Freud originally believed Julius a casualty of the primal
scene. In the dream's re-creation of the negative oedipal revision,
Freud accounts for the loss of his brother in terms of his four-year-
old wish for their father's love. Freud had taken Julius's death as an
indication both of Jacob's violence in the primal scene and of the
extent of Jacob's love for Julius. Desirous of the father's love,
Sigismund wished to be in Julius's place. The consolation Freud
wished to give his father in the original revision was to make up for
the loss of Julius by putting himself in Julius's place in the primal
scene. The wish for substitution is implicit in the story of *Odin's
Trost* to which Freud refers in his associations. This dangerous wish
is reversed in the last episode of the *Count Thun* dream. To be like his
father, whom Freud perceived as tender and destructive in primal
scene activity, Freud now promises to be tender to his father—as

the Marshall was to Julian Bouffler in *A Boy's Sorrows* at the symbolic and sexualized moment of the boy's death. The reader will recall that it was this work that elicited Freud's two childhood memories.

As in *A Boy's Sorrows*, Sigismund's developing relationship to his father is condensed in the Odin story. The association to one-eyed Odin announces the presence of the basal image theme one-eyed doctor into this dream's construction of the revised primal scene. The eye-penis equation that symbolized the one-eyed doctor's instinctual force is revived in Freud's association to the glass urinal: the urinal reminds him of an eye glass or the lenses tried on a peasant by an optician. Freud's association to *Odin's Trost* also shows how Freud connected the loss of one eye with the death of Julius. Guilty for wanting to kill his son Loki, Odin visits the Norns, who compel him to sacrifice one of his eyes and then teach him the limits of his power as a father. On his return from his visit to the Norns, Odin announces that he will no longer be called *The All Father*. He will be *The Son of All*. This recognition of his relation to fate is Odin's consolation. The consolation Freud offers his father is a similar sonship, with Freud himself becoming the tender father. Moreover, the Odin story reverses a boy's ambivalence to his father and his creation of good and bad father images; for Odin's story is a tale of good and bad sons. This ambivalence mirrors Freud's splitting of his own father image between Jacob Freud and the one-eyed doctor.

In his associations to the last portion of the dream Freud wrote of the reversal of roles he felt his father suffered in his final illness. ". . . A tragic requital . . . lay in my father's soiling his bed like a child during the last days of his life; hence my appearance in the dream as a sick nurse" (*Standard Edition*, vol. IV, p. 217).

This association reunites the alternate primal couple. The one-eyed doctor is the victim, the nurse tends him, and Freud identifies himself in both figures. Associatively recreating and revising the original primal scene, Freud gains control of it in this negative oedipal fantasy of mastery. As master he destroys Julius, as he imagined his father had done, though in this later life fantasy Julius and Jacob are identified through their weakness and submission to the powerful father of the revised primal scene. Controlling the situation through his urethral discharge, Freud wakes as the plastic image of his micturating penis, identified with his father's, is about to wash away Julius, inseminate the nurse, and show his father his power.

The piece of primary process thinking at the center—the fantasy—is the 4-year-old's take over of the primal scene. Thinking and experiencing anchor the oedipal fantasy in the body's reality, for thinking and experiencing are the same at the moment one wakes from a dream of micturating. In this context the equation of thinking and experiencing refers to the micturition that appears to the masturbating oedipal child's mind to be the essence of the father's power.

In his final association, the unity of thinking and experiencing reminded Freud of "a strongly revolutionary literary play by Oskar Panizza (*Das Liebeskonzil*, 1895)," in which God the Father is ignominiously treated as a paralytic old man:

In his case will and deed were represented as one and the same thing, and he had to be restrained from cursing and swearing by one of his archangels, a kind of Ganymede, because his imprecations would be promptly fulfilled (*Standard Edition*, vol. IV, p. 217).

This play—the plot of which is summarized by Grinstein—is based on a negative oedipal revision of the primal scene. In the play God is on the verge of killing the humans for their debauched sexual acts. It is the day before Easter (the time of the year that Freud associated with Julius's death); God is restrained from killing the humans by his sexless, beautiful angelic companion. Freud described this angel as a kind of Ganymede. In this version of the negative oedipal story, Freud identifies with the Ganymede figure who is so like Julian Bouffler. In Grinstein's summary,

. . . [God] complains that He has become old and blind and wishes that He could die as He will never be any better. The cherub caresses God and is sympathetic to His complaints about His feet being crooked and His legs burning with pain. With great sensuality, God takes the head of the cherub into His hands. As He presses His wet face against the cherub's cheek, they embrace and kiss each other.

The scene is interrupted by the entry of a winged messenger, who informs God that Naples is a "boiling pit of lust." Morality has been completely abandoned, the Holy commandments are being mocked, and phallic worship is being carried out in public. Women are running around in the nude and men are in a constant state of sexual excitement. In fury, but with great difficulty, God rises from His throne and, raising His fist, threatens to crush the humans. The cherub, however, beseeches Him not to do this as then there will be no more human beings. God must be restrained since, being God, His imprecations would be promptly fulfilled. Thinking it over for a long time with His mouth open, God finally agrees with the cherub that He cannot do this because He is too old to create (Grinstein 1980, p. 152).

We can see how this story of negative oedipal fulfillment relieved Freud. As the sicknurse of the dream, Freud must have identified with the cherub, whose job it was to tend God the Father and save humanity. Freud's wish, here, is to stand between Julius and his father's wrath, just as the cherub placed himself between God and humanity. The fantasy behind the association is that Freud would produce a tender response from the father, and so avert the destructive response that had sent Julius to his death. Moreover, his fantasy of supplanting Julius is a fantasy of saving Julius and so relieves Freud's guilt for desiring the death of the sibling who had supplanted him.

In Paniza's play, God is portrayed as syphilitic. Syphilis is a revenge transmitted through women for sexual violence authorized by the bad father, the pope, Alexander VI, a Borgia. Fantasying himself as the cherub, Freud expresses a wish to tend his good old father kindly, and not bring down the scourges of mankind on him as the human women in the play would do; for these women are Salomé and Lucrezia Borgia, and their dramatic function is the transmission of syphilis.

Freud's last association to the phrase "thinking and experiencing were the same thing," expresses the common creator's fantasy of creating "something out of nothing":

The phrase "thinking and experiencing were one and the same thing" had a reference to the explanation of hysterical symptoms, and the "male urinal" belonged in the same connection. I need not explain to a Viennese the principle of the "Gschnas." It consists in constructing what appear to be rare and precious objects out of trivial and preferably comic and worthless material . . . I had observed that this is precisely what hysterical subjects do: alongside what has really happened to them, they unconsciously build up frightening or perverse imaginary events which they construct out of the most innocent and everyday material of their experience. It is to these fantasies that their symptoms are in the first instance attached and not to their recollection of real events, whether serious, or equally innocent. This revelation had helped me over a number of difficulties and had given me particular pleasure. What made it possible for me to refer to this by means of the dream-element of the "male urinal" was as follows. I had been told that at the latest "Gschnas"-night a poisoned chalice belonging to Lucrezia Borgia had been exhibited; its central and principle constituent had been a male urinal of the type used in hospitals (*Standard Edition*, vol. IV, p. 217).

In this Freud describes the whole construction of the *Count Thun* dream. Constructed out of the most ordinary experience, it makes something of nothing, and with the poisoned chalice refers to a fantasy construction of the female genitals. The dream makes a fetish of the violets and the *Mädchenfänger* out of genetically worthless (fecal) precursors, and the female shape of the male urinal makes a bisexual genital of worthless *Gschnas* association and ordinary pieces of hospital paraphernalia.

Since, as Grinstein observes, Lucrezia Borgia was a character in *The Love Council* play, the male urinal may refer to a female receptacle that poisons through the spread of syphillis. Through his negative oedipal identification with this kind of woman Freud sees that it is possible to weaken the powerful father rather than to succumb to him. This, then, is the negative oedipal fantasy that Freud produced while standing on the train platform preparing to set off on his vacation. By dreaming the fantasy, Freud made it an object of his scientific interest. He learned that hysterical symptoms are a response to a fantasy element that arouses both anxiety and excitement. The symptom is the fulfillment of the oedipal fantasy condition in which thinking and experiencing must be the same. Freud ends his account of this dream with an apology for the one symptom he clearly produced in this way:

One might, I think, be inclined to suppose that these sensations were the actual provoking agent of the dream; but I would prefer to take another view, namely that the desire to micturate was only called up by the dream thoughts (*Standard Edition*, vol. IV, p. 218).

The Creator's Resolution of the Oedipal Dilemma

Freud's two train dreams show the fluid, fluctuating alternative versions of his revision of the original primal scene imagery. Here, as always, the significance of the oedipal reorganization of the mind's basal imagery is profound. The mother- and father-identified basal oedipal constructs determine the nature of subsequent experience. For these twin constructs produce alternative possibilities for revising long-term memory.

As we have stated, in each new construct formation the drives are rechannelled. The original primal scene evokes and tames the disparate aggressive and libidinal drives in such a way that aggressively cathected objectivity and libidinally cathected experience are sundered. As in one version of the primal scene a child is killed, in the other version, a child is created: the two versions of the primal scene structure the sense of reality vis-à-vis libidinal and aggressive forces. The normal resolution of this primal bedrock image split is the development of a sense of identity that excludes either the destruction or creation of new life. In the future creator's case, however, the individual devotes him or herself to the alternative proposition that it is possible for the infant to either create or destroy new life as the infant might create or destroy his or her own consciousness through very special efforts. The resolve to identify the self as creator/destroyer now coexists with the normal resolution of infantile development.

This description implies a syndrome of creators in which basal splits in mental life are maintained side by side with normal resolutions of development. In the oedipal period of life, a new identity serviceable for the latency period is developed as part and parcel of the process of resolving the oedipal conflicts. In the

creator's syndrome, however, a channel of nonresolution is maintained. The creator's method for maintaining this nonresolution is
described by Greenacre (1971) as a system of collective alternates.
In Greenacre's view the creative personality holds a plethora of
imaginative possibilities. As one oedipal irresolution is played off
against another, the anxiety and the exposure to the drives never
becomes so intense as to be overwhelming. This is an apt description
of Freud's situation. He maintained a bisexual attitude that allowed
him a maximum flux of empathic identifications with which to
explore the world. This creative response to the oedipal developments split off from his normal resolution. His creative response
was felt to be an artificial identity; for as a person involved in the
creator's syndrome maintains a split in his sense of identity, his
hypertrophied imagination performs any role in any fantasy. The
identity of one who commands the realm of fantasy continues into
latency, and the latency age creator maintains an identity that
parallels that of the ordinary latency child, the subject of the
following chapter.

6

Freud's Latency

The reconstruction of Sigismund Freud's psychological latency begins with a study of his dream of *The Botanical Monograph*. The *Monograph* dream occurred between March 10 and March 15, 1898. In letter #84 (March 10th, 1898), Freud responded to a letter from Fliess: "It was no small feat on your part to see the dream book lying finished before you" (Kris 1954, p. 246). Freud's own fantasy of completing the book, and his thoughts about how its completion would effect his ambition, stimulated the production of the dream. In his associations to the dream Freud wrote:

I had had a letter from my friend (Fliess) in Berlin the day before in which he had shown his power of visualization: "I am very much occupied with your dream book. I see it lying finished before me and I see myself turning over its pages." How much I envied his gift as a seer! If only I could have seen it lying finished before me (*Standard Edition*, vol. IV, p. 172).

While the image of the completed book was a powerful stimulus to the production of the dream, another stimulus was that having completed a chapter of *The Interpretation of Dreams*, Freud needed to do more work before he could complete the following chapters.

In his next letter to Fliess, #85, written on March 15, 1898, Freud announced that he was sending Fliess the first chapter he had

written—Chapter Two of *The Interpretation of Dreams*. The writing
of Chapter Two is thus contemporaneous with the dream of *The
Botanical Monograph*. Letter #85 refers to some of the contents of
the chapter: Freud's Irma dream and the dream of his uncle with the
yellow beard. These two dreams are filled with references to Freud's
ambition, they secretly indict Fliess's incompetence and treat him
as an inferior oedipal rival. They exhibit latency-derived feelings of
self-justification aroused in response to guilt over the wishes
expressed in the dreams. Having had recourse to the collective
alternates as a means of avoiding resolution of his oedipus complex,
Freud needed to justify to himself the vitality of his oedipal
ambition to triumph over his own father and transferential sur-
rogates for him.

Little did Fliess know the extent of the destructive impulses
against him that were represented in these very dreams. Nor did
Freud fully understand the origin of his aggressive wishes expressed
in Chapter Two:

The two dreams described will reappear in later chapters, where the partial
interpretations will be completed. I hope you will not object to the candid
remarks in the professor-dream. The Philistines here will rejoice at the
opportunity of being able to say that I have put myself beyond the pale. The
thing in the dream which will probably strike you most will be explained
later (my ambition). Remarks about *Oedipus Rex*, the Talisman fairy-tale
and perhaps *Hamlet* will also come in. First I must read more about the
Oedipus legend—I do not know what yet (Kris 1954, p. 248).

Yet the dreams contained the very oedipal materials Freud needed
to understand in order to complete the book. These were the family
romance themes embodied in *Oedipus Rex* and *Hamlet*. They
represent the aggressively cathected creative impulses of the
latency-age child, for in the family romance fantasy the creative
child disguises his oedipal wishes by imagining that the parents
toward whom his taboo wishes are directed are not his real parents
after all. If his parents are not his "real" parents, then his wishes
will no longer be incestuous or parenticidal.

What Freud was to discover about *Oedipus Rex* was not only
that, "The story of Oedipus is the reaction of the imagination to
these two typical dreams" (*Standard Edition*, vol. IV, p. 264)—the

dream of lying with the mother, and the dream of killing the father—but that the oedipal motifs animating creative work often originate in the family romance dreams of the latency-age creative child. Shakespeare's motive in writing Hamlet—like Freud's own in writing about the oedipal underlayer of Hamlet—was the fulfillment of a family romance-disguised wish for the death of his father. It was in this connection that he pointed out that Shakespeare's father had died just prior to his writing *Hamlet*. Not only had Freud's own father died in the prelude to Freud's undertaking *The Interpretation of Dreams*, Freud's special interest in *Hamlet* derived from his sense that understanding his identification with Hamlet would be a key to understanding his own creative drive as it manifested itself incompletely surmounted oedipal strivings. As Freud read *Hamlet*, the play was not about revenge so much as it was about Hamlet's inability to commit revenge. This inability Freud traced to Hamlet's guilt over his wish for his father's death. In *The Interpretation of Dreams* Freud wrote that *Hamlet* attempted to interpret the deepest layer of impulses in the mind of the creative writer" (*Standard Edition*, vol. IV, p. 266).

What was true of Shakespeare was true of Freud. The oedipal-aggressive wish to kill the father commands a retinue of wishes for the actualization of aggressive drives. If Freud could write about his oedipal aggression—and thereby actualize it—he could write about and actualize any derivative of aggression. In March of 1898 Freud realized that if he could unlock the mystery of his own death wishes, he would be free to complete the dream book. Thus, his own creativity was on Freud's mind between March 10th and 15th, 1898, when he had the dream of *The Botanical Monograph*. The dream expresses Freud's ardent wish to be free to complete his dream book. The roots of the dream wish spring from the early latency-age family romance, aggressive fantasy of being an exception to the rules that govern other individuals.

The Dream of The Botanical Monograph

I had written a monograph on a certain plant. The book lay before me and I was at the moment turning over a folded colored plate. Bound up in each copy there was a dried specimen of the plant, as though it had been taken from a herbarium (*Standard Edition*, vol. IV, p. 169).

The dream is manifestly an image of Freud examining his dream book. As we know he had sent the chapter containing the *Irma* dream, entitled "Analysis of a Specimen Dream" to Fliess around this time.

The apposition of colored plates and dried specimens, contrasting the vividness of experience with the dryness of memories that have been robbed of their effect is a major theme in Freud's analysis of this dream. As a botanical monograph the dream is itself a flower of Freud's imagination—composed in reaction to his anxiety that the material he already had on hand for the dream book, all the other specimens, would illustrate his own insufficiency. The flower imagery that pervades this dream, directly and in disguises, is restitutional, as all fetishes are restitutional for what is feared to be missing, or worse—destroyed—in experience. In turning over the "Specimen Dream of Psychoanalysis," for instance, Freud must have wondered at all the life experience and memory that was enshrined there, and he must have worried whether his aggression, and his ill-treatment of the patient, Irma, would emerge, and be clear to the reader. As Freud looked over his *Irma* dream, he must also have thought about Fleischl, who died through abuse of the plant coca, which Freud had wanted to make the vehicle of his latency-derived ambition to become a great man.

ASSOCIATIONS TO THE DREAM OF
THE BOTANICAL MONOGRAPH

That morning I had seen a new book in the window of a bookshop, bearing the title *The Genus Cyclamen*—evidently a *monograph* on that plant (*Standard Edition*, vol. IV, p. 169).

This neutral, dream-inciting image must have been linked with Freud's wish that it might be his own monograph, the dream book. Its colored plates must have been equated with his own vivid dreams. The book tempted him. Freud had an expensive habit of buying monographs for himself—instead of flowers for his wife. The temptation must have been perpetual, for in another section of *The Interpretation of Dreams* Freud described a similar dream:

I dreamt one night that I saw in the window of a bookshop a new volume in one of the series of monographs for connoisseurs which I am in the habit of buying . . . (*Standard Edition*, vol. IV, p. 268).

For Freud, book buying was accompanied by guilt. In his associations to the dream he wrote:

Cyclamens, I reflected were my wife's *favorite flowers* and I reproached myself for so rarely remembering to *bring* her *flowers* which was what she liked (*Standard Edition*, vol. IV, p. 162).

Freud contrasted this with his wife's generosity in bringing him his favorite flowers, artichokes, frequently. Freud related an anecdote of a Frau L., whom he had treated some years earlier. Frau L. had been disappointed when her husband "forgot" to give her birthday flowers. Depriving a woman of flowers points to the fetishistic dynamic of Freud's screen memory of his and John's snatching the flowers away from Pauline-Anna. The screen memory paper was on Freud's mind, for he mentioned it in connection with the following screen memory—itself an association to the dream and a representation of the dynamics of Freud's early latency:

It had once amused my father to hand over a book with coloured plates (an account of a journey through Persia) for me and my eldest sister to destroy. Not easy to justify from the educational point of view! I had been five years old at the time and my sister not yet three; and the picture of the two of us blissfully pulling the book to pieces (leaf by leaf, like an *artichoke*, I found myself saying) was almost the only plastic memory that I retained from that period of my life. Then, when I became a student, I had developed a passion for collecting and owning books, which was analagous to my liking for learning out of monographs: *a favorite hobby*. (The idea of "favorite" had already appeared in connection with cyclamens and artichokes.) I had become a *book-worm*. I had always from the time I first began to think about myself, referred this first passion of mine back to the childhood memory I have mentioned. Or rather, I had recognized that my childhood scene was a "screen memory" for my later bibliophile propensities. (Cf. my paper on screen memories.) (*Standard Edition*, vol. IV, pp. 172–173).

Freud's reference to the first time he began to think about himself is interesting, for we know he dates the beginning of continuous self-observation to latency, approximately the age of 6. It could not be too far from the truth to conclude that Freud's first self-realization is that he had a passion for reading books. Thus the screen memory associated to this dream is a structure that simultaneously contains, represses, and represents the derivatives that went into Freud's passion for books.

Elements in this screen memory are essential to an understanding of Freud's latency. First, the father's permission to tear the book apart is taken as if it were permission both to satisfy his curiosity about his sister's genitals and to fulfill his wish to dispose of the unwanted sibling altogether. In the essay on Goethe's childhood, we saw that Freud's passion for taking something to pieces and throwing the pieces away derived from his death wish toward Julius. Second, the element of pulling apart refers to masturbation, as Freud himself interpreted in his screen memory paper. Thus Freud's guilt over his bibliophile habit is guilt over a habit that is the one primary addiction. Third, the fact that Freud exercised his passion on a travel book, points to Freud's latency dreams of adventurous conquest. Fourth, Freud's passion for learning and reading strongly colored his latency.

The permissive or justifying aspect of this memory screens the aggressive current that runs through it. The aptness of the memory as an association to the dream is that at the time of the dreaming Freud begins a new lap in the journey of conquest in which there will be no authority except the truth he discovers. In this screen memory Freud neutralizes his father's authority, deflowers his sister, and rids himself of unwanted siblings.

Continuing the aggressive aspects of his oedipal fantasies into latency, Freud's favorite latency reading centered around battles of conquest. Anything was allowed in books. For, during his latency

Freud's psychic-life was organized around family romance fantasies of his own greatness. Not having shattered his oedipal complex, Freud, like other latency-age creators, refused to accept his father's authority. Rather than replace it with the authority of his teachers or of society, Freud indulged fantasies of retribution for his father's disgrace at the hands of the Christians. Thus he justified his fantasied usurpation of power.

In his reading, Freud was enthralled with Hannibal and Moses, Semites who redeemed their people and whose aggression was justified because it was deployed in the service of their people. By means of family romance fantasies, Freud avoided the shattering of his childhood oedipal wishes. Freud's study of books, his acquisition of books, and ultimately his writing of books became the means of actualizing the family romance motif of his latency.

While the self-observing quality of this dream turns it into a specimen too, as a species of latency thought, the dream represents a fantasy of overcoming all rivals on the way to becoming an all-conquering hero. The dream received reinforcement both from the screen memory, which referred to a variety of latency fantasies, and from a later oedipal, early latency-derived fantasy that Freud had entertained the night before the dream. The fantasy is contained within Freud's account of an earlier opportunity he had had to make a great discovery:

Once, I recalled, I really *had* written something in the nature of *a monograph on a plant*, namely a dissertation on the coca-plant, which had drawn Karl Koller's attention to the anaesthetic properties of cocaine. I had myself indicated this application of the alkaloid in my published paper, but I had not been thorough enough to pursue the matter further. This reminded me that on the morning of the day after the dream—I had not found time to interpret it till the evening—I had thought about cocaine in a kind of daydream. If I ever got glaucoma, I had thought, I should travel to Berlin and get myself operated on, incognito, in my friend's [Fliess's] house by a surgeon recommended by him. The operating surgeon, who would have no idea of my identity, would boast once again of how easily such operations could be performed since the introduction of cocaine; and I should not give the slightest hint that I myself had a share in the discovery. This fantasy had led on to reflections of how awkward it is, when

all is said and done, for a physician to ask for medical treatment for himself
from his professional colleagues. The Berlin eye-surgeon would not know
me, and I should be able to pay his fees like anyone else. It was not until I
had recalled this daydream that I realized that the recollection of a specific
event lay behind it. Shortly after Koller's discovery, my father had in fact
been attacked by glaucoma; my friend Dr. Konigstein, the ophthalmic
surgeon, had operated on him; while Dr. Koller had been in charge of the
cocaine anaesthesia and had commented on the fact that this case had
brought together all of the three men who had had a share in the
introduction of cocaine (*Standard Edition*, vol. IV, p. 170).

Freud's fantasy of submitting to the unknown eye doctor is a
variant of the negative oedipal revision of the primal scene. The
fantasy was stimulated by an intimate conversation Freud had the
night before with Dr. Konigstein. In it, according to Freud, he made
an ardent, self-justifying plea for maintaining his habits. Their
discussion included the propriety of charging doctors' wives for
treatment. In his associations to this dream, Freud noted that his
Irma dream was also a dream of self-justification. Then—as in his
conversation with Dr. Konigstein—Freud wanted permission to
continue his unique psychoanalytic treatment of hysterical patients.
The common affect in seeking permission ties Dr. Konigstein to
Freud's father in the screen memory. Freud's latency belief that he
must be an exception derives here from negative oedipal themes;
Freud's fantasy of submitting to an eye doctor under the cloak of a
secret identity reveals the underlying negative oedipal revision of
the primal scene. The morning fantasy of submitting to the eye
doctor is a continuation of the previous night's conversation with
Dr. Konigstein. Thus Freud's friend Konigstein here represents a
latency version of the one-eyed doctor. An opthalmic surgeon who
has operated on Freud's father for glaucoma, he had been assisted by
Freud in performing some surgery that made use of cocaine
anaesthesia. On this occasion Freud acted as Dr. Konigstein's
assistant in enucleating a dog. At the time they did not carry their
research far enough to get credit for the discovery of cocaine as an
anaesthetic agent in performing human surgery. If they had, Freud
felt, he would already have fulfilled his latency fantasy of becoming

a great man. Thus, in the fantasy of submitting to the eye doctor as a patient who would pay, Freud was elaborating on his negative oedipal, latency fantasy of submitting to a great man in order to become great himself. It is in this sense that Freud submits himself to Dr. Konigstein's judgment.

The meaning of cocaine is overdetermined in this fantasy. As Freud indicated, cocaine is a powder derived from flowers. Symbolically, then, cocaine represents the essence of flowers. Moreover, in "Über Coca" and in a famous letter to his future wife, Freud wrote that coca is a drug that will restore potency and enhance the vigor of men and women. Thus Freud perceived this special flower essence as a kind of chemical fetish. In the morning fantasy Koller is the equivalent of the bad one-eyed doctor, while Konigstein is the good one.

Fantasies of damage and aggression lurk behind every element of Freud's morning fantasy. Freud goes in the fantasy to Fliess's house in Berlin. This alludes to operations that Fliess had performed on Freud's sinuses with the aide of cocaine, and also to an operation Fliess had performed on Irma, the subject of Freud's specimen dream. That operation, although Freud did not admit it quite openly to his associations to the *Irma* dream, had ended almost fatally for Irma. Fliess had left a piece of iodoform gauze in Irma's sinus, leading to infection, and to further severe symptoms when it was removed by another specialist. Sharing a neurosis around nasal pathology with Fliess and having sent Irma to him, Freud felt he was a collaborator with Fliess in his treatment—or mistreatment—of Irma.

The whole notion of using cocaine therapeutically, fraught with magic and fetish imagery as it is, includes a great deal of aggressive and hostile memories and fantasies. Freud could not have a conversation with Konigstein without thinking about Fleischl, whom Freud felt may have been a casualty of his own ambition to make himself great with the use of cocaine.

Each specimen memory of Freud's attempt to become great alludes to damage that Freud may have caused. His hobbies, his analyses, his researches, and his writings had, he thought, all damaged women, or sibling figures or father figures. The quality of

damage is seen in another memory Freud beings into association
with the dream coming from later in his latency:

There was a *dried specimen of the plant* included in the monograph, as
though it had been a herbarium. This led me to a memory from my
secondary school. Our headmaster once called together the boys from the
higher forms and handed over the school's herbarium to them to be looked
through and cleaned. Some small worms—bookworms—had found their
way into it. He does not seem to have had much confidence in my
helpfulness, for he handed me only a few sheets. These as I could still
recall, included some crucifers. I never had a specially intimate contact
with botany. In my preliminary examination in botany I was also given a
crucifer to identify—and failed to do so (*Standard Edition*, vol. IV, p. 171).

This incident sheds more light on the earlier screen memory
from Freud's fifth year. Freud felt some guilt over destructive
aspects of his fantasy of deflowering his younger sister. He
disclaimed any intimate knowledge of her anatomy. In this memory
he identified himself through the master's eyes with the bookworms.
This is a reference to the intrusive little boy's penis. Since Freud
was generally a fine student, we must take his inability to recognize botanical specimens as a symptomatic disclaimer of aggressive
fantasies of exploring his sister's genitals.

Freud's compulsion to confess is revealed in his allusion to the
patient—her name was Flora—he was discussing with Konigstein
the day before. Freud's attitude toward Flora needed justification,
for Freud wanted to cathect her as he had cathected Anna in the
screen memory of the book:

What, it may be asked, would have happened if . . . the patient we had
been talking about had been called Anna instead of Flora? (*Standard
Edition*, vol. IV, p. 176)

In another section of *The Interpretation of Dreams*—dealing
with the direct contribution of infantile material to the form the
dream takes—Freud indicated directly that this dream took root in a
late oedipal fantasy of aggressively dismembering the female genitalia:

. . . in the course of my analysis of the dream of the monograph on the genus Cyclamen, I stumbled upon the childhood memory of my father, when I was a boy of five, giving me a book illustrated with colored plates to destroy. It may perhaps be doubted whether this memory really had any share in determining the form taken by the content of the dream or whether it was not rather that the process of analysis built up the connections subsequently. But the copious and intertwined associative links warrant our accepting the former alternative: cyclamine—favorite food—artichokes; pulling to pieces like an artichoke, leaf by leaf (a phrase constantly ringing in our ears in relation to the piecemeal dismemberment of the Chinese Empire)—herbarium—bookworms, whose favorite food is books. Moreover I can assure my readers that the ultimate meaning of the dream, which I have not disclosed, is intimately related to the subject of the childhood scene (*Standard Edition*, vol. IV, p. 191).

The Interpretation of Dreams is built on specimen scenes of carnage. The dream of *The Botanical Monograph* demonstrates in its manifest simplicity what a binding of aggression occurs in latency. All of the affect is tightly bound in the manifest rendition of the dream, just as all of the oedipal aggression is absorbed into themes of social morality in latency. This and Freud's interest in soldiery and conquest during latency are revealed in Freud's final comments on this dream which contain an image that is itself a general metaphor for the interpretation of the dream:

Let us, for instance, take the dream of the botanical monograph. The thoughts corresponding to it consisted of a passionately agitated plea on behalf of my liberty to act as I chose to act and to govern my life as seemed right to me and me alone. The dream that arose from them has an indifferent ring about it: "I had written a monograph; it lay before me; it contained colored plates; dried plants accompanied each copy." This reminds one of the peace that has descended upon a battlefield strewn with corpses; no trace is left of the struggle which raged over it (*Standard Edition*, vol. V, p. 467).

This is the advent of the latency mind. The dried specimens are the bound oedipal fantasies and memories of early childhood. Each period of early childhood leaves only screen memories as traces of basal constructs. We can see that the screen memory that caps the oedipal period opens to exercise its influence on Freud's subsequent fantasy life and on his creative work.

Peace on the Battlefield: Freud's Middle Latency

The "peace on the battlefield," was the result of the repression that accompanied the onset of latency. Sigismund's early reading centered on battlefield heroes, triumphant conquests, and justified aggressions. These materials he was later to connect with his wishes to enter Rome. In *The Interpretation of Dreams* he discovers that the origin of his enthusiasm for Hannibal is the books he read between the ages of 6 and 7:

I believe I can trace my enthusiasm for the Carthaginian general a step further back into my childhood; so that once more it would only have been a question of transference of an already formed emotional relation on to a new object. One of the first books that I got hold of when I had learned to read was Thiers' history of the Consulate and Empire. I can still remember sticking labels on the flat backs of my wooden soldiers with the names of Napoleon's marshals written on them. And at that time my declared favorite was already Massena (or to give the name in its Jewish form, Manasseh). (No doubt this preference was also partly to be explained by the fact that my birthday fell on the same day as his, exactly a hundred years later.) Napoleon himself lines up with Hannibal owing to their both having crossed the Alps (*Standard Edition*, vol. IV, pp. 197–198).

Another book that carried Freud into the martial realm of his family romance was the Bible, specifically the *Phillipson's Bible*. (*Die Israelitische Bibel*). There is evidence—in the form of a note Freud's father included with a gift of the second edition of this bible which Jacob made his son when he was 35—that Freud had been given this book to read when he was 6 or 7 and had just begun to read. The imagery of its lavish woodcuts appealed to the boy's imagination. While writing *The Interpretation of Dreams*, Freud recalled a dream from his latency that relied on imagery from *Phillipson's*. The dream condenses events from the middle period of Freud's latency. Like a screen memory, it represents the dynamics of an era.

A Failure of Repression in Latency

In *The Interpretation of Dreams* Freud dates the dream to his seventh or eighth year, but the dream imagery alludes to the death of Freud's maternal grandfather, which took place when Freud was nine-and-one-half years old. For this reason, it seems likely that the dream occurred when Freud was between 9½ and 10, and that it refers to early episodes of failures of repression, even perhaps to anxiety dreams from earlier in Freud's latency.

The dream is clearly an oedipally revised primal scene dream. Part of its imagery stems from Freud's repeated entries into his parents' bedroom for the purpose of using the chamber pot. On another of these occasions, Freud's father ordered the child out of the room as he attempted to witness parental intercourse. The anxiety in this dream indicates that Freud's latency was disturbed by a failure to lay his oedipal wishes to rest.

The Dream of The Bird-beaked Figures

Freud introduces the dream in this way:

It is dozens of years since I myself had a true anxiety-dream. But I remember one from my seventh or eighth year, which I submitted to interpretation some thirty years later. It was a very vivid one . . . (*Standard Edition*, vol. V, p. 583).

By saying it took place dozens of years earlier, Freud is trying to push the dream as far back into the past as he can. Although Freud suspects that the dream took place when he was 7 or 8, the reference to his grandfather's death suggests that the dream must have occurred when Freud was around 9 years old. The implication is that dozens of years later Freud had still not resolved the dynamics represented in the dream.

I saw my beloved mother, with a peculiarly peaceful, sleeping expression on her features, being carried into the room by two (or three) people with bird's beaks and laid upon the bed. I awoke in tears and screaming, and interrupted my parent's sleep. The strangely draped and unnaturally tall figures with bird's beaks were derived from the illustrations to Phillipson's Bible (*Standard Edition*, vol. V, p. 583).

Strachey, the Editor of the *Standard Edition*, points out in a footnote that the fourth chapter of Phillipson's *Deuteronomy* shows several Egyptian gods with bird's heads. This reinforces Freud's statement that the figures "must have been gods with Falcon's heads from an ancient Egyptian funerary relief" (*Standard Edition*, vol. V, p. 583). A glance at these falcon-headed people shows them to be one-eyed and phallic—imagistic representations of a figure essential to Freud. In association to the dream Freud indicates that in his childhood the falcon's heads represented penises and intercourse. For the German slang for copulating is *vögeln*, as he was taught by one Phillip, the son of a concierge, who was Freud's playmate in Freiberg.

The punning associations to the name Phillipson may be a key to understanding this dream, for the imagery of the mother's peaceful appearance replaces another image of the mother as passionate. This is strongly reminiscent of the screen memory of the 2½-year-old Sigismund standing in front of the empty cupboard (Kasten) screaming for his mother, who suddenly appears looking slim and beautiful. In that scene Philipp, Freud's half-brother, was the sexual instructor, jokingly telling the young boy that his mother-nurse had been boxed up. That primal pun stood simultaneously for the ideas that his mother was dead, that she was pregnant (going into confinement), that she had had intercourse with the father (been "knocked up"), and that she had been imprisoned in a box. The fact that Freud alluded to another Phillip as his sexual instructor indicates that even as a young child he had been informed of the method of copulation, possibly by his brother Philipp, and that he had enough information to connect that with the primal scene and with pregnancy. In regard to the early screen memory Freud wrote that he had concluded that Philipp must have impregnated his mother. In that fantasized case, Freud himself could also have been Philipp's son.

In his discussion of the childhood anxiety dream Freud states that the expression on his mother's face had been copied from the view of his grandfather's face in his terminal coma. This Freud interprets as an indication that a dream process of secondary revision had substituted the grandfather's partial image in order to portray the mother as dying rather than in the midst of a passionate sexual scene. He ends his recollection of the dream with the interpretation that,

The anxiety can be traced back, when repression is taken into account, to an obscure and evidently sexual craving that had found appropriate expression in the visual content of the dream (*Standard Edition*, vol. V, p. 584).

In the continuation of his text, Freud associates this anxiety dream with another one dreamt by a patient. Freud's dynamic understanding of this patient's anxiety dream is strongly suggestive of dynamics in his own case:

A 27-year-old man . . . reported that when he was between 11 and 13 he had repeatedly dreamt (to the accompaniment of severe anxiety) that a man with a hatchet was pursuing him; he tried to run away, but seemed to be paralyzed and could not move from the spot. . . . In connection with the hatchet, he remembered that at about that time he had once injured his hand with a hatchet while he was chopping up wood. He then passed immediately to his relations with his younger brother. He used to ill-treat this brother and knock him down; and he particularly remembered an occasion when he had kicked him on the head with his boot and had drawn blood, and how his mother had said: "I'm afraid he'll be the death of him one day." While he still seemed to be occupied with the subject of violence, a recollection from his ninth year suddenly occurred to him. His parents had come home late and had gone to bed while he pretended to be asleep;

soon he had heard sounds of panting and other noises which had seemed to him uncanny, and he had also been able to make out their position in bed. Further thoughts showed that he had drawn an analogy between this relation between his parents and his own relation to his younger brother. He had subsumed what happened between his parents under the concept of violence and struggling; and he had found evidence in favor of this view in the fact that he had often noticed blood in his mother's bed (*Standard Edition*, vol. V, pp. 584–585).

As Grinstein suggests, the thematic similarity of the explanation of this man's anxiety dreams with these of Freud's own anxiety suggests that Freud's dream of his mother with the bird-beaked figures referred to an experience of the primal scene, which Freud had repressed (Grinstein 1980, pp. 457–459). The grandfather's death must have stimulated oedipal wishes and, beyond that, preoedipal fantasies of killing Julius in a revivified image of a violent primal scene. The image of serenity on the mother's face replaces the excitement and commotion of arousal. "I remember that I suddenly grew calm when I saw my mother's face, as though I had needed to be reassured that she was not dead" (*Standard Edition*, vol. V, p. 584). Having gone into his parents' room, Freud reassured himself that his mother was neither dead nor having intercourse—but it may be surmised that she was pregnant. He had received similar reassurance in the Kasten screen memory of his mother's becoming pregnant with a revenant of Julius. Amalie was pregnant, not dead. Occurring some time after Freud was 9½, when his mother was pregnant with Alexander (who was born when Freud was 10) the anxiety dream of bird-beaked figures revived the dynamics of Freud's early childhood.

Given that this screen memory containing a reference to Philipp first occurred to Freud when he was about 10 years old, it can be reconstructed that when Freud was about 10 years old, he experienced a failure in repression, which expressed itself in an anxiety dream. In this dream, or series of dreams, the one-eyed doctor was again seen in an act of primal intercourse with his mother, which destroyed old life (whoever might get between the primal couple) and created new. So memorable a dream must have functioned as a screen memory to express dynamic themes connected with entrance into a new stage of psychic life. Probably the failure in repression was determined by neuropsychological factors which ended the more subdued aggressive phase of latency and ushered in the preadolescent phase.

Preadolescence (*Ages 10 to 12*)

Freud commenced secondary school at the age of 9½. He was a diligent, independent student, who showed from the beginning a preference for studying monographs and other materials beyond the required reading: "At the 'Gymnasium' (Grammar School) I was at the top of my class for seven years; I enjoyed special privileges there and had scarcely ever to be examined in class," Freud wrote in *An Autobiographical Study* (*Standard Edition*, vol. XX, p. 8). In this way he established his independent intellectual authority. Scholarship became the realm of his ambition.

As he became a scholar, Freud began to feel that his own learning outstripped his father's. In his preadolescence, from the ages of 10 to 12. Freud felt that his father was weakening while he himself was strengthening. Soon after he began school, he took a new model for himself. Sigismund found a friend in Heinrich Braun, two years older and destined to become a leading political figure among the social democrats in Austria. Freud modelled his own sense of masculine strength on Braun's. Emulating Braun's interest in the social world, Freud wished to become a lawyer.

Implicit in the identification with Braun was Sigismund's wish to surpass his father.

In the pregymnasium days, Jacob Freud had been unable to pursue his trade with much success in Vienna. The family received economic help from Amalie Freud's relatives. When Freud was 9½ or 10, however, the family moved into a new and larger dwelling in Vienna. It would seem that since Freud started the gymnasium, and the family was able to move to better living quarters in the period immediately after the maternal grandfather's death, the family must have profited from some sort of legacy which paid for the new residence and Sigismund's education. Scattered details about the Freud family's life during this period indicate little economic distress, although the preceding years in Vienna appear to have been somewhat difficult.

While in these years Sigismund consciously believed himself to be surpassing his unsuccessful father, derivatives of his identification with his father were not to materialize until later. As an adult he was to identify with his father as a man who needed financial help from his wife's family. In later years, attempting to downgrade the help he received from his wife's family which finally allowed his long projected marriage to get under way, Freud borrowed money from such doctor friends as Breuer and Flieschl who had superior means.

As in earlier years, during his preadolescence Freud perceived his father's weakness as the result of anti-Semitism directed toward Jacob.

One would hardly guess it from looking at me, and yet even at school I was always the bold oppositionist, always on hand when an extreme had to be defended and usually ready to atone for it (Ernst Freud 1975, p. 202 letter to Martha Bernays, Feb. 2, 1886).

Wanting to liberate his father from the Christian forces that crippled him, Freud identified with Hannibal, who in overreaching also suffered defeat on the road to Rome. As a guilty, overreaching scholar he identified also with Winckelmann, an intellectual warrior who also met his death attempting to reach Rome.

It was on my last journey to Italy, which, among other places took me past Lake Trasimene, that finally—after having seen the Tiber and sadly turned back when I was only fifty miles from Rome—I discovered the way in which my longing for the eternal city had been reinforced by impressions from my youth. I was in the act of making a plan to bypass Rome and travel to Naples, when a sentence occurred to me which I must have read in one of our classical authors: "Which of the two, it may be debated, walked up and down his study with the greater impatience after he had formed his plan of going to Rome—Winckelmann, the Vice-Principal, or Hannibal, the Commander-in-Chief?" I had actually been following in Hannibal's footsteps. Like him, I had been fated not to see Rome; and he too had moved into the Campagna when everyone had expected him in Rome. But Hannibal, whom I had come to resemble in these respects, had been the favorite hero of my later school days. Like so many boys of that age, I had sympathized in the Punic Wars not with the Romans but with the Carthaginians. And when in the higher classes I began to understand for the first time what it meant to belong to an alien race, and antisemitic feelings among the other boys warned me that I must take up a definite position, the figure of the semitic general rose still higher in my esteem. To my youthful mind Hannibal and Rome symbolized the conflict between the tenacity of Jewry and the organization of the Catholic church (*Standard Edition*, vol. IV, p. 196).

Freud's justification of his determination to redeem his father was further aided by the birth of his brother Alexander when Freud was 10. Freud influenced his family to name the new sibling Alexander by making an impassioned speech for the Macedonian military hero, thus justifying his preadolescent ambition. The birth of this brother further buried Freud's residual regrets for Julius's death. Freud's impassioned speech in the family council showed his learning to be in the service of the family fortune. Thus, while early in his latency Freud had viewed his father as permissive, he later thought of him as weak. This latter view upheld Freud's continuing belief in his own specialness and in his fantasy of changing the world.

Continuing his association to his identification with Hannibal, Freud presented the following recollection from this period:

I may have been ten or twelve years old, when my father began to take me with him on his walks and reveal to me in his talks his views upon things in the world we live in. Thus it was on one such occasion that he told me a story to show me how much better things were now than they had been in his days. "When I was a young man," he said, "I went for a walk one Saturday in the streets of your birthplace; I was well-dressed and had a new fur cap on my head. A Christian came up to me and with a single blow knocked off my cap into the mud and shouted: "Jew! get off the pavement!" "And what did you do?" I asked. "I went into the roadway and picked up my cap," was his quiet reply. This struck me as unheroic conduct on the part of the big man who was holding the little boy by the hand. I contrasted this situation with another which fitted my feelings better: the scene in which Hannibal's father, Hamilcar Barca, made his boy swear before the household altar to take revenge on the Romans. Ever since that time Hannibal had had a place in my fantasies (*Standard Edition*, vol. IV, p. 197).

The father's story is an allegory of why the family had to leave Freiberg; they had left because of religious persecution. At this time Freud's wish to return to his birthplace became charged with justifiable aggression and condensed with a wish to conquer Rome.

Although the anecdote of the 50-year-old father's referring to himself as a young man was consciously charming, the preadolescent boy was oblivious to the self-knowledge contained in the mature man's remarks. Even the mature Freud who retold the anecdote seems unaware of his father's self-knowledge and of his father's attention to the boy's education. The 11-year-old Freud was filled with the thrill of his own potential as a man in the world. The expanding self-image of the young creator seems to blow past the mature image of his father, who has nowhere to go but the inevitable decline into physical decrepitude. In his preadolescence Freud developed the attitude which was to support later remarks to the effect that his father had tried many ventures, none quite successfully.

The preadolescent Freud's unconscious assumption of superiority emerges at the end of "A Disturbance of Memory on the Acropolis":

The very theme of Athens and Acropolis in itself contained evidence of the son's superiority. Our father had been in business, he had had no secondary education, and Athens could not have meant much to him. Thus what interferred with our enjoyment of the journey to Athens was a feeling of filial piety (*Standard Edition*, vol. XXII, p. 247).

Indeed, Freud's father had been in the sexual business since his adolescence, having a wife and a son to support by the time he was 17.

Preadolescent Derivatives in Freud's Creativity

It is commonly believed that Freud's ability to write *The Interpretation of Dreams* stemmed from the understanding and resolution of his own Oedipus complex achieved in the aftermath of his father's death. Although understanding and resolution of the Oedipus complex contributed to his achievement, these were not the only causes of Freud's success. In the aftermath of his father's death, useful derivatives of other developmental periods were stimulated as well. What follows is a discussion of the derivatives of Freud's preadolescent period as contributors to *The Interpretation of Dreams*.

Freud's ambivalently held belief in his superiority to his father was reinforced in the aftermath of his father's illness and death in late October 1896. During the period of his father's illness, Freud was much concerned with his own state of health, which he felt might also be failing. After a few months had gone by, however, Freud began to feel more optimistic about his own prospects, and the preadolescent feeling revived in him that his father's weakness and mortality provided him with reasons to show strength for both of them.

His reaction to his father's decline in stature during the son's preadolescence, and the son's response to his father's decline, illness, and death during the son's fortieth year, indicate that Freud felt as if he shared a certain fund of masculine strength with his father and that, as the strength of one increased, the strength of the other decreased. These kinds of feelings were particularly important when Freud was remodeling his sense of personal identity as a maturing boy just prior to his adolescence. The sense that he alone was the man of his extended family and the sole support of some dozen dependents increased Freud's awareness of his own importance in the months after his father's death. It was in those months that Freud determined to understand the psychology of the dream process. Thus the writing of *The Interpretation of Dreams* had strong roots in Freud's preadolescent need to assume the strength of a recognizedly important man. While Freud's wish to become a professor took on added significance in the months after his father's death, the facts that a professorship had been denied him because he was Jewish and that Karl Lueger's anti-Semites had taken charge of the government in 1897, gave Freud more reason to feel that his battle for recognition was to be waged against the same forces that had weakened his father.

The Dream of The Uncle with the Yellow Beard

Because the wish to become a professor and the need to unravel the structure of the dream process were on Freud's mind in the late winter of early 1897 these wishes were major factors in the construction of the *Uncle* dream. This dream and the *Irma* dream form the backbone of Freud's initial work on the dream book. The *Irma* dream established in Freud's mind that dreams are all unconsciously wish fulfilling. In this period, the *Uncle* dream established that there was a second psychical agency, a censoring agency which was as important as the unconscious wish in the formation of the dream. One of the major associations to the *Uncle* dream refers to an incident from Freud's preadolescent period in which Freud first developed the wish to become a minister of the government. That memory served a decisive function in the formation of the *Uncle* dream, because it provided a basis in the original structuring of the censoring agency in Freud's own mind. Understanding the function of his own censoring agency allowed Freud to circumvent its power through analysis of it. The *Uncle* dream is thus a formal problem-solving dream. Its job is to suggest the existence of both psychic agencies. Proving the existence of two agencies is the wish-fulfilling function of the dream.

The dream of the yellow-bearded uncle was instigated by a visit on the day before the dream from a colleague who informed Freud that his name was to be put before the ministry in nomination of a professorship. Knowing that anti-Semitism in the government militated against fulfillment of the recommendation, Freud suppressed his excitement:

On the morning after this visit I had the following dream, which was remarkable among other things for its form. It consisted of two thoughts and two pictures—each thought being succeeded by a picture. I shall, however, report only the first half of the dream here, since the other half has no connection with the purpose for which I am describing the dream (*Standard Edition*, vol. IV, p. 137).

This prologue shows the form in which a thought is represented twice, once as a verbal residue, once as a picture. This gave Freud reason to believe that a single idea could be represented by or conveyed into more than one system. Since this is a morning dream, it seems likely that the *Uncle* dream is hypnopompic and that the pictorial image is directed toward holding onto sleep wishfully while the verbal equivalent is directed more toward consciousness, i.e., toward an acceptance of waking. In that sense the repetition implies a conflict between sleeping and waking. The phallic imagery of the picture indicates that it is probably a REM dream accompanied by an erection:

I. . . . My friend R. was my uncle.—I had a great feeling of affection for him.

II. I saw before me his face, somewhat changed. It was as though it had been drawn out lengthways. A yellow beard that surrounded it stood out especially clearly (*Standard Edition*, vol. IV, p. 137).

ASSOCIATIONS TO THE DREAM OF
THE UNCLE WITH THE YELLOW BEARD

The elongated face, the phallic luster, and the emphasis on the beard indicate that this is a penile image. Freud associates the image with a number of men: his friend, his uncle, his father, and himself. In association to the beard imagery Freud thinks of the color changes undergone by black beards turning grey, changes which his beard, and that of his friend, were at the time of these associations undergoing. Equating the change in color with a decline in masculine strength, Freud superimposes his own image on those of other men—particularly his father's—in order to emphasize a phallic likeness. At the same time his dream aims to show the similarity between his own inevitable decline in phallic stature and the declines of his predecessors. The theme of ambition and remodelling the self-image in the likeness of increased or decreased strength evokes the wish to become a professor.

"R. was my uncle." What could that mean? I never had more than one uncle—Uncle Josef. There was an unhappy story attached to him. Once—more than thirty years ago—in his eagerness to make money, he allowed himself to be involved in a transaction of a kind that is severely punished by law, and he was in fact punished for it. My father, whose hair turned grey from grief in a few days, used always to say that Uncle Josef was not a bad man but only a simpleton (*Standard Edition*, vol. IV, p. 138).

In a footnote Freud mentions that he actually had five uncles, not one. Therefore it must be that the uncle he had in mind was the one closely attached to his father, his father's brother. The memory, going back over 30 years, refers to Freud's latency. The exaggeration of his father's hair turning grey in a few days must stand for a change in Freud's attitude about his father occurring consciously over a few days. Thus the reference to economic hardship and the loss of status refers to Freud's father, and to the change in Freud's feelings about his father's status during his latency.

Freud traced his preadolescent wish to take on the power that belongs to the social authorities:

My parents had been in the habit, when I was a boy of eleven or twelve, of taking me with them to the Prater. One evening, while we were sitting in a restaurant there, our attention had been attracted by a man who was moving from one table to another and, for a small consideration, improvising a verse upon any topic presented to him. I was dispatched to bring the poet to our table and he showed his gratitude to the messenger. Before inquiring what the chosen topic was to be, he had dedicated a few lines to myself; and he had been inspired to declare that I should probably grow up to be a Cabinet Minister. I still remember quite well what an impression this second prophecy had made on me. Those were the days of the "Burger" Ministry. Shortly before, my father had brought home portraits of these middle class professional men. . . . There had even been some Jews among them. . . . The events of that period no doubt had some bearing on the fact that up to a short time before I entered the University it had been my intention to study law; it was only at the last moment that I changed my mind (*Standard Edition*, vol. IV, pp. 192–193).

As always, Freud's manner in telling the tale conveys the sense of the very young man's understanding of events.

Politically there was a great difference between the Burger Ministry of Freud's preadolescence and the Lueger Ministry 30 years later. Freud had established the possibility of admitting wishes to become politically great to his consciousness when he was 11, and the same intensity attached to the latter-day wish to become a professor. In the reminiscence of celebrating the Burger Ministry, Freud's father celebrates the fact that his son will have an opportunity to make advances in the world that were denied him.

Analyzing the dream, Freud became aware of his ambivalence toward his own father and toward father figures in general. In his associations he realized that the dream was denigrating two "esteemed" Jewish colleagues, who had been refused professorship, by equating them with his uncle. One was too simple; the other had a blot on his record. He realized that in doing this he had identified himself with the Minister who had the power to accept or reject recommendations put before him.

With regard to Freud's understanding of the dream process, what is important here is the extended analogy he makes between the dream censorship and the political censorship. As a writer whose works may be read by the censoring ministry, Freud uses phrases like "denominational consideration" to indicate the reason he did not expect to be appointed professor. He doesn't want to come out and say, "because I am a Jew."

A similar difficulty confronts the political writer who has disagreeable truths to tell those in authority. If he presents them undisguised, the authorities will suppress his words—after they have been spoken, if his pronouncement was an oral one, but beforehand, if he had intended to make it in print. A writer must be aware of the censorship, and on its account he must soften and distort the expression of his opinion. . . . The fact that the phenomena of censorship and of dream-distortion correspond down to their smallest details justifies us in presuming that they are similarly determined. We may therefore suppose that dreams are given their shape in individual human beings by the operation of two psychical forces (or we may describe them as currents or systems); and that one of these forces constructs the wish which is expressed by the dream, while the other exercises a censorship upon this dream-wish and, by the use of that censorship, forcibly brings about a distortion in the expression of the wish (*Standard Edition*, vol. IV, pp. 143–144).

Enlivened by conflicting affiliations to both agencies, Freud's dream of *The Uncle* is full of ambivalence. The dreamer shifts between an identification with the authority and an identification with the aspirant. He makes the aspirant stronger and the authority weaker, and then he makes the authority stronger and the aspirant weaker. The fluctuating identification is rooted in Freud's pre-adolescent relationship with his father. In the dream it is represented by the process of superimposition in the visual imagery:

What I did was to adopt the procedure by means of which Galton produced family portraits: namely to projecting two images on to a single plate, so that certain features common to both are emphasized, while those which fail to fit in with one another cancel one another out and are indistinct in the picture. In my dream about my uncle the fair beard emerged prominently from a face which belonged to two people and which was consequently blurred; incidentally, the beard further involved an allusion to my father and myself through the intermediate idea of growing grey (*Standard Edition*, vol. IV, p. 293).

No doubt a great host of other figures hide behind the common likeness. One thinks of the original Joseph, Joseph Pur, the original for the one-eyed doctor; and of Joseph Breuer, a colleague from whose likeness Freud was actively disengaging himself by writing *The Interpretation of Dreams* without him. One thinks also of Fliess, who, during these years, is a true composite figure, a true collective audience who stands for the object of every transference. Fliess's figure stands behind the ambivalence of all these dreams, including this one. In one footnote to this dream added in 1911, trying to explain the element of affection that is admitted to consciousness while all the hostility is barred, Freud referred to Fliess:

While I was engaged in working out a certain scientific problem, I was troubled for several nights in close succession by a somewhat confusing dream which had as its subject a reconciliation with a friend whom I had dropped many years before. On the fourth or fifth occasion I at last succeeded in understanding the meaning of the dream. It was an incitement to abandon my last remnants of consideration for the person in question and to free myself from him completely, and it had been hypocritically disguised as its opposite (*Standard Edition*, vol. IV, p. 145).

At the time of the present dream Freud was still trying to separate his own self-image as a man from the image of his father. As is apparent, guilt over oedipal wishes to destroy his father was not the sole dynamic called into play in Freud's restitutional reaction to the loss through the production of his dream book. Noteworthy among Freud's reactions to his father's death, as he began to actively degrade the source of his father's authority, was a revival of preadolescent attachment to his father. Reconstructing Freud's preadolescence, we see the pubertal boy gradually developing the hirsutism characteristic of males. His conflict centered on reconciling feelings of identity with a father he experienced as stronger and weaker than himself. The reasons for Jacob's ambivalent assimilation into Austria's social and political structure were increasingly salient to Sigismund as his own social assimilation became more significant. At this point, his father's sins and his father's Jewish defense against his sins became directly relevant to Freud's life. Freud's prehistory came into play on the threshold of his adolescence. In one further association to the dream about his uncle, Freud says: ". . . I recalled an anecdote I had often heard repeated in my childhood. At the time of my birth an old peasant woman had prophesied to my proud mother that with her firstborn child she had brought a great man into the world." The family's patent artifice concerning Freud's birth circumstances set a tone of social mythology, compensating the family for the social sin involved in Sigismund's conception. Sensing his father's fault,

Freud could either decide to become a lawyer and overcome his
father's social sins, or he could choose a career in which he would
attempt to penetrate the mythology of his past. Freud's uncle in the
dream was an image of his father's fault. In this degradation, Freud
used Fliess as an intermediate figure of identification with his
father. Thus Freud's motives in writing *The Interpretation of Dreams*
were to strengthen his father's image as it remained imbedded in his
self-image, while overcoming the father in the writing of the work.

7

Early Adolescence
(Ages 13 to 15)

The work Freud did on *The Interpretation of Dreams* in the late summer of 1898 revived the conflicts of his early adolescence. These he portrayed in the dreams of the period, which naturally constituted the material of his self-analysis. After the summer vacation in 1898, work on *The Interpretation of Dreams* was temporarily halted. In order to continue writing the book, Freud needed to understand the contribution of puberty to the development of neurotic symptoms and to understand the parallel between dream formation and symptom formation—in his own life and then in more general terms. His analysis of the *Three Fates* dream, most probably dreamed on the night of his return to Vienna in 1898, finally unlocked the role of puberty and adolescent masturbation in symptom formation. After analyzing this dream, Freud was nearly able to complete *The Interpretation of Dreams*.

Freud returned home after a great deal of travel in August and September of 1898. He had set off at the time of the *Count Thun* dream in early August. According to Jones (1953, p. 334) Freud first visited Fliess, and then set off with his live-in sister-in-law, Minna, for a brief excursion to the Italian Alps. At the end of this excursion he joined his wife, Martha, and his children for two weeks before going on an extended tour with his wife. Because Martha developed a gastric disturbance at Ragusa, she remained at the hotel in Ragusa while Freud went on from Ragusa to Cattaro. Returning, Freud rejoined his wife at Ragusa for a trip to Spalato and Trieste. Then, still bothered by abdominal discomfort, Martha returned to Aussee and the children. Freud continued alone through northern Italy and finally returned home alone. These details form the background for Freud's return to Vienna—on which occasion he dreamed the *Three Fates* dream.

The details of the trip to Ragusa, a conversation with a stranger, and an analysis of forgetting the name of Signorelli and of the painter of The Last Judgement at Orvieto combined to form the residue that stimulated the *Three Fates* dream. A letter (#96) to Fliess (dated September 22, 1898 and written just a few days after Freud's return) reflects the dynamics that stimulated or were about to stimulate the dream. Taking liberties with names had been a main expression of these dynamics. Forgetting names had been another:

> I could not remember the name of the great painter who painted The Last Judgement at Orvieto . . . I forgot the name of Signorelli during a short trip into Herzegovina, which I made with a lawyer from Berlin (Freyhau), with whom I got into a conversation about pictures. In the course of the conversation, which aroused memories which, as I say, evidently caused the repression, we talked about death and sexuality (Kris 1954, pp. 264–265).

The dream's stimulus was a repressed evocation of Freud's adolescent fixation on his old concatenation of sex and death. In *The Interpretation of Dreams*, Freud uses *Three Fates* to illustrate the connection between adult experience and childhood material. However, the material which caused the repression in Ragusa derived its significance not from its childhood origin, but from the meaning Freud attached to the material during adolescence:

> When I was six years old and was given my first lessons by my mother, I was expected to believe that we are all made of earth and must therefore return to earth. This did not suit me and I expressed doubts of the doctrine. My mother thereupon rubbed the palms of her hands together—just as she did in making dumplings, except that there was no dough between them— and showed me the blackish scales of epidermis produced by the friction as

a proof that we were made of earth. My astonishment at this ocular demonstration knew no bounds and I acquiesced in the belief which I was later to hear expressed in the words: "Du bist der Natur einen Tod schuldig" [Thou owest Nature a death] (*Standard Edition*, vol. IV, p. 205).

An effective reenforcer of repression, this memory testifies to the fact that the 6-year-old understood his mother's performance as a threat. He would have to give up his childhood masturbation or suffer the same consequences that Julius had suffered: he would have to submit to the "Last Judgment." Memory of this lesson must have been revived in adolescence when rubbing the hands together produced semen—an ocular demonstration which, when it is first performed, fills the beholder with astonishment and with fear of the Last Judgment. As we shall see in the *Three Fates* dream, a figure who stands for the mother links Freud's childhood masturbation with the adolescent masturbation that is the dream's main topic; the dream was to initiate a struggle (which lasted through the end of 1898) to understand how sexuality and fear of death could lead to symptoms when they are linked in adolescent masturbation.

The struggle led ultimately to a reconstruction of the central conflicts of Freud's own adolescence. Understanding adolescent sexuality took time. In his next letter to Fliess (dated September 27, 1898), Freud reviewed the details of a new case; he neglected an etiology which points to adolescent masturbation guilt in favor of an etiology of childhood masturbation due to conflicts over bedwetting:

The occasion for the outbreak of his condition, which has persisted since his 14th year, was provided by the death of his brother and the death of his father in a psychosis. He feels ashamed of being seen walking the way he does, and thinks that is natural. He patterns himself on a tabetic uncle; the current popular aetiology of tables (sexual excess) caused him to identify himself with him when he was a boy of thirteen (Kris 1954, p. 266).

Recognizing the patient's identification with a victim of sexual excess, Freud somehow avoided making a connection between the 13-year-old's masturbation and his identification with his uncle.

The connection between his shame and his gait was a correct one. Several years ago, when he had gonorrhea, which was naturally noticeable from his walk, and several years before that, he was hampered in walking by constant (aimless) erections. There is also a deeper cause for the shame. He told me that the last year when the family was living by the River Wien (in the country), the Danube suddenly started rising, and he had a panic fear that the water would come into his bed (Kris 1954, p. 266).

From this point Freud traced the patient's neurosis to bedwetting shame, and even further back into infancy. He failed to connect the aggressive fantasies of adolescent masturbation with the formation of symptoms after the deaths of the young man's brother and father.

Unable to understand the relationship of fantasy to dreaming and symptom formation, in letter #99 on October 23, Freud complained that the dream book was at a standstill:

In any case I am not in a state to do anything else, except study the topography of Rome, my longing for which becomes more and more acute. The dream book is irremediably at a standstill (Kris 1954, p. 269).

In letter #101 on January 3, 1899, Freud suggested that evidence began to solve the riddle of adolescence through his work on the "Screen Memory" paper—itself an example of self-analysis. This letter was written after a visit by Fliess, so the piece of self-analysis that culminated in the "Screen Memory" paper appears to have been started in the aftermath of the visit.

First of all I have accomplished a piece of self-analysis which has confirmed that fantasies are products of later periods which project themselves back from the present into earliest childhood; and I have also found out how it happens, again by verbal association.

The answer to the question of what happened in infancy is: Nothing, but the germ of a sexual impulse was there (Kris 1954, pp. 270–271).

As was characteristic when Freud made a new discovery—in this case that adolescent masturbation fantasy revises past versions of sexuality—he gave it preeminence over all past discoveries he had made. He was very excited with his finding as can be seen in the letter as he continued it the next day which is filled with images that evoke erection and ejaculation:

> . . . the thing is growing. There is something in it. It is dawning. In the next few days there will certainly be something to add. . . . All I shall disclose to you is that the dream pattern is capable of universal application, and that the key to hysteria really lies in dreams. I understand now why, in spite of all my efforts, I was unable to finish the dream book. If I wait a little bit longer I shall be able to describe the mental process in dreams in such a way as to include the process in hysterical symptom-formation (Kris 1954, p. 271).

In letter #103 on January 30, 1899, Freud commented:

> Puberty is coming more and more into the center of the picture, and the fantasy key is substantiating itself. (Kris 1954, p. 274).

Finally, having expressed (in letter #104) his fantasy of moving to Berlin where he could be always with Fliess, in letter #105 Freud synthesized his ideas on the role of adolescent sexuality in symptom formation. He had developed an understanding of adolescence, masturbation fantasy, dreams, and hysteria. He was ready to go ahead and complete the writing of *The Interpretation of Dreams*. It is noteworthy that each advance in his thinking during the previous six months had coincided with some fantasy of joining completely with Fliess.

> It is not only dreams that are fulfillments of wishes, but hysterical attacks as well. This is true of hysterical symptoms, but it probably applies to every product of neurosis—for I recognized it long ago in acute delusional insanity. Reality–wish fulfillment: it is from this contrasting pair that our mental life springs. I believe I now know the determining condition which distinguishes dreams from symptoms that force their way into waking life. It is enough for a dream to be the wish-fulfillment of the repressed thought; for a dream is kept apart from reality. But a symptom, which has its place in actual life, must be something else as well—the wish-fulfillment of the repressing thought. A symptom arises where the repressed and the repressing thoughts can come together in the fulfillment of a wish. A

symptom in its character of a punishment, for instance, is a wish-fulfillment of the *repressing* thought, while self-punishment is the final substitute for self-gratification—for masturbation (Kris 1954, p. 277).

This insight allowed Freud to complete *The Interpretation of Dreams.* He now understood the sense of reality accompanying masturbation fantasy. Having unlocked the dynamics of his own adolescent masturbation in "Screen Memories," Freud was able to relate symptom formation to masturbation fantasy and dreaming. The riddle had been hard to unlock, for with few exceptions from age 13 until almost age 30, masturbation must have been Freud's only sexual gratification. Cathected intensely, its pleasures long remained a deliberate mystery.

Masturbation and the Young Creator

In the maturational process, hormonal changes result in the development of secondary sex characteristics. In males these changes culminate readiness for physiologically productive orgasm. Together with the physical changes in the body, the new experience of pleasure provokes a change in the basic neuropsychological identity structure. The remodeling of identity requires an intense creative effort throughout adolescence. For the future creator the fantasy of producing a work comes to be equated with the sought-after identity change of becoming a person capable of engaging in sexual fulfillment. This engenders a sense of longing represented in masturbatory fantasy and in creative work.

For the young writer the culmination of masturbation fantasy is equated with the act of writing; the completion of the work with orgasm. The sensation and physiological concomitants of the excited and orgastic state become equated with the content of the writing. The intellectual defenses and guilt associated with the masturbation fantasy conflict with the instinctual pressure of the writing, and the compromise solution to the conflict is a new form of thinking that may be characterized as the *sexual metaphor*. The sexual metaphor pervades the young creator's thinking.

A sense of pretense based on the nature of the fantasy state during adolescent masturbation, moreover, pervades the future creator's developing identity sense. For whenever there is a major increase and change in the nature of the libidinal drive, the whole organization of personal identity is affected. These are the times in life when a major neuropsychological process is invoked, bringing the past into the present again in the full intensity of its affective reverberation. All of these creative elements, as well as the change in Freud's feeling of identity are expressed in the *Three Fates* dream.

In his adolescence Freud underwent an intense reorganization of the image themes that animated his mental life. For Freud, as for other creators, the adolescent masturbation wishes were raw and undefended. Thus Freud was strongly aware of his sexual desire for his mother. The irrepressible wish led to the fear of death: the wish to penetrate to the inside of his mother's body led the adolescent to fear the chasm into which his fixation suggested Julius had disappeared. The disturbing concatenation of sexual pleasure and death imagery polarized Freud's emotional life. During his adolescence Freud developed a strong wish for a male friend with whom he could share his emotional life and so avoid or protect himself from entering too deeply into a dangerous relationship with a woman. The derivatives of that attitude were to be seen in Freud's illusion of Fliess's companionship in his deepening researches into the origin of the energy for the dream book.

At the turn of the year 1899, when Freud was reformulating his theory of the dynamic opposition of sex and death, he wrote to Fliess:

I live gloomily and in darkness until you come, and then I pour out all my grumbles to you, kindle my flickering light at your steady flame and feel well again; and after your departure I have eyes to see again, and what I look upon is good (Kris 1954, p. 272).

In this biblical image of visual creation Freud announced that he had found the solution to his problems of creativity. In the primal light of his self-knowledge Freud understood that his own instincts were the source of his masturbation pleasure and pain. The man from Berlin must have reminded Freud of Fliess, who was also from Berlin, and with whom Freud had talked at length of death and sexuality, the primal qualities of life. In the conversation with the man from Berlin, Freud had identified the conjunction of death and sexuality as the "Turkish" motif because, as Freud wrote in a contemporaneous essay, a Turk would rather die than have to do without his sexual pleasure (*Standard Edition*, vol. III, p. 292). The *Three Fates* dream analyzes the Turkish motif into the earlier elements from which it was derived.

The Dream of The Three Fates

Tired and hungry after a journey, I went to bed, and the major vital needs began to announce their presence in my sleep; I dreamt as follows:

I went into a kitchen in search of some pudding. Three women were standing in it; one of them was the hostess of the inn and was twisting something about in her hand, as though she was making Knödel [dumplings]. She answered that I must wait till she was ready. (These were not definite spoken words.) I felt impatient and went off with a sense of injury. I put on an overcoat. But the first one I tried on was too long for me. I took it off, rather surprised to find it was trimmed with fur. A second one that I put on had a long strip with a Turkish design let into it. A stranger with a long face and a short pointed beard came up and tried to prevent my putting it on, saying it was his. I showed him then that it was embroidered all over with a Turkish pattern. He asked: "What have the Turkish (designs, stripes . . .) to do with you?" But we then became quite friendly with each other (*Standard Edition*, vol. IV, p. 204).

Freud's presentation of his associations to this dream resemble those of a model analytic session, or series of model sessions. The associations, like the words of a poem are linked in a self-interpreting structure of allusions and themes. Here even minor seeming references—one to a line from Goethe's autobiography, for instance—ramify meaningfully in the structure of the entire "session."

Dealing with the structure of Freud's adolescent identity and with the precursors to that identity, this material is highly "overdetermined." That is to say the identity issues form a coherent mass of complexes radiating from the core of Freud's accumulated bedrock experience. As a result, Freud's associations to *The Three*

Fates emerge as image themes revolving like satellites around the center of Freud's identity. The dream, like adolescence itself, is a search for the common determinants of identity. Because these are the associations of personality marked by the creator's syndrome, a tension between Freud's identity as an individual and his identity as a creator presents itself in the associations to this dream.

The developing creator feels a sense of guilt as he realizes that he has an ulterior motive for involving himself in his experiences. It is his wish to find out what is common to human experience so that he can make use of that in his creative expression. The equation of the central women in Freud's life with the three Fates is an example of that mechanism:

In connection with the three women I thought of the three Fates who spin the destiny of man, and I knew that one of the three women—the inn-hostess in the dream—was the mother who gives life, and furthermore (as in my own case) gives the living creature its first nourishment. Love and hunger, I reflected, meet at the woman's breast. A young man who was a great admirer of feminine beauty was talking once—so the story went—of the good-looking wet-nurse who had suckled him when he was a baby: "I'm sorry" he remarked, "that I didn't make better use of my opportunity" (*Standard Edition*, vol. IV. p. 204).

The adolescent sexual wish for the mother is clear in this. The shaping of the Knödel therefore has a sexual significance ulterior to its relationship to the issue of hunger. In this understanding, the dream is a prototype for the fantasy that accompanies a first ejaculation. The experience of first ejaculation connects the feeling of individual identity with an awareness of the boy's biological origin.

Functional Phenomena in the Dream of The Three Fates

The functional phenomena determining and revealed in the form of this dream recapitulate the dynamics of Freud's psychological adolescence. The association vital to this explication is that

Freud associated the putting on of a condom to the putting on of the
overcoat. The identity of the two acts—putting on an overcoat and
putting on a condom—equates the body with the penis. The penis
represents the body of the dreamer in the dream. The penis is, in
fact, the central image of the dream. The relation of this image to the
dream's functional phenomenon is the relationship of erection to
sleep. Because a penile erection accompanies an REM dream, and
because the amplitude of the erection is often represented directly
in the dream imagery, it is likely that this pleasure-seeking dream is
an REM dream. In this functional context, the equation of the penis
with the dreamer's ego may be used as a guide to the progress of the
dreamer's ego through this dream.

In the opening of the dream, Freud wants to ejaculate, but the
wish is frustrated. The inn-hostess's manipulation of something in
her hands represents the dreamer's wish for stimulation of his
penis, his wish for direct gratification. The "guest" is told to wait.
Being told to wait in the dream is an indicator of anxiety. As an
anxiety prototype, the necessity to wait or to defer pleasure points
to a whole range of adult symptomatic difficulties with the sexual
process. Thus, in the functional context, going off with a sense of
injury indicates the adult dreamer's feeling of diminution in his
sense of potency with the arrival of anxiety. The amplitude of the
erection diminishes at this point. Putting on an overcoat protects
the dreamer's hurt feelings while it guards his penis from possible
injury. But putting on the overcoat is also an image of penetration.
To the adolescent mind the condom may even be a vaginal object.
While the first overcoat's excessive length indicates the diminution
of the adult dreamer's erection, it also illustrates the younger ego's
feeling that the adult woman is too large for him. His surprise that
the coat is trimmed with fur is surprise at the presence of pubic hair.

In the next phase of the dream, the dreamer puts on another
overcoat. Following the functional phenomena, it is likely that the
erection's amplitude has increased again, possibly through the
introduction of a new fantasy directed toward a new sexual object.
While this overcoat contains the Turkish design—an allusion to the
conjunction of sexuality and death which arouses anxiety—it
belongs to the phallic stranger who now appears in the dream. The

other man's coat is the image of the other man's body, the image of his penis.

A compromise is about to be reached. The dreamer becomes friendly with the other man, who thus reinforces the image of the dreamer's own strength, allowing his penis to remain erect. At the same time the wish to penetrate is suspended and so is the sense of danger.

Recall that Freud had gone travelling with his wife, that his travel with her had been stopped short by her illness, and that Freud had found a travelling companion with whom he discussed death and sexuality. Freud's sexual wishes toward his wife had been interrupted by her illness. The other man may be taken as yet another reincarnation of the male companion who would help Freud deflower, for the first association to this dream takes Freud back to the age of 13:

When I began analyzing this dream, I thought quite unexpectedly of the first novel I ever read (when I was thirteen perhaps); as a matter of fact I began at the end of the first volume. . . . The hero went mad and kept calling out the names of the three women who had brought the greatest happiness and sorrow into his life. One of these names was Pélagie (*Standard Edition*, vol. IV, p. 204).

The affective cry, *Pélagie*, is an expression of the pleasure and pain a woman brings to a man, and it is equated in this way with a cry of sexual passion. In the context of these associations, though, the cry should be understood as Freud's 13-year-old response to his own awakened passions; undoubtedly it relates to a memory of his own first productive masturbations. This, in turn, evoked Freud's primal connection of intercourse with death as it had been oedipally defended in the "screen memory" paper.

It is significant that the memory relates to a name and to a novel. Referring to the first novel he had read means that the book was a novel experience for Freud. The fantasy attending productive masturbation became a novel experience too; suddenly the fantasy's intensity increased, and the sense of actualization attending the fantasy was augmented as the fulfillment of the fantasy coincided with a simultaneous orgasm. This new quality—adolescent fantasy prelude to orgasm—required the institution of a new kind of reality-testing. The fantasist learned to maintain that while the masturbation fantasy could be realized, it is pretense in fact. Thus the sense of pretense became a central quality in the productions of Freud, the adolescent creator.

The *Three Fates* dream illustrates the significance Freud attached to pretense as masturbatory fantasy. One of Freud's chief clues to the dream's meaning was "plagiarism," a word he associated to *Pélagie*. Plagiarism is destruction of an author's identity, and in Freud's *Pélagie* the name is broken down into a series of basal signifiers. Even the articulemes become meaningful. This process of grammatical dedifferentiation represents a larger process of wished-for dedifferentiation of the dreamer's identity in the process of the dream. In associations to a second part of the dream Freud identified himself as a thief who stole overcoats from the university lecture hall as lectures were going on. This is dream reference to plagiarism, to stealing ideas, to treating them as if they were his own. Having seen the sexual significance of putting on the overcoat, we realize that plagiarism is a sexually derived symptom.

The theme of plagiarism then is tied to the fantasy of stealing pleasure from women and identity from men. In his associations to the dream, Freud shows plagiarism to be a derivative of adolescent fantasy. For Freud, plagiarism was tied both to the act of writing and to the feeling of stealing pleasure. Freud's tendency in his writing was to want to attribute ideas to other persons. This is a transformation of Freud's guilty belief in his own priority. For example, when Freud was studying the dream literature during the fall of 1898, he claimed that he had little to learn from those persons who had attempted to understand the meaning of dreams before him, although he was uneasy about this contention. Among Freud's expressions about plagiarism in this dream is one in which Freud associatively confessed to a little borrowing. The connection can be seen through the coincidence of the *Pel* root which Freud associated to the presence of the same root in alliterative associations of a predecessor.

(*Pelagie—plag*iarizing—*plag*iostomes . . .) connected the old novel with the case of Knödel and with the overcoats, which clearly referred to implements used in sexual technique (cf. Maury's alliterative dreams) (*Standard Edition*, vol. IV, p. 206).

The case of Knödel mentioned above refers to an incident of plagiarism, told to Freud by his lecturer in his pathology. The plagiostomes connect with fish bladders, which were used as condoms. The reference to Maury quoted in *The Interpretation of Dreams* indicates that Maury's associations convey a declaration about the connection between dreams and hysteria, a concept known to be of critical importance to Freud's sense of intellectual priority:

Maury himself gives two excellent instances of dreams of his own in which dream-images were linked together merely through a similarity in the sound of words. He once dreamt that he was on a pilgrimage (*pele*rinage) . . . he found himself visiting *Pel*letier, the chemist, who . . . gave him a zinc shovel (*pel*le) (*Standard Edition*, vol. IV, p. 58).

Freud included the material from Maury in his chapter, "The Scientific Literature on Dreams," in order to show how sound association could link dream images. Maury called such a linkage of images a *délire*—similar to the spontaneous and automatic mental acts that one finds in hysteria. Maury's connection of dreams and hysteria, particularly by a description of mental acts that might be automatic, must have threatened Freud's sense of priority.

In this connection, a look at the novel Freud mentions will shed further light on Freud's adolescent conflict, and also on the origins of his attempt to find a solution to the equation of death and sexuality through the compromise of writing. Grinstein (1980, pp. 179–190) identifies the novel in question as *Hypatia* by Charles Kingsley, published in 1853. This novel touches all the instinctual issues that were on Freud's mind in adolescence. The protagonist, 18-year-old Phillammon, tries to become a monk while in the grip of instinctual forces that evoke his passion toward two women. The first, Pélagie, the incarnation of voluptuous sensuality, turns out to be a reincarnation of a sister of Phillammon's from an earlier era when brother and sister had lived in Greece. The second woman, Hypatia, evokes in him an equal passion. Although she possesses great beauty, it is her mind that attracts him. She wants to reenact the Greek myths. She is learning incarnate, the mind symbolized, less real than life—she is *Hypatia*, the book.

Both women arouse the adolescent's feelings of sexuality and sense of danger. Hypatia represents a search for the origins of the meaning of life; Pélagie represents the wish for pure carnal pleasure. Both are sister figures for the adolescent hero. A third woman, Miriam, turns out to be Pélagie's Jewish mother. Pélagie's Jewishness is treated as a major source of her carnality. In the novel the tension between the two kinds of women is mirrored in the tension between Judaism and Christianity. Two kinds of monks represent a tension between bound and unbound Christian aggression directed against expressions of sensuality.

Hypatia's fate is to be torn apart by a Christian mob led by "Peter the Reader," a monk-critic who has realized that her passion for learning has the same carnal roots as those shown by Pélagie in a dance of passion. In the aftermath of unleashed aggression, Phillammon enters a quiet life as a monk searching for his wisdom. After a long period of renunciation, he is finally reunited with his sister Pélagie. They die together in an embrace signifying the consummation of their love in death.

The Greek theme in the story derives from the underlying myth of Orestes and Iphigenia; Hypatia and Pélagie are aspects of the mythological Iphigenia. Phillammon is equated with Orestes.

The appeal to Freud was obvious. Like Phillammon, young Freud tried to intellectualize and sublimate his passions and to create an aesthetic-philosophical system. Again, like Phillammon, Sigismund tried to substitute brotherhood for the love of women. Indeed throughout his adolescence Freud warned his friends against the danger of early physical involvement with women. The thrust of each warning was that involvement would put an end to pursuits of the mind.

Having thought of Pélagie, Freud's analysis of the dream led to more and more concrete nominal associations. His own identity, his own name, and the identity and names of his friends became allusions to concrete forms of gratification. For example,

—and now for the dumplings—the *Knödel*! One at least of my teachers at the University—and precisely the one to whom I owe my histological knowledge (for instance of the *epidermis*)—would infallibly be reminded by the name *Knödel* of a person against whom he had been obliged to take action for plagiarizing his writings. The idea of plagiarizing—of appropriating whatever one can, even though it belongs to someone else—clearly led on to the second part of the dream, in which I was treated as though I were the thief who had for some time carried on his business of stealing overcoats in the lecture rooms. I had written down the word "plagiarizing" without thinking about it, because it occurred to me; but now I noticed that it could form a bridge (Brücke) between different pieces of the dream's manifest content (*Standard Edition*, vol. IV, pp. 205–206).

These associations are organized like those in an analytic session. Plagiarizing connected the first part of the dream to a second part. Evoked as if incidentally, the theme of stealing gratification is profoundly connected with the mood of the session Freud has been conducting. For he finds he has been stealing gratification from men and women alike. Further analysis of the dream shows that he has been turning people into concrete representations of their names as a way of subtly stealing gratification from people by placing them in his fantasy world. That process derives from adolescent masturbation fantasy, which is in itself the making of other people into possessions of a fantasy life. It is only a step from the first theft to the intellectual crime of stealing their ideas.

In connection with plagiarism, Freud referred to purchases made on the trip with his wife at Spalato. Apparently Freud felt that, with his wife's help, he might have taken advantage of the shopkeeper, Popovic.

The stranger with the long face and pointed beard who tried to prevent my putting on the overcoat bore the features of a shop-keeper at Spalato from whom my wife had bought a quantity of Turkish stuffs. He was called

Popovic, an equivocal name. . . . Once again I found myself misusing a name, as I had already done with Pélagie, Knödl, Brücke, and Fleishl. It could scarcely be denied that playing about with names like this was a kind of childish naughtiness (*Standard Edition*, vol. IV, p. 207).

Popo is a child's word for "bottom." Freud continued his confession, first justifying his reduction of names to pleasure representations, and then adding his own name to the list:

But if I indulged in it, it was an act of retribution; for my own name had been the victim of feeble witticisms like these on countless occasions (*Standard Edition*, vol. IV, p. 207).

As mentioned earlier, "Freud" means "joy" or "delight." In the dream's context of identifying himself with the male organ, Freud must mean sexual pleasure. Freud continued,

Goethe, I recalled, had remarked upon people's sensitiveness about their names: how we seem to have grown into them like our skin. He had said this apropos of a line written on his name by Herder: "Der du von Gottern abstammst, von Gother oder vom Kote"—"So seid ihr Gotterbilder auch zu Staub" (*Standard Edition*, vol. IV, p. 207).

In a footnote Strachey writes,

The first of these lines comes from a facetious note written by Herder to Goethe with a request for a loan of some books: "Thou who are the offspring of gods or of Goths or of dung—(Goethe, send them to me!). The second line, a further free association of Freud's, is taken from the well-known recognition scene in Goethe's *Iphigenie auf Taurus.* Iphigenia, hearing from Pylades of the death of so many heroes during the siege of Troy, exclaims: "So you too, divine figures, have turned to dust!" (*Standard Edition*, vol. IV, p. 207).

The image of identity growing into names like "our skin" is an image of erection: the erect penis grows into the skin of its identity. As a sexualized image the reduction of identity to dust shows the sexual product as a kind of dust. This accords with his mother's lesson that we all return to dust. The whole sexual experience of ejaculation, growing into the skin of the penis, the manipulation of the penis, and the discharge of semen, with the sensation more intense than any previously known, is a radical identity-changing experience. The reduction of identity from names to body products— Fleischl-meat, Knödl-breast/penis, Freud-pleasure/penis, Goethe-excrement—shows the nature of the pleasure process as it reduces identity-consciousness to more elemental forms, making the process of masturbation as it demonstrates the discharge of energy seem an entropic lesson of fate.

Another parallel theme in the reduction of life to death is the sequence of associations Freud makes from Fleischl to a scene of Fleischl's skin flaking away as a result of his addiction to cocaine injections. Freud associated cocaine with the same sating of needs he expected from the inn-hostess. Using cocaine to find satisfaction was an example of the primary addiction, masturbation, in a derivative form.

The overdetermined nature of the identity lesson Freud presents us with in his associations to the *Three Fates* dream is nowhere more clear than in Freud's association to Goethe's autobiography. As Grinstein (1980) notes, the themes of that autobiography are almost identical with those of *Hypatia*. Even Pélagie seems associatively connected to the autobiography—in the doctrine of Pelagius, which was important to Goethe. Pelagius did not believe in original sin. Thus masturbation need not find moral justification if one believes in the doctrine.

As we know, Freud took Goethe as an identity model for himself, so that he must have felt that he was trying to plagiarize— steal—Goethe's identity. Parallels between his own life and Goethe's were important to him. Freud identified with Goethe's assumption that he was incontestably his mother's favorite, with his unconscious wish to do away with his siblings, and with his guilt over the death of a younger brother. Goethe had had an unrequited love for a girl named Gretchen in his adolescence, Freud had such a love for Gisella Fluss. Goethe had an extremely close friend in his adolesence, whom he called Pylades from the myth of Orestes and Iphigenia. Freud had a similar friend named Silberstein. Goethe had as a later confidante, a one-eyed doctor, Herder. Herder had a swelling of one eye which eventually became disfiguring. Goethe had a terrible ambivalence for his mentor, and older Freud had his Fleischl.

The fact that the theme of Iphigenia appears in Goethe's work and in Freud's association to the dream, and that it is so central to *Hypatia*, shows the overdetermined interweaving of Freud's associations to this dream. Grinstein, concerning the latter part of the autobiography, appears to confirm this:

Later, Goethe reveals his reaction of vexation to the pirating of his ideas (plagiarism) about Faust by Wagner. . . . Among the various topics which Goethe mentions in this work are Pelagianism and the doctrine of Pelagius. Shortly after this, Goethe discusses his Iphigenia, and later a bilateral cataract operation on a patient who became blind from a complicating infection, (Grinstein 1980, p. 173).

The theme of adolescent masturbation guilt is present in Freud's associations to the dream. Freud ended his session of associations to the dream with a statement to the effect that he had thought of the most revolting forms of punishment for the sexual and plagiaristic crimes that were the hidden wishes behind the manifest dream. Fleischl's fate and the fate of Julius turned to dust in the primal chasm were images of the ultimate punishment. Castration and enucleation must have been intermediate to the final complete reduction to dust.

The Adolescent Beginnings of Freud's Writing

The analysis of the *Three Fates* dream reveals that Freud used an intellectual defense to substitute the pleasure of books for the adolescent pleasure of masturbation. During this period he transferred his interest from historical, aggressively cathected war chronicles to libidinally cathected romances. At the age of 13 or 14, Freud became interested in becoming a writer himself.

An examination of some of his adolescent aphorisms shows that Freud tended to identify the mind in general with the extended sexual metaphor. In this sense Freud began to identify his own name as a particular extended metaphor of his mind. Thus, as we saw in *The Three Fates* his own name "Freud" became for him a generalized sexual metaphor for a whole range of possible sexual pleasures. As a metaphor for developing adolescent identity, the sexual metaphor is as close to masturbation fantasy as it is to accomplished sexual performance. Freud was able to bridge the gap between performance and fantasy with an unusual creative flair.

From the beginning of his writing career in early adolescence, Freud identified the writing process with the act of free association. Writing was identified with the discharge process itself. When Freud was 13 years old, he read an essay that was to have lasting effects in his creative method and in his discovery of the psychoanalytic process. The essay was Ludwig Borne's "The Art of Becoming an Original Writer in Three Days." Reference to the work appears in "A Note on The Prehistory of the Technique of Analysis" (*Standard Edition*, vol. XVIII, pp. 262–265). The article, written anonymously by Freud (over the letter *F*), refers to Freud as Professor Freud. Professor Freud favored this technique when he wished to reveal intimate personal knowledge of himself. The screen memory paper is an outstanding, but hardly unique example of this technique in action. In "A Note on the Prehistory of the Technique of Analysis" Freud disguised his authorship to write about the origins of the psychoanalytic technique as secretely and unwittingly plagiarized through a process he called "cryptamnesia."

While this work pretends to be a refutation of Havelock Ellis's contention that Freud's method of free association is an artistic method rather than a scientific one, Freud admitted that the psychoanalytic method is in fact artistic, for he writes that Ludwig Borne's short essay was decisive in his development of the technique of free association. Freud quotes Borne:

. . . for three days on end write down without fabrication or hypocrisy, everything which comes into your head. Write down what you think of yourself, of your wife, of the Turkish War, of Goethe, of Fonk's trial, of the

Last Judgment, of your superiors—and when three days have passed you will be quite out of your sense with astonishment at the new and unheard of thoughts you have had. This is the art of becoming an original writer in three days (*Standard Edition*, vol. XVIII, p. 265).

It is remarkable that even the imagery here, the Turkish motif, Goethe, the Last Judgment, the astonishment at something new and unheard of, all seem to relate to *The Three Fates*. As a piece of reconstruction then, this article adds Borne's essay to the associational matrix of that dream. This notion is further authenticated by F:

When Professor Freud came to read this essay of Borne's, he brought forward a number of facts that may have an important bearing on the question that is under discussion here as to the pre-history of the psychoanalytic use of free associations. He said that when he was fourteen he had been given Borne's works as a present, that he still possessed the book now, 50 years later, and that it was the only one that had survived from his boyhood. Borne, he said, had been the first author into whose writings he had penetrated deeply (*Standard Edition*, vol. XVIII, p. 265).

Thus, like *Hypatia,* which initiated Freud into the mysteries of a new world, Borne's essay remained deeply ingrained in Freud's mind. (In fact, in a letter to Ferenczi dated April 9, 1919, Freud mentioned the Borne book gift as having occurred at the age of 13, the same age at which he read the novel) (Eissler 1978, p. 73). Freud confirmed that some of the other essays in the volume had remained in his mind, even though he had no recollection of the essay on writing. One of the essays that Freud remembered was entitled "The Fool at the White Swan Inn." One wonders if this is akin to the inn where Freud found himself in the *Three Fates* dream. Freud ends this short paper with the statement,

Thus it seems not impossible that this hint may have brought to light the fragment of cryptamnesia which in so many cases may be suspected to lie behind apparent originality (*Standard Edition*, vol. XVIII, p. 265).

Freud's confession to Havelock Ellis, the sexual detective, referred to Borne's work, which had been pivotal in Freud's adolescence. It must be that free association became a metaphor and a derivative of masturbation fantasy flowing freely to gratification. Thus, in the context of a study of Freud's adolescence, it is significant that Freud first mentioned Ellis in the same letter to Fliess on January 3, 1899 in which he noted that he had worked out the connection between adolescent experience and earlier fantasies:

. . . something from . . . Mr. Havelock Ellis, an author who concerns himself with the subject of sex and is obviously an intelligent man . . . deals with the connection between hysteria and sexual life, begins with Plato and ends with Freud. He gives a great deal of credit to the latter (Kris 1954, p. 271).

Even at this early date, Freud connected Ellis with his claim for originality and authenticity. The importance to Freud of whether he really knew what he was talking about concerning sexual matters derived from Freud's adolescent sense that he was exaggerating his manhood. This is an identity theme that preoccupied Freud during his early adolescence. Thus it became important to Freud that he change his official school registration name from the Hebrew, child version, Sigismund, to the official, grown-up, German version, Sigmund. According to Eissler:

He signs his letters Sigismund. In the annual reports of his school he is at first referred to as "Sigismund Freud": as Dr. Eva Laible of Vienna has told us, "Sigmund Freud" does not appear there until 1870 (Eissler 1978, p. 325).

Some Aphorisms of the 15-Year-Old Sigmund

An examination of some aphorisms of the 15-year-old Freud, produced for his school magazine, confirms that the adolescent Sigmund was attempting to erect a barrier of intellectualized masculine identity against the onslaught of his instincts, for this is both the topic and content of his aphorisms' wit. The "Random

Thoughts," as they were titled, appear in translation in Eissler (1978, p. 325):

1. Gold inflates man like air a pig's bladder.
2. The worst egoist is the one to whom it has never occurred to think himself one.
3. Some men are like a rich mine that has never been thoroughly explored. Others write "debit and credit" over their thoughts as they do over their linen, and impale every little worm that gets lost in the wilderness of their brain.
4. Some men are iron ore, other fools' gold and fools' silver.
5. Every larger animal surpasses man in something, but he surpasses them all in everything.

Concerned with the theme of identity, these aphorisms are first a commentary on man's tendency to inflate his sense of importance. Second, the content of the imagery relates to elemental substances that are made into metaphors of an individual's identity. Third, there is a moral structure invoked against those men who inflate themselves in arbitrary and artificial ways. Clearly, these themes express Freud's 14 to 15-year-old struggle to develop a sense of identity strong enough to contain the burgeoning instinctual turmoil he was feeling.

The very fact that he wrote the aphorisms shows that Freud attempted to use a intellectual identity to defend himself and to express himself. The images of the mines, mining, and substances that come from mines evidence Freud's concern for the creative process. Something physical from deep within the earth or within one's body is equated with the formation of a new thought. The transformation of the physical image of creativity—masturbation and its fantasy—to an extended metaphor of the creative process, anticipates the intellectual-creative sublimation Freud later employed.

These notions are validated by the *Three Fates* dream, for in the adolescent-derived imagery of that dream primal dust refers both to the ejaculant and to the composition of the body as it decays and dies. In his paper, "The Theme of The Three Caskets," similar imagery conveys the basic relationship of death and sexuality. In that paper Freud analyzed the meaning of Bassanio's choice in Shakespeare's *The Merchant of Venice*. There lead, the simplest of the elements, signifies a lack of pretense. Gold and silver inflate a man artificially, while simple lead, which is mute, stands for a woman with no artifice. Freud also pointed out that like Portia, the simple, direct Cordelia conveys the truth of mortality to her father, King Lear. Cordelia embodies Ananke, the fate of Necessity, which Freud wrote his mother had introduced to him by ocular demonstration.

"The Theme of the Three Caskets" reveals fairly direct derivatives of Freud's basal-image theme primal fantasy that death and life intermingle deep within the center of the woman's nature, within her womb. The matrix of elements, dirt itself, becomes a basal-image theme of Freud's adolescence, providing the raw material for his essential masturbation fantasies, and ultimately for the sublimations that make an extended metaphor of his masturbation fantasies.

8

Middle Adolescence
(*Ages 15 to 18*)

In 1899, Freud's analysis of his own puberty affected his relationship to Fliess and determined a change in his feeling of personal identity as a writer. This allowed him to write "Screen Memories" and then to go on to complete most of the rest of the clinical portions of *The Interpretation of Dreams*. Both Freud's writing and the work on which Freud and Fliess collaborated—especially during their congresses—constituted a common symbolic object, much as the love of Gisella Fluss as an object of inspiration had constituted an intermediate love bond between Freud and his adolescent companion, Silberstein.

Freud's close friendship with Edward Silberstein during the middle years of his adolescence was a precursor of his later relationship to Fliess. What's more, the Academia Espanola Castellana, the secret society the two adolescent friends shared, is the prototype of the letters and congresses with Fliess that served Freud well he developed his identity as an adult writer. Freud and Silberstein shared common reading and writing, a common mythology, a world view, and sexual excitement over the image of Gisella Fluss:

We were friends at a time when one sees in friendship not a diversion and an advantage but at a time when one needs a friend to live with. We spent all the hours of the day together when we were not at school. Together we learned Spanish, had our own mythology and code names, which we derived from a conversation of the great Cervantes. In our Spanish reader we once found a facetious philosophical dialogue between two dogs lying comfortably outside a hospital door, and we adopted their names. In our talks and letters, he was called Berganza and I Cipion. How often did I address him in a letter: Querido Berganza and signed: tu fidel Cipion, perro en el hospital de Sevilla. Together we founded a peculiar learned association, Academia Espanola Castellana. We collected an extensive humorous literature that can certainly still be found among my old papers; we shared our frugal dinners and we never got bored in one another's company (Stanescu 1971, p. 197).

Freud's literary correspondence with Silberstein contained a shared eroticization of writing. The world they created was heretical. In the manner of Cervantes, they debunked the common romantic notions of their era. Yet their good adolescent fun was a vehicle for the feeling of love between them—so much so that Freud burned all his portion of the correspondence in 1883, after his relationship to his future wife had taken hold. A letter from Freud to Silberstein when Freud was 19 years old shows, in unmistakeable terms, the real love Freud felt for Silberstein:

I really believe we shall never part, though we became friends from free choice, we are so attached to each other as if nature would have made us blood relations. I think we are so far gone that we love in one another the whole person as he is, not only, as it was earlier, his good features. I am afraid that even if, through an unworthy deed, you should appear tomorrow completely different from the image I had conceived of you, I still could not cease to wish you well (Stanescu 1971, pp. 205–206).

A similar expression of unending devotion appeared in Freud's correspondence with Fliess in the early part of 1899 as Freud began to actively separate himself from Fliess. As in the relationship with Silberstein, the written had been the medium in which Freud and Fliess expressed their love.

"Screen Memories": *A Prelude*

In 1899, during the season that always reminded Freud of Julius's death, Freud and Fliess held an Easter congress in Innsbruck, an Alpine town. Both were as filled with intense hope for the future as the fields themselves were full of flowers. Freud had looked forward to the congresses with Fliess as an opportunity to share his love of his creative work. He even entertained fantasies of moving to Berlin to have Fliess always available as a collaborator. He alludes to this fantasy in a letter (#104):

I am perfectly serious about a change of occupation and residence. It is a pity those plans are just as fantastic as "Easter in Rome" (Kris 1954, p. 276).

Letter #105, written in anticipation of the Easter congress, contains derivatives of Freud's old fantasy of simultaneous masturbation in which the two male participants deflower a common object. In addition the letter contains the essence of Freud's discovery that adolescent masturbation fantasies and the response to them hold the key to linking dreams and symptom formation. Also included is material illustrating a contemporaneous intensification of Freud's creative imagery. The intensity of the communication in the letter, the nature of the imagery, and the emphasis on feelings of identity show that Freud was preparing for a creative regression and identity change in the service of completing *The Interpretation of Dreams*. The following citation from letter #105, included in Schur's biography of Freud, but not in other sources of Freud's letters, shows Freud struggling, still unsuccessfully, to synthesize his creative and ordinary identities:

Well, the same thing is happening to you, so I do not need to feel ashamed. You, too, start letters on the 11th which you continue only on the 16th, and on the 16th you can write about nothing other than one tremendously huge piece of work, entirely too hard for the powers of a poor human being, which has a hold on every stirring thought, and eventually sucks up all faculties and susceptibilities, a kind of neoplastic tissue which infiltrates into the human one and finally replaces it. My lot is almost better—or worse. Work and gainful professional activity coincide in my case. I have turned completely into a cancer. The neoplasm likes to drink wine in its latest stage of development. Today I am supposed to go to the theatre, but this is ridiculous—like trying to graft on top of the cancer. Nothing can adhere to it, and so from now on the duration of my life is that of the neoplasm (Schur 1972, p. 193).

In the same letter Freud shows his knowledge of the dynamic meaning of deflowering:

Do you know why our old friend E. turns red and sweats whenever he sees a certain class of acquaintance, particularly at the play? He is ashamed, no doubt; but of what? Of a fantasy in which he figures as a "deflower" of every person he comes across. He sweats as he deflowers because it is hard work. . . . Moreover, he can never get over the fact that at the University he failed to get through in botany; so he carries on with it now as a "deflower". . . . And why was it that at Interlaken, when he was 14, he masturbated in such a peculiar attitude in the W.C.? It was so that he could get a good view of the Jungfrau; since then he has never caught sight of another—or at all events of her genitals (Kris 1954, p. 278).

Thus, letter #105, written in anticipation of the congress with Fliess at the Alpine town of Innsbruck, contains all of the imagery and identity themes that coalesced in "Screen Memories." The strong oral imagery present in that paper is also present in the reference to the cancer of Freud's creativity imbibing wine. As in the paper visual imagery is heightened—in anticipation of the congress. The oral and visual imagery, the reference to masturbation, to deflowering, to the fear of the woman's genitals, the castration imagery, the book as a restitution, even the cancer imagery as a restitution for missing anatomy, all coalesce in "Screen Memories." This paper is a retroactive screen for Freud's change in identity feelings in his adolescence. Perhaps the screen memory that first returned to Freud in his adolescence recurred before the congress with Fliess; perhaps it recurred more fully during the congress under the influence of the Alpine flowers and the excitement of the meeting. The intensity of the meeting with Fliess had the effect of inciting further change in Freud's identity and stimulating both the production of "Screen Memories" and disinhibition of further work on *The Interpretation of Dreams.*

In the first letter written after the congress at Innsbruck, #107, May 28, 1899, Freud wrote optimistically,

. . . I have sent the screen-memories to Ziehen at Jena. . . . The dreams, however, have suddenly taken shape without any special reason, but this time for good (Kris 1954, p. 281).

Yet a decade later, in a discussion with Bleuler as to whether or not the International Congress should be at Innsbruck, Freud demurred, on the grounds of "horrid memories" (Jones 1955a, p. 73). The change of attitude must have originated in Freud's realization that his fantasy of working in collaboration with Fliess represented a fantasy of their deflowering a woman together. After the decisive congress, with the screen memory analyzed, Freud recognized that he could write whatever he pleased. He no longer needed the permission to deflower he had originally received from his father when he tore the Persian travel book apart in the company of his sister.

"*Screen Memories*"

"Screen Memories" offers an unobstructed view of Freud's middle and late adolescence. In his self-analysis and in the self-analytical letters to Fliess, Freud reconstructed identity-forming events of his early life. As time passed, Freud's reconstructions became intertwined with his work on *The Interpretation of Dreams.* Finally, "Screen Memories" carried his reconstruction through his adolescence up to the life of the mature creator who was finishing *The Interpretation of Dreams.* In the screen memory paper, Freud gives us a notion of the manner in which he went about his creative work and his reconstructions. Following Freud, we shall use "Screen Memories" as a window into Freud's adolescence, and then amplify the information in the direction of more complete reconstruction with the aid of letters Freud wrote in adolescence.

The first trauma "Screen Memories" conceals—and expresses —is the one present at the time of its writing. In Innsbruck Freud was re-experiencing derivatives of the basal adolescent fantasy of simultaneous masturbation over a common object in his relationship with Fliess. All along, their common object had been Freud's text, *The Interpretation of Dreams.* Now they focused on the production of "Screen Memories." The object of their most intense discussion must have been the memory itself. In the context of the revival of Freud's adolescent wishes for a fellow academician, the memory with its massed fields of flowers represented a revival of Freud's adolescent investment of Nature with a fetishistic substitution for the genitals that he felt were missing in female nature. The imagery took on literary significance as the equivalent of the orgastic completion of *The Interpretation of Dreams.*

The paper contains a play of imagery and a hierarchy of fantasies:

Yet I can remember quite well for what a long time afterwards I was affected by the yellow color of the dress she was wearing when we first met, whenever I saw the same color anywhere else! . . . Do you not suspect that there may be a connection between the yellow of the girl's dress and the ultra-clear yellow of the flowers in your childhood scene? "Possibly, but it was not the same yellow. The dress was more of a yellowish brown, more like the color of wallflowers. . . ." At a later date, while I was in the Alps, I saw how certain flowers which have lighter colors in the lowlands take on darker shades at higher altitudes. Unless I am greatly mistaken, there is frequently to be found in mountainous regions a flower which is very similar to the dandelion, but which is dark yellow and would exactly agree in color with the dress of the girl I was so fond of (*Standard Edition*, vol. III, pp. 313–314).

Here the later date would be 1899, when Freud was writing the paper.

The element on which you put most stress in your childhood scene was the fact of the country-made bread tasting so delicious. It seems clear that this idea, which amounted almost to a hallucination, corresponded to your fantasy . . . (*Standard Edition,* vol. III, p. 315).

Freud comes to the conclusion that he had projected two current adolescent fantasies back into the past upon the childhood scene, and that it was this process that amplified the sensuous intensity of the original scene. This certainly provided him with further insight into the process of dream formation. Freud identified the fantasies:

. . . in the family where I was staying there was a daughter of fifteen, with whom I immediately fell in love. It was my first calf-love and sufficiently intense, but I kept it completely secret. After a few days the girl went off to her school (from which she too was home for the holidays) and it was this separation after such a short acquaintance that brought my longings to a really high pitch. I passed many hours in solitary walks through the lovely woods that I had found once more and spent my time building castles in the air. These, strangely enough, were not concerned with the future but sought to improve the past (*Standard Edition*, vol. III, p. 313).

The last statement is noteworthy. The restitutional desire to improve on the past reverberates throughout the paper. Restitution, moreover, is a quality of masturbation fantasy. The theme of missed opportunities that are restored in fantasy is an active organizing principle in the formation of such fantasies. Clearly, the intensity of longing for what has been lost spurs new identity formation. In the changed identity of adult life, the mature person either takes advantage of opportunities or no longer considers the pleasures sought as valid and worth seeking.

In this regard it is significant that during the writing of "Screen Memories" Freud was in the final stage of revising his own identity in the direction of an acceptance of himself as a mature creator. In this context we can make sense of Freud's deceptive allusion to himself in the paper as a 38-year-old man. At the time of the screen memory paper Freud was 43. For the preceding five years, beginning with his *Project for a Scientific Psychology*, Freud had been remaking his identity as a creative investigator of the mind. In this paper Freud objectified the process of self-revision.

The process of self-objectification, which Freud took as the significant element in a screen memory, is clearly demonstrated in the paper, for Freud pulled together all of the significant elements in his early childhood under the aegis of a need to reconstruct it. The themes of identity change, intense recollection of the past, and self-objectification are intimately and structurally linked. Thus Freud recollected his whole past on the threshold of his maturity, just as he had recollected his whole past when he was an adolescent in the throes of identity change at age 16. The screen memory itself refers to an age just past infancy when an earlier version of identity recapitulation and objectification must have been occurring.

The restitutional element, as well as the masturbatory fantasy of having help in deflowering, is also present in Freud's reference in the paper to the time when he was looking forward to becoming an adult. In connection to his trip to England at age 19, Freud wrote,

But I believe that my father and uncle had concocted a plan by which I was to exchange the abstruse subject of my studies for one of more practical value, settle down, after my studies were completed, in the place where my uncle lived and marry my cousin. No doubt when they saw how absorbed I was in my own intentions the plan was dropped; but I fancy I must certainly have been aware of its existence. It was not until later, when I was a newly-fledged man of science and hard pressed by the exigencies of life and when I had waited so long before finding a post here, that I must sometimes have reflected that my father had meant well in planning this marriage for me, to make good the loss in which the original catastrophe had involved my whole existence (*Standard Edition*, vol. III, p. 314).

This fantasy, in which Freud is to have help in obtaining his love, was not consciously recognized by Freud as he told it. However, the restitutional quality is included in the fantasy of having help in deflowering. The comprehensive movement toward a reorganization of the past under the aegis of new identity is thus seen in this fantasy, as is his defense against the involvement with the incestuous object through his involvement with books.

In "Screen Memories" Freud went on to relate the sexual significance of his two fantasies:

Taking flowers away from a girl means to deflower her. What a contrast between the boldness of this fantasy and my bashfulness on the first occasion and my indifference on the second (*Standard Edition*, vol. III, p. 316).

. . . the most seductive part of the whole project for a young scapegrace is the picture of the wedding night (*Standard Edition*, vol. III, p. 316).

Can you make any sense of the idea of being helped in deflowering someone? (*Standard Edition*, vol. III, p. 319).

Freud failed to answer that directly. Instead he analyzed the masturbation symbolism in another person's screen memory of breaking off a branch. This association, then, is further evidence that help in deflowering is part of a masturbation fantasy.

The reason Freud needed help in deflowering is evident in the imagery of the screen memory. The knife that delivers the delicious black bread also represents the inherent danger in approaching the "castrated" genitals in search of gratification. The restitutional quality—making up for what is missing in experience—is seen as the black bread that replaces the stolen flowers. The black bread appears then to be a fetish image of satisfaction.

Freud's Adolescent Love for His Muse: Gisella Fluss

There is considerable evidence in the letters Freud wrote as an adolescent in the aftermath of his experience with Gisella to substantiate the view that Freud took Gisella as a dangerous object of his adolescent masturbation fantasy and that he managed to transform her image into a more benign and inspiring presence in his mind. The evidence points to Gisella becoming a shared symbol of bisexual inspiration uniting Freud and his friend Silberstein.

Freud and Silberstein developed an eponym for Gisella, Ichthyosaura. In the intimacy of the learned correspondence of the Academy Castellana she was familiarly known as Ich. The name Ichthyosaura was derived from a phallic and dangerous prehistoric sea creature whose prominent teeth were set in a wide-open jaw. It was, associatively, appropriate to a girl whose last name, Fluss, meant "river" in German.

Despite his disclaimer in "Screen Memories," Freud had established contact with Gisella as early as the age of 14. In a letter to Emil Fluss written when Freud was 16 years old, he referred to an incident involving Gisella and Edward Silberstein that had occurred two years previously on the occasion of an earlier trip of Freud's to Freiberg:

I want to tell you of a little incident which happened two years ago and which is very similar to yours. You will remember that at the time of my first visit to Freiberg . . . I was accompanied by my friend Silberstein. In significance and intellect we two represented only a minute fraction of a large group whose star was "Ichthyosaura." When we visited the weaving-mill, my friend absentmindedly touched one of the machines with his hand. What did Ichthyos do? She whipped his hand away and uttered an alarmed "Don't, this is dangerous." What conclusion would you draw from it? A wrong one I am sure, for nothing justifies the assumption that her concern was love's child (to put it poetically and befitting the subject matter). The explanation is simple. She had often read about factory accidents; when she noticed my friend's movement, they sprang to her mind, and almost instinctively she obeyed the impulse of her kind-hearted nature (E. Freud 1969, p. 422).

In the same letter Freud had been declaiming about the need to keep young women ignorant of the sensual basis of desire. It is a letter full of gentle yet distinct sexual metaphor. In its context Freud's seemingly irrational remarks about Gisella's action may be assumed to include the presence of a far more intimate fantasy. The admonition to watch out, not to touch the dangerous machine was fantasied as a warning to avoid masturbation or sexual contact. Gisella pulls Edward's hand away. The wonder of it is that she touched his hand spontaneously. The touch is at least equal in its sensous imagery to the dire warning—you could lose your hand, you could lose a vital part of your body, you could even die!

Another of Freud's papers indicates that Gisella was a star in yet another eye than Edward's or his own. In his notes to the *Rat Man* case (*Standard Edition*, vol. X), Freud added three exclamation points to the emergence of the same Gisella as the focus for the Rat Man's adolescent masturbation fantasy. The Rat Man had even made a verbal formula of Gisella's name—an obsessive utterance— to spare himself retribution for his masturbation: "Gisellamen." Following Gisella with *amen* was supposed to ward off evil. Like all symptoms though, the formula also contained symbolic gratification, as the intermediate word linkage was condensed to *samen* and one step further to semen.

Formation of the Screen

In letters to Emil Fluss written in the wake of his visit to the Fluss family, Freud formed the screen described in the screen memory paper. The letters document the coalescence of intense intrapsychic imagery and emotion with sensuous impressions. Venting the condensing imagery, the letters themselves became the vehicle for a change in Freud's objective identification of himself. In the letters he adopted an ironic style and a narrative voice indicative of his assumption of the identity as a writer.

The fact that "Screen Memories" referred to the last of several trips to Freiberg as the only one indicates a stringent defensive process in operation against the passion and psychic change involved with the last trip, which was the one in which Freud had taken Gisella as his love object. The creative process of Freud's identity change can be followed by taking Freud's remarks in the paper and his letters in sequence after Gisella left for school. The first letter, to Silberstein, shows the adolescent Sigmund trying to grapple with his loss and his feeling of lost opportunity, manfully, and with intellectual understanding of the situation. But, as is the case with any creative response, the loss could not be solved with the answers at hand.

On September 4th, 1872, still at Freiberg, Freud wrote to Silberstein:

She left Wednesday, not without some slight deceit, which for quite some time annoyed me. I took leave sadly and went to Hochwald, my little paradise, where I spent a very pleasant hour. I quieted all my turbulent thoughts, and am only slightly startled when at table Mother mentions the name of Gisella. The sentiment for Gisella appeared like a nice day in spring, but my nonsensical "Hamlethood," my shyness, prevented me from indulging in refreshing conversation with the partly naive, partly educated, young lady. One day I shall explain to you fully the difference between this sentiment and another passion. For the moment, I merely wish to say that it was in conflict between ideal and reality and that I am unable to ridicule Gisella (Stanescu 1971, pp. 202–203).

In this statement Freud showed his introspective knowledge of an oedipal condition that he was to discuss later in an article aptly titled "On the Universal Tendency to Debasement in the Sphere of Love" (*Standard Edition*, vol. XI, pp. 179–190). In that article Freud discussed what could well have been his relationship with Gisella Fluss, and he concluded that the affectionate current attaching to the original love object must be separated from the sensual current awakened in adolescence. Debasing is a defensive means of splitting the object, in effect producing a madonna-prostitute split that becomes fixated through adolescent masturbation fantasies, isolating the prostitute image as the object of the sensual current.

Freud's conflict over Gisella led him into an adolescent regressive process of identity transformation in the attempt to find some resolution. This transformation and Freud's continuing attempt to prevent himself from debasing Gisella are documented in Freud's subsequent letters. The regressive searching, characteristic of the creative process, took Freud back into a world of his past experience.

The image that Freud discovered was a narcissistic one, an image of a barely pubescent, and therefore phallicized, girl who became available as a sexually composite image of inspiration. The image of a young girl served as an intermediate, linking Freud's own image as a pubescent boy with the image of Gisella as an alternative object choice for his mother. A 12-year-old blond girl with striking brown eyes served to form a terribly vivid screen image that stood for the transformation in Freud's identity.

Two weeks after the letter to Silberstein acknowledging his affection for Gisella, Freud wrote a letter to Emil Fluss that shows Freud's love for Gisella in the process of transforming his identity. This screen-building letter to Emil (September 18, 1872) described Freud's epiphany in vivid detail, as it documented the course of Freud's passion from the time Gisella had left Freiberg. The train trip is reported in minute detail. Freud exhibited heightened powers of observation on this trip. The intensity of observation that was to be transformed into the visual intensity of the screen memory begins to displace the driven passions that had preceded the train trip. This train trip—like earlier ones and later ones—focuses Freud's passions. The primal scene is the prototype for the extreme sensory openness, the ready accessibility of memory, and of the readiness to transform identity while seeing the self objectified. Freud's masturbatory passion of adolescence makes a simultaneous experience of his earlier love of Pauline-Anna and of the primal scene imagery that had preceded that love.

The whole experience of the adolescent epiphany is destined to become a new fixation point for the creator, revealing the kind of sensory openness, and the availability of memory and of passion, that is present in the moment when new identity—prototype of the work—is created. The sensory details of the young girl on the train, her yellow hair, her brown eyes, are magnified in the formation of the screen memory. The same sensory overdetermination of proximal detail is involved in the formation of the fetish object. Indeed the whole phallic composition of the young girl comprises an aspect of the formation of an intrapsychic fetish. The screen memory is formed out of sensory impressions of the girl, Freud's own reflection in the glass of the train window, and the scenery of the landscape moving past the train.

By the time he reached the train, the identity change brought about by falling in love with Gisella had reached the point where Freud's whole past was available for revision. As he says in "Screen Memories" of the time following Gisella's departure,

I passed many hours in solitary walks through the lovely woods that I had found once more, and spent my time building castles in the air. These, strangely enough, were not concerned with the future but sought to improve the past. If only the smash had not occurred! If only I had stopped at home and grown up in the country and grown as strong as the young men in the house, the brothers of my love! And then if only I had followed my father's profession and if I had finally married her—for I should have known her intimately all these years! I had not the slightest doubt, of course, that in the circumstances created by my imagination I should have loved her just as passionately as I really seemed to then (*Standard Edition*, vol. III, p. 313).

Thus Gisella had taken on the significance of his whole lost childhood. The longing for that past cannot to be set to rest without some change in the structure of identity. The train trip recreating early loss of his past childhood, also sexualized, provided Freud with the moment of epiphany when his identity changed.

In "Screen Memories," Freud makes a rhetorical transition that reproduces the moment of engaging the gaze of the young girl. That moment of rapt identity, the narcissistic prelude to object love, is embodied in Freud's singular image in the paper. The image of the eyes engaged, the reflected face, carries the beholder back to an earliest awareness of love engaged:

The assertion that a psychical intensity can be displaced from one presentation (which is then abandoned) on to another (which thenceforward plays the psychological part of the former one) is as bewildering to us as certain features of Greek mythology—as, for instance, when the gods are said to clothe someone with beauty as though it were with a veil, whereas *we* think only of a face transfigured by a change of expression (*Standard Edition*, vol. III, p. 308).

The Screen-building Letter of September 18, 1872

Freud began the letter to Emil Fluss with the word ''confidential.'' His greeting in the letter is ''Dear new friend.'' The letter was not to be shared with Gisella, though one feels Freud hoped that it would be. A love for Emil sprang up with the love for Gisella. As confidant, Emil is brought into the fantasy of intimacy with Gisella. Unconsciously he is equated with the brother figure, John in the screen memory of the paper, who helps to deflower:

I am writing to you as promised, to tell you about my journey from my old home-town. But God knows what whirlwind blew me so fast from Freiberg to Vienna! I have lost almost all my recollection of past events, submit to everything as if dazed—questions, caresses, congratulations—and don't open my mouth (E. Freud 1969, p. 420).

Freud experienced a powerful new wave of repression, much like the one that overtook him when he was 3 years old and first leaving Freiberg. The trip away then recapitulated his experience of leaving in the first place. Freud continued:

I'll have a hard time finding my way about in my memories of yesterday. I shall confess the unvarnished truth to you—but to you alone, and I trust that no one will be allowed to see what was not meant for him to see. But should this happen nevertheless and you are unable to prevent it, then please do not tell me about it (E. Freud 1969, p. 420).

After this allusion to Gisella, Freud set his first image into the letter. It is an image of repulsion. It is a face transfigured by boils from which Freud wanted to look away. No doubt this is a case of upward displacement.

Our first travelling companion was a poor soul, her face terribly transfigured by boils. I tried to force myself to stay in order not to hurt the poor girl, but my plight became more and more unbearable, and when to top it all she started to speak and lifted her head scarf, repulsion won out over the forebearance I owed a suffering human being (E. Freud 1969, p. 420).

Then Freud produced another image of disgust, this time directed at a whole family including a Czech maid. These people represent Freud's own family at the time of their leaving Freiberg. Each member of the family received a dose of Freud's venom:

I ended up in the company of a most venerable old Jew and his correspondingly old wife, with their melancholy langorous darling daughter and cheeky young "hopeful" son. . . . Now this Jew talked in the same way as I had heard thousands of others talk before, even in Freiberg. His face seemed familiar—so was the boy . . . kept by his adoring relatives in the belief that he is a great talent. . . . A cook from Bohemia with the most perfect pug-face I have ever seen put the lid on it. I have enough of this lot. In the course of the conversation I learned that Madame Jewess and family hailed from Meseritsch: the proper compost-heap for this kind of weed (E. Freud 1969, p. 420).

Freud put a lid on his whole past by making it disgusting; ending, in fact, with an image that this typical family is literally "shit," while he himself with his powers of observation has travelled far beyond them. With these images of negative beauty suitably repressing Freud's longing for the past, Freud suddenly picked up a proximal, screening image in the present. The image was heir to all the intensity of abandoned love, reinforced by the new drive of adolescence:

Leaving Prerau two beautiful stars glistened at me. Now you will stop and put two fingers to your lips—the stars were two lovely eyes. But let me tell you everything in proper sequence without omitting anything (E. Freud 1969, p. 420).

Again the eyes; Freud's image of the primary world returned in all its grandeur. Freud makes Emil more than a voyeur, more than a confidant. He actually brings Emil into the scene as a participant.

. . . next to the nervous woman sat her 12-year-old daughter with the face of an angel and features so neutral that she might still have turned into a beautiful page (boy). The girl ate far more leisurely than her mother, and after each mouthful let her shy brown eyes wander over her fellow-diners.

But before my first hunger had been appeased and I could allow myself
time to look firmly into the brown eyes, the anxious mother had carried her
off . . . (E. Freud 1969, p. 420).

Here is the formation of the composite, bisexual, narcissistic
ideal, suitable to represent the adolescent's search for an ideal image
of beauty to reflect his own mind. The 12-year-old's just pubescent
but preadolescent phallic-composite mirrors Freud's mind. Her
image becomes the source of beauty with which Freud began his
account. Finding the girl eating is another link to the screen
memory image of Pauline eating black bread. The image of her
gratification makes the girl-boy into a Pauline-like sibling with
whom one should share. The image of the angel is thus overdetermined. It refers to a dead person, a young boy, someone who does
not exist except in ideal form: it refers to Julius.

At the same time, angels have another symbolic significance.
Such winged creatures, composites sexually and aesthetically, are
classically used as muse representations by creators. The overdetermination of the image makes it a symbolic vehicle for Freud's
new identity as a creator, for this letter is Freud's announcement of
his true vocation. He has become a writer, and Emil is his first
audience.

Freud continued, making a story of his attempt to make eye
contact with the fair creature:

I stood by the window, lying in wait for a glimpse of the blonde head with
the large questioning eyes. Soon it appeared again, and even the worst of
the noise could not make me take my eyes off her. The wind swept gaily
through her thick, blonde, short, curly hair. Thus two hours flew by like a
minute.

But then the head was withdrawn and I could only see it when the train
stopped at a station where the platform happened to be on the same side as
our windows. That is not to say, however, that I passed the time any less
pleasantly. I waited and hoped, and in between thought of Freiberg. Until
now I had had no time to let the six weeks pass in review (E. Freud 1969,
p. 420).

Thus we see that Freud interweaves his experiences at Freiberg
with the image of this girl's face, which was reflected where he could

see his own. The past and the present join seamlessly in his excited reverie. The word "now" in the last sentence suggests moreover that Freud reexperienced the formation of the screen even as he wrote about it. Then Freud pledged to keep the blond girl's image fresh in his mind by looking for it among the faces of Vienna:

Finally, I arrived in Vienna. Once more I saw the nervous mother and the blonde girl and I vowed to keep on the lookout for her among the milling crowds of Vienna. . . . Should you in your next letter ask for the story about Ich, which I have not yet told you, I shall not refuse (E. Freud 1969, p. 420).

Ten days later Freud appeared secure in his new identity as a somewhat detached writer. When Emil tried to encourage Freud to further fantasize about the girl by saying that it was no mere coincidence that she sat on the same side of the carriage as Freud, Freud pooh-poohed him:

You do indeed attach more significance to my little adventure than I did myself. I don't think you will ever see me in the role which you hinted at in your letter just received— . . . that she sat on the same side was coincidence; that she looked out of the window as persistently as I did was not; but I believe the curiosity may have been mutual. After all, if someone fixes us intently with his eyes, we usually return the glance with equal intensity. As far as this is concerned, therefore, I'm afraid I have to blow your lovely castle in the air to bits (E. Freud 1969, p. 421).

Characteristically, Freud had invited Emil into the midst of his fantasy, to help him deflower the girl. When Emil responded by encouraging Freud to do just that, Freud responded that it was Emil's fantasy. The idiom here, "building castles in the air," is the same idiom Freud used in "Screen Memories" to describe his daydreams about Gisella in the forest. Here we have additional evidence that the phrase does indeed have a direct sexual content.

Not only did Freud detach himself from the sexual significance of his own basal, adolescent fantasy, by the time of this letter he showed that he had relegated the past he had longed for far away from himself, for he went on in the letter responding to Emil's request that he talk about his life before the visit to Freiberg with:

This whole period is as remote to me as can be, however much it once seemed part of me. I have thrown myself heart and soul into the future . . .

But if you want me to entertain you with reports about Ichthyosaura, let me tell you that there was more irony, yes mockery, than seriousness in this whole flirtation. You were never present at a meeting of the "Spanish Academy" (the name of our two-member society). But had you heard how the poor creature was torn to shreds, you would have had a different picture of "our" relationship to her (E. Freud 1969, p. 421).

Thus in ten days Freud had restructured his personality further. Gisella had become a mere stimulus to Freud's irony. But that irony, of course, is the center of his style. The image of tearing the creature to shreds reminds one of the screen memory where the flowers are torn away from poor Pauline. Tearing a creature to shreds, Freud would later agree, is an image of disposing of an unwanted younger sibling. The renunciation of the real relationship allows Freud to replace his conflicts about Julius and about the alarming nature of women with an ironical posture that substitutes the creative for the real self.

The Natural Scientist

With the development of a professional identity, the individual achieves a sense of perspective by which life's problems can be gauged. When the perspective fails, however—which is to say, when the prevailing method of problem-solving does not reduce conflict to manageable levels—then the creative solution is to begin a search into the roots of the identity that is structuring consciousness. In Freud's case it is easy enough to see how his prevailing intellectual themes were related to the structuring of the defensive processes that entered into his character formation and overcame the basal emotional themes with which he had contended.

Freud completed his middle adolescent identity change with his career decision to become a natural scientist. This decision contained and expressed the identity themes that Freud had built up in the years of his childhood. In particular it contained and expressed Freud's "naturalistic" adolescent passion for Gisella Fluss. Toward the age of 17 Freud developed a passionate intellectual curiosity about nature and its origins, and especially about evolution and evolutionary theory. His interest in Greek and Latin myths, containing the dynamics of all his overcome instinctual passions, developed into a more general interest in philosophy.

As his final exams in the gymnasium were approaching, Freud struggled with the decision to become a natural scientist. In the letter of March 17, 1873, to Emil, Freud coyly hinted that he would soon have an important announcement to make. He was so coy in fact that Emil thought that Freud must be referring to some romantic decision. Insofar as Freud equated women with nature, it was a romantic decision indeed. In his next letter (May 1, 1873), just before his 17th birthday, Freud released the tension:

Of which "relationship" did I, in your opinion, speak so meekly and dejectedly? Did I not perhaps refer to it as "an event," a plan? It is the latter and does merit the term "event" in the sense of intending to be sensational or arousing surprise. I was not more specific at the time, partly because of the suspense, which would have greatly flattered me, partly because I was not yet sure of myself. Today it is as certain and as fixed as any plan can be. . . . Now I can also speak freely. When I lift the veil of secrecy, will you not be disappointed? Well, let's see. I have decided to be a Natural Scientist and herewith release you from the promise to let me conduct your lawsuits. It is no longer needed. I shall gain insight into the age old dossiers of nature, perhaps even eavesdrop on her eternal processes, and share my findings with anyone who wants to learn . . . (E. Freud 1969, p. 424).

The imagery is revealing as usual; Freud will be entering the primal scene, spying on mysterious, sexual secrets, bringing others into the scene with him. His plan is a safe one. It sets him a long course of study which will remove the temptation of getting involved prematurely with a woman. Years later Freud reaffirmed the sexual origin of his choice of a scientific career. In "An Autobiographical Study" he wrote:

Under the powerful influence of a school friendship with a boy rather my senior who grew up to be a well known politician, I developed a wish to study law like him and to engage in social activities. At the same time, the theories of Darwin, which were then of topical interest, strongly attracted me, for they held out the hopes of an extraordinary advance in our understanding of the world; and it was hearing Goethe's beautiful essay on Nature read aloud at a popular lecture by Professor Carl Bruhl just before I left school that decided me to become a medical student (*Standard Edition*, vol. XX, p. 8).

The essay to which Freud referred is permeated with revised primal scene imagery. To understand Freud's excitement with it, we must understand that as a gymnasium student Freud saw Bruhl as the first of what was to be a long line of scientific mentors whose job was to induct him into the mysteries of life. Freud had already taken Goethe as an idealized creator whom he wished to emulate. Thus Freud's experience of hearing the essay almost on the eve of his final gymnasium examinations was of great significance.

In the essay, Nature is presented as an omniscient woman, all-giving, but ruthless. Having the power to create and to destroy, Nature is both entirely real and the essence of illusion. Though she is a woman, Nature enters into the identity of every person, male or female, as she enters into the voices of the one who writes the essay and the one who reads the essay. Nature even has self-knowledge: "She has analyzed herself in order to enjoy herself" (Wittels 1924, p. 31). In short, Nature is equated with all of the qualities of the human mind. Such a theme for universal identification, promising as it does complete intellectual satisfaction, contributed to Freud's development of a posture that allowed him to entertain thoughts and feelings regardless of their psychodynamic origin.

The study of evolution had a special meaning for Freud's intellectual organization. The attempt to trace the origins of life back to their beginnings, the idea of the survival of the fittest, and the search for some ultimate purpose in the arrangement of life forms simulated the kind of mental regression needed to get into touch with the source of new ideas when old ones failed. Undoubtedly Bruhl was a character in Freud's unconscious fantasy that some wise older doctor, unafraid of the mysteries of life, would lead him back into the past where the source of Julius's failure to survive a process of natural selection would be revealed in its full sexual significance. But as Freud became more confident of understanding evolution through his own efforts and his own researchers, Bruhl became a figure he pitied more than honored.

Thus on March 6, 1874, after almost a year of study at the university, Freud addressed Emil:

I hope to see you hale and hearty at Bruhl's on Sunday. As regards him, you must not take amiss a confession I have to make in black and white. I caused you—perhaps in years to come as a peaceful citizen, you will say I incited you, to attend his lectures. But I could, after all, judge the man only by what he had said, and not by what he was going to say . . . the man is getting old, and with advancing age the bilious, nihilistic tendency in him grows excessively. . . . Very probably his achievements have not kept pace with earlier expectations and aspirations. . . . Of Darwinism, which last year he supported in several of his lectures, he declares that it does not contribute to the natural science student's understanding of nature(!) (E. Freud 1969, pp. 426–427).

9

Late Adolescence
(*Ages 19 to 21*)

The process by which Freud made the transition to the adult self-identification as a natural scientist involves an understanding of the fate of his late adolescent impulses for bisexual exploration. The loss of his muse—Gisella—flooded his mind with bisexual impulses, the sublimation of which increased his intellectual passion. When the sublimation was completed, he immersed himself in physiologic-anatomic investigation, which contained these bisexual drives.

It was necessary for Freud to consciously appreciate these impulses in order to complete the last stage of the journey of *The Interpretation of Dreams*. This he did in his analysis of the dream of *Dissecting My Own Pelvis*, for this dream recapitulated the organizing events of Freud's late adolescence and worked through the unresolved feelings that inhibited the publications of *The Interpretation of Dreams*.

Ichthyosaura

News of Gisella Fluss's impending marriage compelled Freud to reorganize his identity. His thoughts about her wedding night put an end to the masturbation fantasies in which she had figured as his bride. The result was the destruction of the personal muse to whom

218

Freud had dedicated his adolescent creative and procreative urges. Freud's renunciation of Gisella was the first part of a new stage in which he would reject the validity of his adolescent imagination. By the time Freud was 19 years old, his internal representation of Gisella Fluss had evolved into a bisexual person. As is usually the case with muse figures, Gisella was represented as a phallic woman. Associated with gratification and with the act of discharge, she was identified with the fantasy process of Freud's masturbation. As muse, as representative of productive fantasy, Gisella was also equated with the experience of productive orgasm.

An image of his own creative urges, Gisella had been deeply involved in the building of Freud's adolescent dreams. In his correspondence with Edward Silberstein in the months before Gisella's marriage, Freud began to expose and analyze the sources of this creature's effect on him. On January 24th, 1875, when he was 19, Freud wrote to Silberstein about Gisella's visit to his sisters:

If you will come here, you will have the pleasure (which cannot be expressed in words, or, at least very feebly and vaguely so) to "touch" Gisella, for which I have neither enough incentive nor opportunity (Freud 1971, p. 203).

Still sharing the simultaneously idealized and denigrated younger girl with a friend, Freud begins to expose the shared fantasy of their joint possession of Gisella, and so begins to weaken for himself the fantasy's dynamic significance. Soon Freud will rationalize what he has found so fearful about women as to require his seeking friendly assistance in fantasying about them.

A letter dated March 27th, 1875, discusses a play by Frederick Hebbel. The play is about Judith and Holofernes. What is fearsome about Judith is that she beheads Holofernes after intercourse. This is an act of symbolic castration.

. . . Very beautiful is his Judith, an eternal problem the strong woman who defies the overwhelming man and avenges the inferiority imparted by her sex (Freud 1971).

It appears that unconsciously Freud believed that his mother should seek revenge for the destruction of her baby and the mutilation of her genitals by the one-eyed doctor, Freud's father's surrogate.

Not ready to risk any direct physical contact with a woman, Freud feels that it is a fraternal duty to warn his friends about potentially mutilating sex. He writes to Silberstein on March 7th, 1875, not long after the conclusion of Gisella's visit:

The indifference with which you mention the first kiss of your "principle" appears to me a bad omen, first because you so easily get kisses and second because you take a kiss so easily. I consider it my duty to draw your attention to a calculation by the famous statistician, Malthus, who proved that kisses tend to multiply in an ever increasing proportion, so that within a short time from the start of the series, the small area of the face does not suffice and they are then forced to migrate. Because of this Malthus is a definite opponent of kisses, and a young national economist should take his authority into consideration (Freud 1971, p. 203).

The clever trope suggests that coitus leads to population explosion and thus threatens the life and nourishment of the parties to the kiss. Thus the image refers to the history of Freud's childhood neurosis: the infantile poverty and greed leading to the destruction of the unwanted sibling. The derivatives of his primal scene construct referred to in the economic metaphor, point to an ever inflating, dangerous sexual energy.

When Gisella married in the early fall of 1875, Freud stopped writing as a member of the Spanish Academy. That Freud had been heavily invested in these writings can be deduced from his destruction of the notes and writings of the society in an *auto-da-fé* before his marriage to Martha—years after the collaboration had come to an end.

I have destroyed all my notes of the past fourteen years, as well as letters, scientific excerpts, and the manuscripts of my papers. As for letters, only those from the family have been spared. Yours, my darling, were never in danger. In doing so all old friendships and relationships presented themselves once again and then silently received the *coup de grace*. . . . I couldn't have matured or died without worrying about who would get hold of those old papers. Everything, moreover, that lies beyond the great turning point of my life, beyond our love and my choice of profession, died long ago and must not be deprived of a worthy funeral. As for the biographers, let them worry, we have no desire to make it too easy for them. Each one of them will be right in his opinion of "The Development of the Hero," and I am already looking forward to seeing them go astray (E. Freud 1969, pp. 140–141).

Before the *auto-da-fé*, however, in an epithalamium of 1875, Freud divested Gisella of phallic qualities, and made fun of her round, female openness:

> Not all too tall was her figure, she did not look like the poplar
> Which by faultless growth aspires straight to the sky.
> Nor like the spruce and the fir, the jewels of the Nordic forests,
> Nor Lebanon's cedar, the classic tree of the Jews,
> But like the highest of all forms, the ideal of figures,
> Her appearance was that of the globe and wonderfully fully rotund,
> Rotund the face with spirited, sparkling eyes,
> Rotund the body's enclosure.
> (Eissler 1978, pp. 473–474)

In another, longer poem on the occasion of Gisella's marriage, Freud again shattered the bond to Ichthyosaura to liberate himself from the identification of his creative drive with Gisella and from the intimacy with Silberstein which had been a necessary part of his relationship to her. The poem destroys the symbol of the academy which was the bond that had united Freud and Silberstein.

Hochzeitscarmen

1. Singe mir, Muse, den Ruhm der Ichthyosauri communes
2. Vormals machtig im Lias und anderen Formationen,
3. Die ein leuchtend Vorbild gewesen der Academia.
4. Und so mögen sie beide das Los vollenden des Lebens,
5. Gleich den Insekten und Wurmern, die unsere Erde bevolkern
6. Ungestorter Atumung begabt und Nahrungsaufnahme
7. Nie vom Gieste beruhrt, das wunscht die Academia.
8. Rund des Leibes Umfassung, und wenn dem Dichter vergonnt ist

9. Schauenden Augs zu dringen, in was gewohnlichen Blicken verhällt
   ist
10. Zweifelt er nicht, dass die Rundung sich bewahre der Formen,
11. Welche dem glücklichen Mann enthuellt der selige Abend.
    (Stanescu 1971, p. 203)

This poem was translated for the present volume by Frank Edler, the philosopher:

Weddingsong

1. Sing me, Muse, the glory of Ichthyosauri communes
2. Once mighty in Lias and other formations,
3. Which was an illuminating model of the academy.
4. And thus they both desire to fulfill the destiny of life,
5. Like the insects and the worms that populate our earth
6. The academy longs for gifted tranquil breathing
7. And satisfaction unaffected by spirit.
8. Around the enclosure of love, and when the poet is granted
9. Sounding eyes to pierce into what is hidden to everyday glances
10. No longer does he doubt that the rounding (out) proves the forms to
    be true,
11. Which the blissful evening reveals to the lucky man.

The title, *Hochzeitscarmen*, is a compound of German and Spanish that symbolizes the union of Freud and Silberstein in thralldom to their muse, Ichthyosaura. Releasing himself from his allegiance to the image of his adolescent masturbation fantasy, Freud analyzes the primitive psychology that has bound him to the image.

Webster's Third International Dictionary defines Ichthyosaura as,

An order of Mesozoic marine reptile most abundant in the Lias (geological period) having an ichthyoid body, elongated snout, short neck . . . eyes very large and protected by a ring of bony sclerotic plates, and numerous conical teeth set in grooves and adapted for catching fish.

Ichthyosaura is a vagina-penis-dentata. In Freud's imagery, the penis-like body with the short neck and the protuberant eye must have been equated with his bedrock image of the one-eyed doctor.

The strategy of Freud's poem is to allude to characteristics of this monster in order to free its inventor of the monster's significance to his unconscious. Insofar as Ichthyosaura was an unconscious image of Freud's self-identity, she served the productive purpose of linking diverse drives for creative purposes. Insofar as Ichthyosaura was an unconsciously determined object of love, she produced anxiety, threatening both castration and death. Thus the poem, like the March letter to Silberstein, uses Ichthyosaura to represent Freud's developing neurosis. The second line for example ties this creature to Freud's past; the third line shows how the phallic luster of the image united Sigmund and Edward, both in their academy and in the knowledge they shared of the dangers attendant upon intimacy with a woman. The reference to "both," in line four, refers equally to Gisella and her husband desiring intercourse, and, at the conscious level, to Freud's and Silberstein's defensive superiority. The intercourse is imaged deep within the soil of the earth, where, womblike or gravelike, sexuality and death are united in a process clearly resembling the Malthusian kiss. In the poem Freud seeks the earliest locale of his pleasure, the comfort of his mother's arms and the inside of her body, where he felt he would experience "gifted tranquil breathing." The union with Silberstein, like the union with Julius, means a sharing of love. The poet, in lines eight and nine, shares the intimacy of penetration with the husband on the wedding night; but the poet is carried into the blissful enclosure only with his sounding (probing) eyes, which are the equipment of the poet, the one-eyed doctor, the man of science. In the end, the poem develops an image of Gisella and her husband in imagined intercourse.

The poem resolved the bisexual affiliation of adolescence. The sign and the agency of his having outgrown the need for Silberstein and Gisella was the 19-year-old Freud's willingness to give up allegiance to the past as it crystallized in the muse of his adolescence. Although not ready to marry, he was able to focus his creative researches in a more adult way. Thus Freud wrote to Silberstein:

Herewith this period ends, here I submerge the magic wand that has contributed to its organization: a new time may commence without secretely active forces, a time that does not need poesy and fantasy.

Nobody may search for a principle in the alluvium and diluvium or elsewhere but in the present, nowhere but among the children of human beings, but not in the grisly primordial past (Eissler 1978, pp. 474–475).

Freud would break the magic wand, the penis of masturbatory fantasy, complement to Ichthyosaura. In continuing his remarks about the wedding poem Freud wrote, that he would, like Prospero,

. . . break my staff, bury it certain fathoms in the earth, and deeper than did ever plummet sound I'll drown my book (Eissler 1978, p. 474).

Having renounced his creative identification with the muse image of Gisella, his adolescent masturbatory story-telling art, and the essential bond of the academy with Edward, it would be years before Freud felt inclined to pick up the essential threads of his creativity. In his relationship to Fliess he would reinvent the academy all over again. In his young manhood, though, Freud threw himself into the work of making himself an adult scientist.

The Sublimation

In late adolescence, Freud sublimated his passions as he began to invest himself with the identity of a man-of-science. Except for translating a volume of John Stuart Mill's philosophy from English into German when he was 20 years old, Freud ceased to exert himself as a man of letters until later in his adult life. In late adolescence Freud immersed himself in the studies of zoology and philosophy. After beginning active research in zoology during his 19th year, Freud stopped taking the philosophy courses, although study of the philosopher Aristotle contributed to his ability to subordinate his artistic interests to his scientific ones. These Freud approached (at the University of Vienna) as a student of evolution. This interest allowed him to make a gradual transition from his long standing, overdetermined interest in nature to an interest in the evolution of the nervous system. Progressing from a study of the genitalia of eels to research into the evolution of the nervous system, Freud developed mechanisms for taming his adolescent passions.

Trieste

In March of 1876, when he was still 19 years old, Freud received a grant to do research under Carl Claus at the Zoological Experimental Station at Trieste. Freud examined and dissected immature eels. His goal was to discover in immature eels the undifferentiated organ that eventually differentiates into the male or female genital. Freud returned to Vienna for the summer semester of 1876. In Vienna he made the acquaintance of Sigmund Exner and Ernst Fleischl, fellows of the Physiological Institute, the latter ten years older than himself. In the fall Freud returned to Trieste, where he continued his research, dissecting up to 400 mature eels to examine their sex organs for micro-histologic characteristics. Upon his return in late 1876 Freud entered the Physiological Institute, where he was to work under Joseph Brucke's supervision for the next six years.

The two trips to Trieste were sexually stimulating. Freud was alone in a warm southern vacation spot doing research on sexual genesis. If he had intercourse before he was married, the chances are it occurred on one or both of these trips. It is not probable that Freud had intercourse before this time, for he is known to have warned his friends of the dangers of intercourse in a way that showed little practical knowledge of sex itself. From other comments it appears that after he settled down to work at the Physiological Institute, Freud applied himself single-mindedly to study and research. There is no evidence of sexual activity at this time. After his engagement at the age of 26, Freud felt great loyalty to his beloved Martha. Thus it appears that the visits to Trieste were the only interlude before Freud's 30th year when he might have performed the crucial experiment with women.

Freud's letter of April 15th, 1876, to Silberstein from Trieste indicates (Freud 1971) that Freud did have intercourse on his mind, and that he experienced a tempestuous conflict over his sexual impulses. Significantly, April 15th was the anniversary of Julius's death, always a day on which Freud was prone to feel his conflicts reverberating to his inner psychic core. Thus, Freud's feelings about Christians as repressive are mobilized and apparent in the imagery of the letter, which recalls Freud's belief that the one-eyed doctor, here perhaps imaged as the pope, would destroy him if he attempted to enter the primal scene. Following Stanescu:

In Trieste on the 15th of April, 1876, Freud launches an attack against the existing order. When describing the stormy sea, which prevented him from enjoying his free Sunday, to which he was looking forward eagerly, he explains the bad weather following a week of glorious sunshine by stating: "The Adriatic sea, perhaps as a true Italian, hates the Pope, the priests and Sundays" (Stanescu 1971, p. 204).

Certainly Freud wanted to be on the promenade on Sunday enjoying the view of the beautiful Italian women. Of the Italian women, whose beauty he regrets he can only appreciate from afar, Freud writes:

Physiologically, I only know they like walking, and as to anatomical investigations—it is unfortunately forbidden to dissect humans (Stanescu 1971, p. 203).

Eels were another story. The letter includes extensive diagrams of the genital anatomy of the eels Freud was dissecting as well as far-reaching evolutionary speculation about the meaning and origin of their sexual anatomy. Here we can see the direct conjunction of Freud's basal image theme of the bisexual or fetishistic anatomy and his awakened interest in Italian women. In later correspondence to his future wife, Freud seemed to speak with a carnal knowledge that indicated something more than the maturation of adolescent fantasy about intercourse.

When Freud returned to Vienna after his second stint at Trieste, he settled in under Brucke's tutelage, content as he wrote in his associations to the *Three Fates* dream to cling to the breast of wisdom. Brucke was the *bridge* to Freud's highly sublimated existence at the Physiological Institute:

. . . the honored name of Brucke (cf. the verbal *bridge* above) reminded me of the Institute in which I spent the happiest hours of my student life, free from all other desires . . . (*Standard Edition*, vol. IV, p. 206).

During the ensuing years Freud's research became the only invested derivative of Freud's interest in the nature of womankind, and the only important recipient of his creative energies.

10

Adult Origins of Freud's Creativity

The task of the creator in his adult life is to weld the twin creative and normal aspects of his identity into a single synthesis through the mediation of socially relevant works (Harris and Harris 1981). Freud was forced to bear witness to the process of identity change which he underwent as he made himself into a mature psychoanalyst. The final stages of Freud's self-analysis coincided with the final stages of writing and revising *The Interpretation of Dreams*. In the work of revising his manuscript—the progressive as opposed to the regressive phase of his creative cycle—Freud passed through the hierarchical stages in the development of his consciousness. Revision recapitulates epigenesis. The final stages of his creative work on *The Interpretation of Dreams* were entirely analogous to the revision of a dream which occurs prior to waking as the dream is set in secondary process terms. Freud's classic dream of completing analysis, the dream of *Dissecting My Own Pelvis*, is a container for Freud's final identity summary as he prepares to wake into the post-*Interpretation* light of his maturity.

In the early years of Freud's adult life he tried to consolidate all aspects of his identity under the framework of his investment in becoming a scientist. Nevertheless this period was not devoid of human feelings, for Fleischl took on the mantle of Freud's close friend, acting as a buffer to Brucke, who was more distant and fearsome in Freud's mind. Research and study became the common bond that tied Freud to a brother figure and a father figure during his early adult years.

Brucke gave Freud the task of studying the histology of certain special spinal cord nerve cells in a primitive species of fish. Just as Freud had studied an undifferentiated form of sexual cell, he now studied an undifferentiated form of nervous cell. During the next six years Freud studied more such problems, primarily with the aid of the microscope. He studied the histology of nerve tissue in the crayfish in 1879, for instance, and examined it again in 1881 (Jones 1953, p. 48).

Freud's work as a researcher invited the basal image themes that had dominated his childhood. Now, at its close, by absorbing power from his studies and from his idealized mentors, by peering through the microscope for hours, days, weeks, months, and years, and piercing the primal obscurity that hid the basic origins of life from him, Freud started to become a one-eyed doctor himself.

If Brucke was the latter day version of the powerful one-eyed doctor, then Fleischl was compounded of Freud's brothers and nephew, Emanuel and Philipp and John. Freud made clear his idealization of Fleischl and his vicarious identification with him as a man of the world in a letter to his fiancée, Martha. The letter is included to illustrate how Freud's adolescent fantasy of receiving help in deflowering had been turned to other ends during Freud's stay at the Physiological Institute. It was only after he met Martha that Freud's sexual drive lost the sublimated quality that characterized it during Freud's years at the Physiological Institute.

Yesterday I went to see my friend, Ernst V. Fleischl, whom hitherto, so long as I did not know Marty, I envied in every respect. But now I have an advantage over him. I believe he has been engaged for ten or twelve years to a girl of his own age, who was prepared to wait for him indefinitely, but with whom he has now fallen out for reasons unknown to me. He is a thoroughly excellent person in whom nature and education have combined to do their best. Wealthy, skilled in all games and sports, with the stamp of genius in his manly features, good looking, refined, endowed with many talents and capable of forming an original judgment about most things, he has always been my ideal, and I was not satisfied until we became friends and I could properly enjoy his value and abilities. . . . Then I looked around his room, fell to thinking about my superior friend, and it occurred to me how much he could do for a girl like Martha, what a setting he could provide this jewel, how Martha, who was enchanted even by our humble Kahlenberg, would admire the Alps, the waterways of Venice, the splendors of St. Peter's in Rome; how she would enjoy sharing the importance and influence of this lover, how the nine years which this man has over me could mean as many unparalleled happy years of her life compared to the nine miserable years spent in hiding and near-helplessness that await her with me. I was compelled painfully to visualize how easy it could be for him—who spends two months of each year in Munich and frequents the most exclusive society—to meet Martha at her uncle's house. And I began wondering what he would think of Martha. Then all of a sudden I broke off this daydream (E. Freud 1975, pp. 11–12).

Just as the aim-inhibited versions of the earlier fantasies allowed Freud to substitute intellectual pursuits for direct forms of gratification, this latter-day version of the adolescent fantasy supplied Freud enough satisfaction to help him achieve stability at the Physiological Institute.

The Threshold of Maturity

Freud's identity-altering major work, *The Interpretation of Dreams*, was the fulcrum that lifted him into his maturity as a creator. The last fixation Freud needed to analyze in order to liberate himself from intellectual inhibition-fixation to adult sublimations. After entering the Physiologic Institute, Freud adapted the Helmholtzian motto that the same principles determine both organic and inorganic processes. In order to become a true scientist of the mind, and to resolve the discrepancy between his creative, artistic approach to life and his scientific objectivity, Freud had to develop a more complete mastery of his emotional psychological world.

The last piece of self-analysis necessary for the completion of the dream book was the analysis of the origins of heterosexual and homosexual character structure. Both heterosexual and homosexual character trends had been sublimated in Freud's devotion to his research, and beyond that the research contained the history of Freud's unconscious development. The final step to completing the dream book required that Freud become aware of the whole sequence of his development up to his present life. One must be aware of the nature of one's entire life and motivations in order to lay a secure foundation for the mature identity.

Even after becoming aware of his psychological history, and of the bisexual fantasies that animated his creative researchers, it was still necessary for Freud to reveal these dynamics to an audience, for in his maturity Freud had to accept his creativity as an aspect of his overall identity as a psychoanalyst. We can see Freud struggling with this problem, and presenting it allegorically within a letter to Fliess on the subject of deciding to publish *The Interpretation of Dreams*. Thus, in letter #107, sent to Fliess on May 28, 1899—the same letter in which Freud announces he has finished "Screen Memories" and that the dream book has taken shape—he says:

I have decided that all the efforts at disguise will not do, and that giving it all up will not do either, because I cannot afford to keep to myself the finest—and probably the only lasting—discovery that I have made. In this dilemma I have followed the rabbi's line in the story of the cock and the hen. Do you know it? A man and wife who owned one cock and one hen decided to celebrate a festival by having one fowl for dinner, but they could not make up their mind which to kill, so they consulted the rabbi. "Rabbi, what are we to do, we've only one cock and one hen. If we kill the cock the hen will pine, and if we kill the hen the cock will pine. But we want to have a fowl for dinner on the festival. Rabbi, what are we to do?" "Well, kill the cock," the rabbi said. "But then the hen will pine." "Yes, that's true; then kill the hen." "But Rabbi, then the cock will pine." "Let it pine!" said the rabbi.
So the dreams will be done . . . (Kris 1954, p. 281).

Metaphorically, the male part of Freud lives on by the decision to publish, while the female part (Fliess) must perish. One last dream, which must have been dreamed around this time, exemplifies Freud's analysis of the remaining obstacles to publishing. This dream of *Dissecting My Own Pelvis* belies Freud's contention that "unfortunately it is forbidden to dissect human beings." This dissection is carried out in public.

The Dream of Dissecting My Own Pelvis

Old Brucke must have set me some task; strangely enough, it related to a dissection of the lower part of my own body, my pelvis and legs, which I saw before me as though in the dissecting room, but without noticing their absence in myself and also without a trace of any gruesome feeling. Louise N. was standing beside me and doing the work with me. The pelvis had been eviscerated, and it was visible now in its superior, now in its inferior, aspect, the two being mixed together. Thick flesh-colored protuberances (which in the dream itself, made me think of hemorrhoids) could be seen. Something which lay over it and was like crumpled silver-paper had also to be carefully fished out. I was then once more in possession of my legs and was making my way through the town. But (being tired) I took a cab. To my astonishment the cab drove in through the door of a house, which opened and allowed it to pass along a passage which turned a corner at its end and finally led into the open air again. Finally, I was making a journey through a changing landscape with an Alpine guide who was carrying my belongings. Part of the way he carried me too, out of consideration for my tired legs. The ground was boggy; we went round the edge; people were sitting on the ground like Red Indians or gypsies—among them a girl. Before this I had been making my own way forward over the slippery ground with a constant feeling of surprise that I was able to do it so well after the dissection. At last we reached a small wooden house at the end of which was an open window. There the guide set me down and laid two wooden boards, which were standing ready, upon the window-sill, so as to bridge the chasm which had to be crossed over from the window. At that point I really became frightened about my legs, but instead of the expected crossing, I saw two grown-up men lying on wooden benches that were along the walls of the hut, and what seemed to be two children sleeping beside them. It was as though what was going to make the crossing possible was not the boards but the children. I awoke in a mental fright (*Standard Edition*, vol. V, p. 452).

ASSOCIATIONS TO THE DREAM OF
DISSECTING MY OWN PELVIS

Freud's final association to this dream is that,

. . . in the dream itself I missed the gruesome feeling ("Grauen") appropriate to it. Now this was wish-fulfilling in more than one sense. The dissection meant the self-analysis which I was carrying out, as it were, in the publication of this present book about dreams—a process which had been so distressing to me in reality that I had postponed the printing of the finished manuscript for more than a year. A wish then arose that I might get over this feeling of distaste (*Standard Edition*, vol. V, p. 477).

This was not true. Thus the statement covered an emotional truth Freud wished to disguise. He *had* postponed analyzing his bisexual fantasies for a year. In this dream's disguised dealing with intercourse and orgasm it appears that Freud did not want to disclose his knowledge of the bisexual impulse. Perhaps he could hardly allow himself to think about it for a long time, while he was reassuring himself that it had not become instrumental in his death—"grauen," growing grey—for, like *The Three Fates*, this dream is full of imagery that equates sexuality and death.

Since this is an anatomical dissection dream, anatomy may be our guide to the functional phenomenon as we follow Freud into the dream's inner mystery. The first dream episode comes to an end as the inner and outer aspect of the anatomy are simultaneously revealed. As a functional phenomenon analogue this represents the wish for vaginal-anal penetration. In the second dream episode, Freud penetrates a house and, to his astonishment, comes out the other side. Again there is the simultaneous double experience. This, anatomically, must be a reference to penetrating the vagina and finding another structure beyond—a fantasy for proceeding beyond the vagina in intercourse.

The last portion of the dream recreates the sexual experience of (1) penetration and (2) intercourse with orgasm in an allegorical way, following the plot structure of a book, or books. Once again Freud is accompanied on his journey by another person. Freud enters the boggy ground of the vagina. Then he penetrates to another structure, the uterus. The opening to the uterus is a window into the very center of Freud's fantasy life. This place, the center of creation, must hold the grave where Julius had been buried, and where he, Freud, might also be buried. If his seeds cross this barrier to make children, the selfsame crossing becomes the seeds of his own destruction. We know that Freud felt that to procreate was to make oneself an ancestor.

This particular dream came after Freud had already decided not to procreate anymore. Entering his middle age, he is becoming grey, and his only new successors will be his works. The change in Freud's position in life is demonstrated in a conversation he had with a woman friend. The conversation with Louise N. was an instigation to the dream. It is noteworthy that Freud was at this stage in a position to entertain a woman visitor. This shows him now a man of the world. The incident stands out in *The Interpretation of Dreams* as rather a departure in Freud's image of his social self. As we can see from the conversation, however, Louise N. issued Freud a metaphorically sexual challenge that discomforted Freud. The discomfort evoked a spate of latent thoughts that gave rise to the dream formation on the night after the visit.

The sexual innuendo challenged Freud's lack of sexual experience or response and was one factor that made the dream recapitulate Freud's earlier and prototypical sexual experience. Issues derived from Freud's anxiety about exposing his sexual secrets in public produced his discomfort with Louise N.:

Louise N., the lady who was assisting me in my job in the dream had been calling on me. "Lend me something to read," she had said. I offered her Rider Haggard's *She*. "A *strange* book, but full of hidden meaning," I began to explain to her. "The eternal feminine, the immortality of our emotions . . ." Here she interrupted me: "I know it already. Have you nothing of your own?"—"No, my own immortal works have not yet been written." "Well, when are we to expect these so-called ultimate explanations of yours which you've promised even *we* shall find readable?" she asked, with a touch of sarcasm. At that point I saw that someone else was admonishing me through her mouth and I was silent. I reflected on the amount of self-discipline it was costing me to offer the public even my book upon dreams—I should have to give away so much of my own private character in it (*Standard Edition*, vol. V, p. 453).

Freud's account of this encounter is interesting—novelistic. Freud responded to Louise N. on two levels. In one sense his response was somewhat weak, for Freud was intimidated by the force of Louise N.'s husband's challenge spoken through his wife's lips. In another sense, by offering Louise N. *She*, Freud was responding with a degree of openness and vulnerability that went far beyond her expectations. What he offered was his own knowledge of the eternal feminine.

After his complaint that to satisfy Louise N. he would have to give away so much of his private character, Freud interrupted his text to issue his favorite caveat:

> Das Beste was du wissen kannst
> Darfst du den Buben doch nicht sagen
> (*Standard Edition*, vol. V, p. 453).

As stated earlier, this quote from Mephistopheles in Goethe's *Faust* translates, "After all, the best of what you know may not be told to boys" (*Standard Edition*, vol. IV, p. 142). This is the same quote that Freud had wanted to use as the "motto" for *The Interpretation of Dreams*, but which Fliess discouraged. The challenge to his masculinity made Freud wish for a helper in the task of penetrating the woman; yet that was not completely acceptable because submission to the man went along with it. This was what could not be disclosed.

Generally the need to prove himself through his writing had always required that Freud expose exactly those feelings the conversation with Louise N. had aroused. Freud's next association was to Brucke, who had once pushed him along both in his research and toward publishing:

Old Brucke came in here appropriately; even in the first years of my scientific work it happened that I allowed a discovery of mine to lie fallow,

until an energetic remonstrance on his part drove me into publishing it
(*Standard Edition*, vol. V, p. 454).

On the threshold of his adult life Freud had submitted to Brucke's
authority, for Brucke also comes into the dream associations by way
of the crumpled silver paper, which reminded Freud of the word
stanniol, and that in turn reminded him of Stannius, the author of a
tract on the nervous system of fishes. Stannius was Freud's guide as
he penetrated the nervous systems of his primitive fishes. Thus, the
silver paper is overdetermined as it alludes to the paper on the
nervous system of fishes that Freud wrote when he was 21 and
subsequently wished that he had thrown away. The silver-paper
imagery is also a representation of inferior sexual products in
Freud's own basal image theme lexicon of symbols.

The paper Freud had written carried out Brucke's research
idea. Furthermore, Brucke presented the results at a scientific
meeting before Freud felt satisfied with it. Thus the paper represents Freud's sexually ambivalent feelings about submitting to
Brucke: in the dream the silver paper covers a hemorrhoid-like
structure. By making an anatomical structure where none existed
before, like the Madchenfänger in the *Count Thun* dream, Freud is
performing the basic creative act. In this case the intrapsychic fetish
produced is suitable to stand for the whole range of oedipal sexual
significants. It represents Freud's anal receptiveness to Brucke, at
the same time that it defends it by making a fleshy protuberance in
place of the anal orifice. In that sense it might be termed a male
fetish. The fish symbolism juxtaposed with this male fetish shows
that the representation leads into Freud's bisexual symbol of
creativity, the image of his adolescent masturbation inspired by
Ichthyosaura.

The dream imagery indicates an affirmation of this whole
hypothesis. Freud analyzed the imagery *in situ* as the crumpled
paper indicating a lack of authenticity had to be "fished out." Freud
was similarly afraid as a young adult investigator that the structure
he found in the primitive nervous system of the fish might have
anatomic presence only in his own mind. In the dream the discovery
of the intrapsychic fetish allows the journey to move on. Thus

Louise N. helped him with the initial penetration in this self-dissection.

Still, Freud tired again, and he had to call on an Alpine guide. As Freud's fourth Rome dream showed, crossing the Alps meant getting to Rome: completing the dream book. Since Brucke has been on Freud's mind in the dream and in the associations, the guide may well be Brucke, who helps him "bridge" the difficult parts of the journey. The images of the cab and a house opening up are signs of Freud's claustrophobia and fear of travel, so it is understandable that he invokes the image of a strong man to guide him. Brucke helped Freud carry the investigation toward an understanding of the functional phenomena of the anatomical dream.

Following the dream journey functionally, Freud finally entered into the heart of his dream world, the furnace of all his imagery, the center of nature, the uterus of the dream. The second of the two Haggard books, aptly entitled *The Heart of the World*, provided Freud with the day residue imagery for this dream center. Freud's associations to this part of the dream refer to the whole history of his bedrock imagery organized as a single mythological theme that encompasses the whole of his childhood. The two Haggard books make an antithesis out of Freud's eternal feminine "nature" and his eternal masculine, which in *The Heart of the World* is imaged as an all-seeing eye. The uterus-grave containing the all-seeing eye comprises the basal elements of Freud's personal adult mythology.

The further thoughts which were started up by my conversation with Louise N. went too deep to become conscious. They were diverted in the direction of the material that had been stirred up in me by the mention of Rider Haggard's *She*. The judgment "strangely enough" went back to that book and to another one, *The Heart of the World*, by the same author, and numerous elements of the dream were derived from these two imaginative novels. The boggy ground over which people had to carry, and the chasm which they had to cross by means of boards brought along with them, were taken from *She*; the Red Indians, the girl, and the wooden house were taken from *The Heart of the World*. In both novels the guide is a woman; both are concerned with perilous journeys; while she describes an adventurous road that had scarcely ever been trodden before, leading into an undiscovered region. The tired feeling in my legs, according to a note which I find I made upon the dream, had been a real sensation during the day-time. It probably went along with a tired mood and a doubting thought: "How much longer will my legs carry me?" The end of the adventure in *She* is that the guide, instead of finding immortality for herself and the others, perishes in the mysterious subterranean fire. A fear of kind was unmistakably active in the dream-thoughts. The "wooden house" was also, no doubt, a coffin, that is to say, the grave (*Standard Edition*, vol. V, p. 454).

The last part of the dream is so much taken with the imagery from these two books that this fact deserves to be explained. Grinstein (1980, pp. 394–421) summarized the two novels in his book on Freud's dreams. In both books a young man just coming of age is given a mission connected with a legacy from his father. In this adult version of the family romance, the young man is a special person who must reclaim a birthright that has been denied all his ancestors. The young man must brave the same perils upon which his ancestors foundered.

The heroes must actualize the mythological structure that is their legacy. This task represents the work of adult identity structure: forming conscious goals and purposes in life. This both heroes must do, despite having been deprived of mother and father. This is the realization every adult has in the course of realizing the distinction of his own consciousness. Each young man is thus taken up with a mission to fulfill himself while fulfilling the family destiny.

Freud identified with this task in so far as it was his task to make his life as a creator harmonious with his identity as a scientist. In order to do this Freud had to develop one overriding perspective that could include both his artistic and his scientific sense of his professional identity. The dream book had to fulfill the requirement to do both. The mythology of the hero's life in each of these novels relates to Freud's own.

Both *She* and *The Heart of the World* pretend to be manuscripts written by a survivor of a two-year-long, perilous, multifaceted series of adventures. In both novels a young man is given a quest to fulfill from a legacy mandated by a dead father. In both novels the hero is a family romance hero whose real parents or ancestors were thwarted in their quest to synthesize a strong nation. In both cases the hero's mission is to reunite some set of opposite forces, which if reunited can give the bearer of the knowledge, and the people governed by the knowledge, a direct participation in a form of greatness, represented by immortality. In *She* the emphasis is on individual immortality, in *Heart* it is on immortality of the social group.

In both cases the hero is given a special object, a fetishistic talisman, to aid him in his search. In *She* it is a scarab, in *Heart* an amulet. In both cases the young man is told about his quest on coming of age. Each undertakes the quest willingly, for each needs to establish the foundations of his identity: both have been brought up without connection to the source of their identity.

In both cases the hero is joined by a relatively normal friend or mentor who is drawn into the quest. Neither hero can love a woman on his own, though together the hero and the alter ego can love a woman. The loyalty of the hero and mentor to one another is the only lasting feeling.

The dénouement is of great importance in both novels. There is a journey toward the center of mysteries in each case, actualized by a revelation. In *She* the hero is offered the opportunity to bathe in a pulsating fire of immortality at the center of a volcano. Having declined, the hero watches his guide bathe in the fire and age before his eyes until her ancient figure is finally reduced to elemental dust. In *Heart* the center of action comprising the dénouement is a special symbolic fabrication. Two halves of an ancient amulet are first reunited forming a "heart." Then the heart is fitted like a key inside a casement, which itself is at the center of a fabulous piece of machinery. The heart glows in its case as a living omniscient eye. At the very end, after the destruction of a newborn baby who was meant to rule the community in the future, in an act of passion the heart, casement and all, is wrenched out of the machine. This opens the sluice gates, and the whole city, built on water, is inundated as the dam releases its contents.

In both cases then the consummation of the story is a release of pent-up emotion (which may be equated with an orgasm) in which destruction is loosed and the central place, the uterus, becomes a grave. The hero, in both cases, has been moved as much by vengeance as by the urge to restore life. In the end nothing is left but the story and a life, which will be an ordinary one for the hero. Thus, these are stories about the life and mission of a creator. He must be in contact with the most primitive and general of his motives in order to accomplish his work.

At the center of his dream life Freud found a burial crypt. Freud's feelings about immortality, which were an important irrational component of his thinking during the years after *The Interpretation*, relate to his identity-organizing fantasy concerning his mother's womb as the burial place for Julius, and the fantasy that the father's primal penis resided in the womb as a central creative or destructive eye catalyzing creation and destruction at the source of life. This primal fantasy holds the center of Freud's psychological integrity.

Although there are many crypts in *She* and *Heart*, there are no wooden houses in either of them (Grinstein 1980). Freud wrote that the wooden house was also:

no doubt, a coffin, that is to say, the grave . . . I had already been in a grave once, but it was an excavated Etruscan grave near Orvieto, a narrow chamber with two stone benches along its walls, on which the skeleton of two grown-ups were lying (*Standard Edition*, vol. V, p. 454).

The image of the grave-uterus suggested to Freud a sense of coincidence between death and sexuality, the dipolar sources of his instinct theory. Orvieto reminded him, as we know from *The Psychopathology of Everyday Life*, of the intimate connection between sexuality and death:

. . . if the repressed thoughts on the topic of death and sexual life are followed up, one will be brought face to face with an idea that is by no means remote from the topic of the frescoes at Orvieto (*Standard Edition*, vol. VI, p. 13).

It was at Orvieto that Freud had a conversation with a stranger about the strange customs of the Turks, who feel that one might as well be dead if sexuality is denied.

Freud ended his explication of the dream with an assertion that the wish substituting the Etruscan grave for his own fear of death, activated during the previous day, was the wish that he might achieve immortality through his works:

Accordingly, I woke up in a "mental fright," even after the successful emergence of the idea that children may perhaps achieve what their father had failed to—a fresh allusion to the strange novel in which a person's identity is retained through a series of generations for over 2000 years (*Standard Edition*, vol. V, p. 455).

The allusion to a wish for immortality through his works, specifically *The Interpretation of Dreams*, or immortality through the continued work of one's children, shows Freud having come to the point of providing himself with a new sense of identity for his maturity which he hopes will endure forever.

The theme of immortality through one's works is the mature creator's essential irrational illusion, hierarchically replacing the whole gamut of bedrock irrationalities that are the legacy of previous developmental periods. The essential irrational nature of the mature age wish for immortality provides a continuing focus for anxiety into old age, when the wish must at last be qualified and resolved if the creator is going to be productive into old age. Freud's mature age fantasy has him peering with one phallic eye, deep into the uterine grave where Julius is buried. The image of two children there—one must be Julius, and the other must be himself—and two men—one must be his father, the other himself—wakes him. In his latter day consciousness, Freud-Fliess, the creator's image of identity was compounded hierarchically by child-Freud-adult-Freud, and child-Fliess-adult-Fliess. The artifice may die as the book itself lives. The only consciousness the real man Freud can control is his own: that is the only real creation of any human being.

After this dream, or at least after Freud's analysis of it, Freud wrote the remaining portions of *The Interpretation of Dreams*. In letter #111 to Fliess addressed on July 17th, 1899, Freud wrote,

. . . I have finished the big task, but there are still 115 little ones. Chapter I of the dreams is in type and the proofs are waiting to be read. . . . On the whole it has been a triumphant year, with many doubts resolved. The only surprising thing is that when long-awaited things at last happen you no longer take pleasure in them. . . . In my good hours I imagine new works, great and small. No introductory quotation for the dreams has suggested itself since you condemned the sentimental one from Goethe. It will have to be a hint at repression; *Flectere si nequeo superos, Acheronta movebo* (Kris 1954, p. 286).

This "motto" for *The Interpretation of Dreams*, translates: "If I cannot bend the Higher Powers, I will move the Infernal Regions." When Freud quoted this in his text of the chapter on dream psychology to illustrate the pressure of what is repressed to reach consciousness, he followed it with his now famous line, "The interpretation of dreams is the royal road to a knowledge of the unconscious activities of the mind" (*Standard Edition*, vol. V, p. 608). The royal road to Rome is paved with Freud's dreams. With this quotation from Virgil's *Aeneid*, Freud announced that his determination has brought him to Rome. He had harnessed the power of his bisexuality, for the quote shows Juno, who speaks it, unleashing Allecto, a Fury, on the camp of Aeneas's allies. The fury is a response to Aeneas's scorn for the Semitic Dido. Schorsky (1980, p. 200) described Allecto as "a Gorgon-like phallic female alive with black and writhing snakes," a bisexual monster.

In the letter Freud continued his references to Roman mythology, showing his thorough understanding of the subject and his mastery of the unconscious, in the following self-satisfied announcement to Fliess:

The ancient gods still exist, for I have bought one or two lately, among them a stone Janus, who looks down on me with his two faces in a very superior fashion (Kris 1954, p. 286).

His identification with this God of January is the sign of Freud's maturity. For Janus looks ahead with one face to all new beginnings and looks back with the other on all that is past. He turns one face to look within himself to what is repressed, what has passed and been transformed, while the other looks to the life to be encompassed. This is an improvement on the two faces Freud had shared with Fliess, for from this time forth Freud renounced the identity of bilaterality and bisexuality. In this renunciation he declares himself independent of Fliess, capable of his own travels in the world.

References

Eissler, K. R. (1978). *Sigmund Freud: His Life in Pictures and Words: A Biographical Sketch*. New York: Harcourt Brace Jovanovich, Inc.

—— (1978). Creativity and adolescence, *The Psychoanalytic Study of the Child*, ed. by Ruth Eissler et al., vol. 33. New Haven: Yale University Press.

Freud, E. (1969). Some early unpublished letters of Freud, *International Journal of Psychoanalysis*, 50:419–427.

—— (1975). *The Letters of Sigmund Freud*, trans. by Stern and Stern. New York: Basic Books, Inc.

Freud, S. (1899). Screen memories, *Standard Edition*, vol. 3. London: The Hogarth Press, 1964.

—— (1900–01). The interpretation of dreams, *Standard Edition*, vols. 4–5. London: The Hogarth Press, 1964.

—— (1901). The psychopathology of everyday life, *Standard Edition*, vol. 6. London: The Hogarth Press, 1962.

—— (1909). Notes upon a case of obsessional neurosis (the rat man), *Standard Edition*, vol. 10. London: The Hogarth Press, 1964.

—— (1912). On the universal tendency to debasement in the sphere of love, *Standard Edition*, vol. 11. London: The Hogarth Press, 1964.

——— (1915). Thoughts for the times on war and death, *Standard Edition*, vol. 14. London: The Hogarth Press, 1964.

——— (1916). The archaic features and infantilism of dreams, *Standard Edition*, vol. 15. London: The Hogarth Press, 1963.

——— (1917). A childhood recollection from *Dichtung und Wahrheit, Standard Edition*, vol. 17. London: The Hogarth Press, 1964.

——— (1918). From the history of an infantile neurosis (the wolf man), *Standard Edition*, vol. 17. London: The Hogarth Press, 1964.

——— (1919). The uncanny, *Standard Edition*, vol. 17. London: The Hogarth Press, 1964.

——— (1920). A note on the prehistory of the technique of analysis, *Standard Edition*, vol. 18. London: The Hogarth Press, 1964.

——— (1925). An autobiographical study, *Standard Edition*, vol. 20. London: The Hogarth Press, 1964.

——— (1930). Civilization and its discontents, *Standard Edition*, vol. 21. London: The Hogarth Press, 1964.

——— (1936). A disturbance of memory on the Acropolis, *Standard Edition*, vol. 22. London: The Hogarth Press, 1964.

Greenacre, P. (1971). The childhood of the artist: libidinal phase development and giftedness, *Emotional Growth*, vol 2. New York: International Universities Press.

Grinstein, A. (1980). *Sigmund Freud's Dreams*, Revised edition. New York: International Universities Press.

Harris J. and J. Harris (1981). *The Roots of Artifice*. New York: Human Sciences Press.

Jones, E. (1953). *The Life and Work of Sigmund Freud*, vol. 2. New York: Basic Books, Inc.

Kris, E. (1954). *The Origins of Psychoanalysis*. London: Imago.

Roazen, P. (1924). *Freud and His Followers*. New York: Alfred A. Knopf, Inc.

Schorsky, C. E. (1980). *Fin-De-Siècle Vienna: Politics and Culture*. New York: Alfred A. Knopf, Inc.

Schur, M. (1972). *Freud: Living and Dying*. New York: International Universities Press.

Stewart, W. A. and L. Freeman (1972). *The Secret of Dreams.* New
     York: Macmillan Publishing Co., Inc.
Stanescu, H. (1971). Young Freud's letters to his Rumanian friend,
     Israeli Annals of Psychiatry and Related Disciplines, 9:197,
     205–206.
Winnicott, D. W. (1953). Transitional objects and transitional
     phenomena, *International Journal of Psycho-Analysis*, 34:89–97.
Wittels, F. (1924). *Sigmund Freud.* New York: Dodd, Mead & Co.

Index

Anal phase, 43–73
  ending of, 62–64
An Autobiographical Study (Freud), 161, 215–216

Balmary, 3, 18, 57, 60
Bedrock images, 7–8, 48
Bernays, Martha, *see* Freud, Martha
Bernays, Minna, 118, 173
Beyond the Pleasure Principle (Freud), 54
Bible, *Phillipson's* (Die Israelitische Bibel), 156–158
Biography, 7–22
Bird-beaked figures dream, 157–161
Bisexuality, 67–68
  of sphinx, 83
Bleuler, E., 200
Borne, L., 191–192
Botanical monograph dream, 145–156
Braun, H., 20, 161
Breuer, J., 22, 29–30, 170

Brücke, E., 21–22, 27, 30, 35–36, 225, 235, 237
Bruhl, C., 216–217

Civilization and Its Discontents (Freud), 68
Clauss, C., 21, 225
Cocaine, 153
Construct, 7
Count Thun dream, 42, 111, 117–138, 173, 236
Creativity, 165–166
Creator
  fixation of, 10
  masturbation and, 178–180
  resolution of oedipal drama, 143–144
Creator's syndrome, 1, 16–17
Crying at the cupboard, 57–62

"A Disturbance of Memory on the Acropolis" (Freud), 164

Early adolescence, 173–195
Edler, F., 222
Ego
  flexibility of, 135–137
  splitting of, 13
Eissler, K. R., 20, 58, 192, 194, 224
Ellis, H., 191–193
Exner, S., 225

Family romance fantasy, 4
Fantasy
  bedrock, 46
  development of oedipal, 75–76
  organizing effect of, 4
  primary, 7
Faust (Goethe), 80, 235
Ferenczi, S., 192
Fleischl von Marxow, E., 21–22, 27, 32, 153, 189, 190, 225, 229
Fliess, W., 25–27, 30–33, 35, 38, 41–42, 67–68, 118, 170–171, 196
  Freud's correspondence with, 1, 2, 23, 26–29, 36, 40, 45–52, 56–57, 63, 75–82, 87–88, 95–101, 145–146, 175–179, 193, 198–200, 231, 241–242
  operation on Freud, 153
  operation on Irma, 153
  separation from, 197
Fluss, E., 19, 21, 64
  Freud's letters to, 1, 205–206, 208, 210–217
Fluss, G., 19, 21, 64, 196, 218–219
  Freud's adolescent love for, 204–210
  marriage of, 220–222
Freud, Alexander (brother), 19
  birth of, 59

Freud, Amalie (mother), 12, 13, 17–19, 58–59
Freud, Anna (daughter), 2
Freud, Anna (sister), 12
  birth of, 18, 58, 62–64
Freud, Dolfi (sister), 19
Freud, Emanuel (half-brother), 3, 12, 44, 56, 58
Freud, Ernst (son), 82, 162, 210–217, 230
Freud, Jacob (father), 12, 17–19, 44
  death of, 26
  expectations for Sigismund, 15, 20
  seductions of, 2–4, 46, 47
Freud, John (nephew), 12, 17, 35, 36, 44–45, 64–66
  departure of, 66
Freud, Julius (brother), 23–26, 28–45, 56, 59, 64, 68, 72–73
  birth and death of, 13–18, 50–51
  death and funeral of, 37–42, 116
Freud, Martha, (wife, *nee* Bernays), 22, 173–174, 225, 229–230
Freud, Mitzi (sister), 19
Freud, Paula (sister), 19
Freud, Pauline (niece), 12, 17, 64–66
Freud, Philipp (half-brother), 3, 12, 44, 56, 58–60
Freud, Rebecca, 3
Freud, Rosa (sister), 19, 80
Freud, Schlomo (grandfather), 12
Freud, Sigmund, 7
  An Autobiographical Study, 161, 215–216
  Beyond the Pleasure Principle, 54
  birth of, 3, 12
  chronology of childhood, 11–14

Civilization and Its Discontents, 68
creativity of, 43–73
  adult origins of, 228–243
death of father, 125
departures, separations, and
  losses of, 66–67
"A Disturbance of Memory on
  the Acropolis," 164
dreams of, 8, 23–42
  the bird-beaked figures, 157–
    161
  botanical monograph, 145–
    156
  Count Thun, 42, 111, 117–
    138, 173, 236
  dissecting my own pelvis, 232–
    242
  Hollthurn, 101–110
  Irma, 148, 153
  my son the myops, 67–73
  news from the front, 53–57
  non vixit, 27–37
  open air closet, 111–119
  riding on a horse, 37–42, 91
  three fates, 173–175, 179–194
  of travel to Rome, 89–92
  the uncle with the yellow
    beard, 166–172
  zehner, 55–57, 61
early adolescence of, 173–195
early childhood of, 17–18
ending of anal phase of, 62–64
family romance fantasy of, 4
Goethe's childhood analyzed by,
  93–94, 150
identification with Goethe, 95
infancy of, 23–42
The Interpretation of Dreams, 1,
  4–6, 8, 17, 23–32, 53–55, 87,

90, 102–188, 196, 200–201,
  228, 230–242
Introductory Lectures, 53
late adolescence of, 218–227
latency of, 145–172
later childhood of, 19–22
letters
  to Ferenczi, 192
  to Fliess, *see* Fliess, W.
  to Fluss, 1, 205, 206, 208, 210–
    217
  to Martha Bernays, 162
  to Silberstein, 1, 2, 196–197,
    207, 219–226
middle adolescence of, 196–216
natural science embraced by,
  214–217
"A Note on the Prehistory of the
  Technique of Analysis,"
  191–192
oedipal dreams of, 97–144
and oedipal mythology, 2, 82–86
oedipal period of, 74–96
preadolescence of, 161–166
primal scene of, 11, 14–17
Project for a Scientific Psychology,
  63, 202
*The Psychopathology of Everyday
  Life*, 1, 28–29, 59–61, 102,
  240
Rat Man, case of, 206
"Screen Memories," 1, 59, 198–
  204
screen memory of, 64–66
self-analysis of, 1, 5, 6
  reconstructions from, 45–48
split father image of, 139
symptoms of, 86–89
Three Essays on Sexuality, 77

Freud, Sigmund (*continued*)
 transitional era of, 33–37
 "The Uncanny," 70, 84
 Wolf Man, case of, 9

Gargantua (Rabelais), 113
Germinal (Zola), 126–127
Goethe
 childhood recollection of, 93–94,
  150
 essay on Nature, 216
 Faust, 80, 235
 Freud's identification with, 95,
  189–190
 Iphegenia auf Taurus, 188
Greenacre, P., 74, 144
Grillparzer, F., *Des Meeres und der
  Liebe Wellen*, 130–131
Grinstein, A., 108, 113, 114, 121,
  123, 125, 127, 130–131,
  140–142, 160, 185, 189,
  190, 238, 240
Gulliver, 113

Haggard, R.
 The Heart of the World, 237–240
 She, 234–235, 237–240
Hamlet (Shakespeare), 73, 146–147
Hannibal, 151, 156
Hebbel, F., 219
Henry VI (Shakespeare), 126
Hercules, 112–113
Die Hochzeit des Monchs (Meyer),
  101
Hoffman, E. T. A., 84
Hollthurn dream, 101–110
Hypatia (Kingsley), 185–186

Ichthyosaura, 218–224
Images

bedrock, 7–8
castration, 63
 of the eye, 24
 Freud's primal scene, 14–17
 reconstruction through, 5–6
 revised primal scene, 11
 split father, 139
The Interpretation of Dreams
  (Freud), 1, 4–6, 8, 17, 23–
  32, 53–55, 87, 90, 102–188,
  196, 200–201, 228, 230–242
 1919 edition, 53–55
Introductory Lectures (Freud), 53
Irma dream, 148, 153

Jones, E., 80, 118, 173, 200
Julius Caesar (Shakespeare), 34–35

Kanner, S., 3
Kingsley, C., *Hypatia*, 185–186
Koller, K., 151–153
Konigstein, 152–154
Kris, E., 13, 26, 28–29, 46–52, 57–
  58, 75–82, 87–88, 95–96,
  98–101, 145–146, 175–179,
  193, 198–200, 231, 242

Late adolescence, 218–227
Latency, 145–172
 failure of repression in, 157
"Die Leiden eines Knaben"
  (Meyer), 113–114, 119
Libido, 78
Das Liebeskonzil (Panizza), 140–142
Lucrezia Borgia, 141–142

Massena, Marshall, 156
Masturbation, 81–82, 92, 150
 adolescent, 175–177
 and the young creator, 178–180

Maury, A., 185
Maxwell, J. C., *Matter and Motion*, 109–110
The Merchant of Venice (Shakespeare), 195
Meyer, C. F.
  Die Hochzeit des Monchs, 101
  "Die Leiden eines Knaben," 113–114, 119
  Die Richterin, 99–102
Middle adolescence, 196–216
Moliere, *Le Malade Imaginaire*, 109–110
Moses, 151
Mountaineering, 55
Mozart, W. A., *Le Noze di Figaro*, 122, 123
Mushrooms, 63
My son the myops dream, 67–73

Napoleon, 156
News from the front dream, 53–57
Non vixit dream, 27–37
Le Noze di Figaro (Mozart), 122, 123

Oedipal drama, 143
Oedipal dreams, 97–144
Oedipal period, 74–96
Oedipus, Freud's attachment to, 82–86
Oedipus complex, 2
Oedipus Rex (Sophocles), 82, 146
Omnipotence, 44–45
Open air closet dream, 111–119

Paneth, J., 22, 27, 30, 34, 38–40
  death of, 26
Panizza, O., *Das Liebeskonzil*, 140–142

Pantagruel (Rabelais), 118
Plagiarism, 184–185
Preadolescence, 161–166
Primal scene, 8–11
  Freud's, 14–17
  interruption of, 115
  negative oedipal revision of, 111
  oedipally revised, 74–96
  positive oedipal revision of, 101–103
  revised, 11
Primary fantasy, 7
Project for a Scientific Psychology (Freud), 63, 202
The Psychopathology of Everyday Life, 1, 28–29, 58–61, 102, 240
Pur, J., 4, 14, 18, 51–53, 170

Rabelais
  Gargantua, 113, 118
  Pantagruel, 118
Rat Man, 206
Reconstruction
  of anal origins of creativity, 43–73
  of Freud's infancy, 23–42
  through images, 5–6
  method and theory of, 7–8, 48–52
Regression, creative, 5–6
Repression, failure of, 157
Restitution, 202
Die Richterin (Meyer), 99–102
Riding on a horse dream, 37–42, 91
Rome, 68–69
  dreams of travel to, 89–92

Salomé, 141
Scar, the, 52–53

Schiller, J. C. F. von, 108–109
Schorsky, C. E., 19, 123, 242
Schur, M., 13, 25–27, 31, 38, 125
"Screen Memories" (Freud), 1, 59, 198–204
Screen memory, 64–66
Seduction theory, collapse of, 46
Self-analysis (Freud's), 1
    course of, 5–6
    reconstruction from, 45–48
Sexual metaphor, 178
Shakespeare, W.
    Hamlet, 73, 146–147
    Henry VI, 126
    Julius Caesar, 34–35
    The Merchant of Venice, 195
Silberstein, E., 20–21, 204–205
    Freud's letters to, 1, 2, 196–197, 207, 219–226
Skiing, 55
Sophocles, *Oedipus Rex*, 82, 146
Sphinx, 83
Stanescu, 197, 207, 226
Strachey, J., 158, 188
Symptoms, 86–89

La Terre (Zola), 127–128
Three Essays on Sexuality (Freud), 77
Three fates dream, 173–175, 179–194
Transitional era, 33–37
Transitional thinking, 9–10, 23–24

Uncle with the yellow beard dream, 166–172
Unconscious, discovery of, 1

Vienna, 19–20
    trip to, 81–82
Virgil, *Aeneid*, 242

Winnicott, D. W., 9, 23
Wittels, F., 216
Wolf Man, 9, 115–116

Zagic, M., 4, 13, 14, 17, 18, 50–52, 60, 66
Zehner dream, 55–57, 61
Zola, E., 126–128